STATISTICS AS A TOOL FOR EDUCATIONAL PRACTITIONERS

Harriet Talmage

University of Illinois
at Chicago Circle

McCutchan Publishing Corporation
2526 Grove Street
Berkeley, California 94704

ISBN 0-8211-1905-2
Library of Congress Catalog Card Number 75-31312

Typography by HMS Copy Service

PREFACE

Educators continually engage in activities concerning evaluation that range from systematically planned research studies to impressionistic reactions. The information acquired is used to make decisions about many aspects of classroom instruction, such as particular teaching strategies, group achievement, progress of students, instructional materials, and students' reactions to the classroom environment. At the building and district levels, the administrators make decisions regarding other facets of the classroom, the school, and the school system: types of school organization that facilitate teaching and learning; textbooks for system-wide adoption; new programs; feasibility of utilizing paraprofessionals; extent of parent and community participation in school decisions; and evaluation of the staff. Each level within the school system requires *evaluation* to assist in making curricular, instructional, and organizational decisions.

> EVALUATION is defined in this book as collecting information systematically and arranging the data in meaningful ways in order to decide from among alternatives and to study the effects of the decision on the educational process.

Teachers and administrators draw from an array of procedures to collect data: many types of observations, self-reporting devices, paper and pencil testing, and a variety of analyses of interaction. All too often the large amounts of data collected have limited value, for educators frequently over-look statistics as a tool to assist in ordering, analyzing, and interpreting the data. By itself a statistic (or any datum) means little. Its utility increases, however, as educators make appropriate use of statistics as a resource for educational evaluation.

Educational practice guided the choice of statistical concepts included in the book. Hence the dialogue chapters have a twofold purpose: first, to intro-duce readers to basic statistical concepts that have direct application to practice; and, second, to interpret the statistics within the educational milieu. The purpose is *not* to expose educators to a comprehensive course in statistics. The reader may find some standard material usually found in in-troductory statistics texts missing. The author made a conscious effort to re-duce, where possible, extraneous statistical concepts that have little relevance for educational evaluation. Topics and statistical concepts follow from prac-tical situations; they are not sequenced in an organizational pattern found in many textbooks.

The book is designed for those concerned about practices in evaluation—teachers, administrators, students of education, psychology, and social work, parents, and members of the community. The flexible instructional format permits differentiated use of the book. Readers with some mathematical background and a familiarity with educational settings can work through the chapters on their own. In advanced education or educational psychology courses the book can serve as a self-instructional supplement. The chapters also provide a ready resource to those who need to brush up on selected topics.

The arrangement of the materials also suits large-group and small-group instruction in teacher education courses that touch on introductory statistics and evaluation. Individual chapters assigned to small groups meet the re-quirements of short-term in-service workshops, or the entire book fulfills long-term in-service program needs. Administrators and teachers consider-ing the evaluation of some portion of their instructional program would find the book a handy reference for planning the study and preparing instruments for obtaining and analyzing data.

The book employs a teaching strategy I call "a self-pacing dialogue." This is not to be construed as a play on words; the reader engages in a dialogue with the author, and the reader controls the pace. Unlike programmed ma-terials, the dialogue permits open-ended responses, unique solutions, and in-dividual conceptual styles for formulating answers. The reader goes beyond a statistical solution. He or she interprets the statistics within the constraints imposed by the realities of the classroom and the school system. An open-ended approach more nearly fits ongoing educational practice than does a single right answer.

In addition to the self-pacing dialogue approach, the text incorporates several other instructional strategies to facilitate learning. First, with gentle prodding, frequent feedback, and the gradual introduction of necessary mathematical and statistical concepts, we build toward a level of mastery needed to use statistics as a tool in classroom and school evaluation. Second, an explanation follows the introduction of statistical symbols. It is marked off from the text for easy reference. The same procedure pertains for mathematical computations and relevant definitions. Third, the case study problems following the appendix permit the reader to apply previous explanations to classroom and school data. The emphasis is on the use of statistics for interpreting data. Agreed upon responses to the study programs can be found following the case studies.

Part I introduces the reader to ways of quantifying performance and products of performances (Chapter 1), to an examination of the obtained data for group and individual performance patterns (Chapters 2 and 3), and to a re-examination of the performance on the basis of statistical data related to central tendency, variability, and the normal distribution curve (Chapters 4 and 5).

Part II (Chapters 6, 7, and 8) looks at the correlation of multiple performance and the extension of the concept of correlation to evaluation instruments. The concepts of reliability and validity are developed to alert educators to sources of error and misinterpretations of data obtained from standardized and teacher-made instruments.

Part III applies the statistical concepts developed in Parts I and II to selected forms of instrumentation most frequently used by teachers and administrators in class and school evaluation.

The materials were pilot tested using a number of classes in educational evaluation. After several revisions, the materials were used by teachers in the field prior to the final revision. The dialogue approach emerged only after cataloging all variations of responses. There is always the possibility that a reader may find a unique, unanticipated answer; only an open-ended approach allows for this possibility.

I would like to thank the many preservice and in-service students who were instrumental in bringing to final form the several versions of the manuscript through their responses and reactions. A special acknowledgment is extended to Professor Robert M. Rippey of the University of Connecticut, Farmington, for his invaluable suggestions, to Professor Terry Denny of the University of Illinois, Urbana, and his doctoral students for their candid comments, and to Professor Herbert J. Walberg for his collegial encouragement and support. In addition, I would like to express my appreciation to my daughter, Gita Talmage, for the many hours she devoted to reacting to the intent of the dialogue approach as well as to her meticulous scrutiny of each problem and response; and to Pat Fox, editor, for her suggestions and scrupulous care in seeing the manuscript through to completion.

GUIDE TO THE USE OF THE DIALOGUE CHAPTERS

Each chapter presents a practical evaluation problem that teachers or administrators frequently encounter. In proposing solutions to the problem, the reader augments the explanation in the text with his or her own experiences. A space is provided for recording the reader's tentative solution. Immediately following the reader's response, the author discusses the most reasonable responses. In some cases there may be as many as three or four alternative solutions. After reading the discussion, the reader is encouraged to reread his or her own comments. Sometimes the reader's remarks will coincide with the author's explanation. At other times the response will have some relevance as a solution, but not go far enough. Or the reader's suggestion may pose an alternative that was not considered by the author. At this point the reader should review the discussion to determine whether he or she has come up with a unique, plausible solution or whether his or her understanding of the problem falls short of the author's intent. Rereading should bring the reader back to the intended direction.

The results of evaluation lead to decision making. The final decision, however, is based on options and consequences and seldom on a single right solution. For each situation, any number of plausible alternatives provide solutions. As the reader reexamines the responses in the light of the subsequent explanation, he must put the response into the real world of the classroom or school system. After carefully examining the alternatives, the reader should base his selection on what is most plausible in his own educational context. It is, in the final analysis, the teacher and the administrator who know the class, the school, and the school system, and the adequacy of the selected explanation is contingent upon their professional judgment.

When a new concept is introduced, the text provides an opportunity to work through the concept. Again, the reader is asked to respond using the concept in new situations. A further explanation follows that response. Single correct solutions pertain to cases dealing with mathematical computations for deriving a statistic.

There are two case studies for each chapter; they draw upon concepts, generalizations, and explanations introduced in the chapter. This permits the reader to work with the new concepts within the context of a practical class or school setting and to develop solutions that require interpretation of statistical and descriptive data.

For teachers and administrators: as you respond to the questions, direct your thinking to your own classroom experiences and the effects at the building and system levels.

For teacher candidates and students of education: as you respond to the questions, direct your thinking to your own experiences as students and as observers, tutors, or participants in some way in a teaching-learning situation.

GUIDE TO TERMS USED

CONTENTS

Part I
Statistics for Analyzing and Interpreting Performance and Products of Performance

Many of the tasks concerned with evaluation involve the use of standard instruments for collecting data or the development of instruments that fit the particular needs of individuals, the class, the school, and the school system. The data thus collected are the focus of analysis and interpretation, which, in turn, give direction to decisions about the individuals, class, school, and system.

The subject of Part I centers on the data in the form of *raw scores* obtained from performance or the product of performance. Methods for quantifying individual performance in the form of raw scores are discussed. The reader is invited to develop descriptive interpretations of the data on individuals and on groups. Graphs and statistical concepts related to central tendency and deviation are introduced to provide the reader with additional tools for analyzing and interpreting the raw scores.

RAW SCORE is the term used for a quantitative value (number) assigned to measurable characteristics, such as a performance or its product. X usually symbolizes a raw score. If one refers to a specific raw score, then a subscript denotes a specific score.

Example: X_2 reads "X sub 2." The numeral 2 stands for the second score, the name of a student, or any designated assignment to the datum.

At the conclusion of Part I the reader should be able to:

1. Quantify performances or their products.
2. Break down a performance or its product into meaningful components.

1

3. Assign weights to components.

4. Interpret individual and group performance on the basis of total scores and subscores.

5. Differentiate between criterion-referenced and norm-referenced performance.

6. Compare interpretation of a performance or its product on criterion and normative standards.

7. Construct coordinate graphs from raw scores.

8. Distinguish between different types of graphs.

9. Interpret data that use nominal, ordinal, and interval scales.

10. Determine the appropriate types of graphs to construct for a given set of data.

11. Calculate central tendency statistics: mean ($\bar{X}$), median (Mdn), and mode.

12. Compute the standard deviation (SD) of a distribution.

13. Apply the short-cut, teacher-made statistic in deriving a standard deviation.

14. Compute a z score.

15. Analyze a distribution from the calculated statistics: $\bar{X}$, mode, Mdn, SD, and z score.

16. Interpret data using the normal distribution curve.

17. Use the table of percent area under the normal curve for obtaining percentiles and z scores.

18. Convert percentiles to z scores, raw scores to z scores and percentiles, z scores and percentiles to stanines, z scores to T scores, and z scores to raw scores.

19. Understand the relationship between a random sample and a population.

20. Analyze and interpret the performance of a random sample using the normal distribution curve and associated statistics.

1.
QUANTIFYING PERFORMANCE AND PRODUCTS OF PERFORMANCE

Teachers dedicated to improving their teaching and their students' learning encounter the fundamental questions of evaluation. What should they look for? How do they go about it? How do they decide if the instruction is effective or if the students are progressing satisfactorily? To carry out an evaluation plan, teachers need to focus on some product or performance, measure it, and come to some value judgment that will assist in planning subsequent instruction. The process of setting objectives, measuring outcomes of working toward the objective, and making a judgment and acting upon it characterizes evaluation.

The above description of the process of evaluation still does not identify what it is that will be measured. A principal glancing around a classroom will observe many things: textbooks, homework papers, the teacher's lesson plans, an oral recitation, a small group of students working together on a report, one student poking another, the teacher frowning on the behavior, a report presented to the whole class, a student's three-dimensional display in one corner of the room, students diligently at work or a lethargic class. Everything the principal sees can be classified in one or two categories—an overt act or a product. The first is labeled performance, and examples of it are the one student poking the other, a lethargic class, or the teacher frowning. The behavior is directly observable. Products, on the other hand, are concrete evidence of previous performances, such as homework papers, the teacher's lesson plans, a display, or a test paper. In this case the behavior is inferred from the product.

The principal can make some gross measurements and pass judgment about the teacher, the classroom environment, and the achievement level of the students. Although the principal may feel he knows enough about what makes a teacher effective, about what constitutes an orderly classroom, and about academic criteria for judging the students' achievement in his school, what usually emerges as evaluation is the principal's subjective reactions. Even if these reactions are valid, he has little basis for making suggestions for improving instruction.

Regardless of the type of behavior, some procedure for quantifying the performance or the product must be considered. To quantify performance or their products, it is necessary to establish a procedure for assigning numerical values in such a way as to be of assistance in improving instruction. Assigning quantitative values does not make evaluation completely objective; it merely removes some of the subjectivity, or it provides a basis for understanding the subjective judgment.

An eleventh-grade social science class is given the assignment of writing an essay on the topic "The Influence of Mass Media on the American Political Scene." The teacher can take one of two approaches to scoring the products: a gut-level subjective reaction or an attempt to bring a degree of objectivity to the scoring. The teacher may have a preconceived standard of performance. In scoring the papers he may decide an individual paper is better than the standard, par with the standard, or below the standard. The teacher makes a broad descriptive judgment. He assigns either a word value (good, fair, not acceptable) or a quantitative value (10 points, 20 points, and so forth).

If the procedure for scoring a product is to improve the quality of an assignment or the students' learning, the basis for scoring the essay should contain information that will identify areas of the product's weaknesses and strengths. The teacher needs to determine what is important for the students to be able to do and to list these as components of the essay. A quantitative value is then assigned to each component. These values are subscores, which, when added together, yield a total score for the essay.

DEVISE A SET OF COMPONENTS FOR THE ESSAY TOPIC ON THE INFLUENCE OF MASS MEDIA. (Consider any aspect of the assignment that may be of importance to the evaluation of the product. Record these components in the spaces provided below.)

—— 1. _____

—— 2. _____

—— 3. _____

—— 4. _____

—— 5. _____

A variety of components may be listed. The components emphasized are dependent on the type of class, the interests of individual students, their weaknesses and strengths, and the learning outcomes the teacher has determined to be important to the class. The components could range from clarity of written expression to depth of analysis of a particular mass medium. The teacher may want to stress documentation of statements or identification of propaganda techniques.

For the most desirable performance, it is best not to have students play the old guessing game: "What does he want me to write about?" The assignment could have been introduced through discussion in which the teacher's expectations are clearly stated: the acceptable format, the extent of reliance on outside materials, and the breadth of coverage.

Points are next assigned to each of the components, which is called *weighting.*

> WEIGHTING is the assignment of quantitative values to subsections or components of a performance or product of performance.

IN THE BLANK TO THE LEFT OF THE COMPONENTS YOU LISTED PREVIOUSLY, ASSIGN WHAT YOU CONSIDER THE APPROPRIATE WEIGHTS. (Place a quantitative value in each space.) INDICATE BELOW ON WHAT BASIS YOU ASSIGNED THE VARIOUS WEIGHTS.

_____

_____

_____

Assigning weights is an important part of preparing data for later evaluation. If you are stressing open-ended exploration of the topic, then more weight would be assigned to this component. If the research nature of the assignment was emphasized, this part would receive more points. Many teachers consider clarity of presentation, accuracy in reporting, and specific content coverage of equal importance.

In the above instance, the social science teacher felt his class needed to learn to focus its attention on relationships. The students should receive the messages delivered via the media and relate these to subsequent political events. The teacher also expected that by the eleventh year students should be able to present their cases clearly. With these objectives in mind, the teacher had a basis for assigning weights to the essay. An essay that met all the expectations could have a total score of 35 points. The example below illustrates this.

Scoring Schedule

____ (*5 points*)   The student cites information from different media.

____ (*5 points*)   The student cites examples of inconsistencies in presentations by the media.

____ (*10 points*) The student shows awareness of subtle influences of the media.

____ (*5 points*)   The essay is written in a clear style.

____ (*10 points*) The student presents a lucid discussion concerning the influence of mass media on politics.

To avoid any uncertainties about the teacher's expectations, the scoring schedule should be available to the students.

There is another way to weight a particular component of an assignment other than by assigning different quantitative values. As an example, on a test in science covering a unit on weather, the teacher included 40 objective test items. The items covered three aspects of weather: forecasting, instruments used in forecasting, and reading weather maps. Because the teacher wanted to emphasize the reading of weather maps, he gave less weight to the other two components, but assigned equal value to each test question.

EXPLAIN HOW THIS CAN BE DONE. _____

_____

_____

_____

- -

The teacher assigned one point to each test item. He adjusted his weighting of the components by writing 20 test items on reading weather maps, 10 items on forecasting, and 10 items on weather instruments. The total score was 40 points, with reading weather maps comprising 50 percent of the total possible points.

Many products or performances to be evaluated represent highly complex skills, levels of understanding, or attitudes. In these cases, merely to list the component is not sufficient for measuring performance or their products. It may be necessary to break down the components into subcomponents for a more detailed analysis.

Principals face such a problem in evaluating the teaching staff. Many types of behavior go into producing effective teaching. In addition, a teacher is evaluated beyond that which is observable in the classroom. The teacher's relationship with other staff members, professional attitudes, work habits, and compliance with reasonable rules are all components of evaluation of teachers. Each of the components must be broken down into subcomponents. Professional attitudes, for example, could include such subcomponents as going beyond minimum professional expectations; maintaining confidentiality of students' personal records; adjusting classroom procedures in light of a school-wide or district situation; accepting constructive criticism; continuing to grow professionally; pilot testing new materials for possible adoption; and accepting professional responsibilities not necessarily stipulated in the contractual agreement.

At the classroom level an intermediate teacher is preparing to evaluate the written communicative skills of his pupils. His components are handwriting, creative expression, and mechanics of the written language. Since these are too broad for making judgments, he breaks down each component into subcomponents. Mechanics, for example, contain such subcomponents as spelling, vocabulary, punctuation, capitalization, and correct word usage.

The teacher now has scores on each subcomponent and component and a total score. Each score serves a particular purpose.

WHAT KIND OF INFORMATION CAN YOU GET FROM EACH SCORE?

Total score: _____

Component score: _____

Subcomponent score: _____

- -

For a complex product or performance, the total score loses much information. It can only give a sketchy picture of the student's ability. The component score gives information on the area of strength or weakness within the particular ability being measured. The subcomponent score is usually for diagnostic purposes. It points up the specific trouble spot within a component.

Two fallacies are associated with quantifying performances or their products. One concerns objectivity versus subjectivity. It must be kept in mind that subjective judgment is not completely avoided by merely assigning numerical values to a product. If the performance or its product is not quantified, however, we cannot proceed with statistical analyses; thus we reduce the amount of information otherwise available for making effective instructional decisions. A second fallacy concerns the restrictions placed on creativity if the performance or its product is quantified. By identifying components too narrowly or too precisely, so the argument goes, creativity, imaginative responses, and novel ideas may go unrewarded. This can be avoided by providing for unique and unexpected responses either within a component or as a separate component.

Case studies 1 and 2 follow the appendix. In the first question of Case 1 and the third question of Case 2 the reader should provide for creative responses on the part of the student.

REFERENCES

Davis, Frederick B. *Educational Measurements and Their Interpretation.* Belmont, Calif.: Wadsworth Publishing Company, 1964. Chapter 1, "Measurement and Its Uses in Schools," is a brief discussion of assignment of measurement values by grouping, ranking, and fixed numerical values.

Dyer, Henry S. "Educational Measurement—Its Nature and Its Problems," in *Evaluation in Social Studies,* ed. H. D. Berg. Washington, D. C.: Thirty-fifth Yearbook, National Council for the Social Studies, 1965. Chapter 1 emphasizes problems related to obtaining quantitative data in educational measurement.

Stevens, S. S. "On the Theory of Scales of Measurement." *Science* 103 (1946), 677–680. The article is a classic discussion of the different scales used in measurement.

Tyler, L. E. *Tests and Measurement.* Englewood Cliffs, N. J.: Prentice-Hall, 1963. Chapter 1 briefly discusses quantification of behavioral characteristics.

2.
DESCRIPTIVE INTERPRETATION OF
RAW SCORES

Now that a performance or the product of a performance can be quantified, what does the number as a value mean? Let us take the case of Ronald, who received a total of 58 points on a task assigned to the class. What do 58 points signify about Ronald's work? If your immediate response is "I don't know," you are on the right track. You will need further information before 58 will have any meaning.

LIST SOME OF THE THINGS YOU WOULD WANT TO KNOW. ____

It makes little difference in what order you think of these items. Each adds meaning to 58.

1. Did you want to know the total possible points on the task? A score of 58 points out of 100 possible points would mean one thing. A score of 58 points out of 60 possible points alters the picture considerably.

2. Did you inquire about the range of the scores? A class range of 0 to

100, 0 to 60, 50 to 100, or 50 to 60 gives a different value to Ronald's 58 points.

3. Did you mention the position of 58 relative to other scores in the class? Ronald's position in relation to his class (the *norming group* in this case) helps to determine the value of his points. The 58 points may fall into either the upper or lower half of the class. It could represent one of the top 10 percent of the scores or a typical score. There is another aspect to the question. If Ronald were a seventh grader, 58 points out of 100 on a seventh-grade mathematics computation test might not indicate a satisfactory level of performance in relation to the seventh-grade class. But if Ronald were a fourth grader, 58 points on the same test would tell another story about his performance.

NORMING GROUP is a designated group whose performance or product of performance on a particular characteristic is used as a standard of comparison.

Examples: Eighth-grade boys at Central Junior High; students enrolled in eastern high schools with less than 1,500 students; primary students from bilingual homes.

---

4. Did you ask about the position of raw score 58 in relation to *frequency?* It helps to know how many other students received 58 points or to know what were the most frequently obtained scores.

FREQUENCY is the number of cases observed for any one score in a set of scores. The statistical symbol f is used to designate the term frequency.

Example: $f = 5$ would mean that five cases having the same score were observed in a set of scores. It does not indicate the raw score.

Position alone will not always give an accurate assessment of performance. This will become evident on examining the three sets of scores shown below. Ronald's raw score is pointed out in each set.

Set A	Set B	Set C
89	89	62
58 (Ronald)	88	60
57	87	59
56	65	59

Set A	Set B	Set C
45	62	58
37	61	58 (Ronald)
37	60	58
32	60	58
25	59	58
24	59	57
23	58 (Ronald)	57
17	32	56

DESCRIBE RONALD'S POSITION IN RELATION TO EACH OF THE ABOVE SETS OF SCORES. (Use such terms as high, low, and so on.)

Set A. _____

Set B. _____

Set C. _____

IS RONALD'S PERFORMANCE MOST SIMILAR TO THE GROUP ON THE TOP, MIDDLE, OR BOTTOM?

Set A. _____

Set B. _____

Set C. _____

If your responses are similar to the following comments, you are on target. In Set A, Ronald is next to the top; in Set B, he is near the bottom; in Set C, he is somewhere in the middle. Although Ronald's position differs in the three sets of scores, when evaluating his performance in relation to the class, we would conclude that in Set A Ronald's raw score is more *representative* of the average than of the top raw score. In Set B, his raw score is more representative of average than the bottom. In Set C, his score is again representative of the average raw score.

REPRESENTATIVE: A representative score is the one most typical of a set of scores. "Typical" and "representative" are used interchangeably. The term "average" is reserved for a statistical concept having a specific quantitative value. See Chapter 4 for a discussion of "average."

---

5. Did you inquire whether "58" represented a measure of learning on a new task, or was it a score on a task where mastery could be expected? Knowing more about the performance expectations or a priori standards would give further meaning to the score. Expanding on the issue of mastery leads to the sixth question.

6. Did you inquire about the *criterion level* of acceptable performance?

A score of 58 may be the highest score in a class out of a total possible score of 80, but the criterion level for acceptable performance could be 75 points.

CRITERION LEVEL is a standard of performance or product of performance that is established on the basis of achievement of the requisite skills or understandings for mastery.

Example: Correct answers to 70 percent of the test items may indicate adequate comprehension on a story at the primary reading level for first graders, but, on the other hand, 100 percent mastery of the requisite skills is required of medical students before they can perform open-heart surgery.

---

7. Did you question whether 58 points represent a subscore on some performance or the total score? The raw score may subsume five subscores. Ronald's 58 points could indicate many things about his performance. He may have earned all his points on two of the components and have responded incorrectly on the three other components.

8. Did you want to know about Ronald's past performance? It may well be that 58 points is at the low end of the class scores, but for Ronald this indicates a sizable increment of progress based on past performance.

9. Check the other responses you might have given. See if the information adds meaning to the raw score.

Information obtained from answers to each of the questions provides additional data for understanding Ronald's performance. And the third, sixth, and eighth questions present information on educational achievement from three different perspectives: the third is normative-referenced (based on a given norming group); the sixth is criterion-referenced (based on a given level of mastery); and the eighth is self-referenced (based on the individual's rate of growth).

A principal, in evaluating his faculty, assigns a number of points to each component making up effective teaching. As he evaluates the scores, he views the performance from three perspectives. He certainly measures a teacher's performance in terms of the whole faculty. The teacher may be considered among the best, may be performing about at the level of most of the other teachers in the building, or may be below par for the group. The "best" for his school could represent only mediocre performance when compared with other schools in the district. The principal also views a teacher's performance from a standard based on what he has found to constitute effective teaching.

He may find a teacher's performance par for the faculty, but still regard the performance inadequate for effective teaching. Finally the principal evaluates performance from the standpoint of improvement, especially in the case of the younger faculty.

The raw score derives its meaning from the context and perspective through which it is examined. The following four chapters introduce mathematical and statistical procedures that extend the analysis and interpretation of a performance or its product in order to enhance educational decision making.

The case studies for Chapter 2 involve the reader in making instructional decisions from a set of raw scores, and, where decisions are not possible to make, to indicate awareness of the type of information needed to make the decision.

REFERENCES

Ahmann, J. Stanley, and Glock, Marvin P. *Evaluating Pupil Growth.* Boston: Allyn and Bacon, 1967. The raw score is discussed (pp. 246-252) as a source of evaluation data. The authors cover the difficulties that arise when one compares raw scores obtained from different sets of data.

Cronbach, Lee J. *Essentials of Psychological Testing.* New York: Harper and Row, 1960. A short section in Chapter 4 (pp. 69-72) deals with interpretation of raw scores.

Ebel, Robert L. "Content Standard Test Scores." *Educational and Psychological Measurement* (No. 22, 1962), 15-25. Ebel discusses the value of the raw score as a source of information. It is essential to know the content from which the raw score serves as a quantitative representation.

Gardner, Eric F. "Normative Standard Scores." *Ibid.,* 7-14. This is a companion piece to the Ebel article above. Gardner discusses the inadequacy of a raw score in providing useful information without considering the raw score in a normative framework.

3.
USE OF GRAPHS IN INTERPRETING RAW SCORES

In Chapter 2 a set of raw scores was ordered from high score to low score, and statements were made on the basis of observation about the relationship among the scores. The reader derived some information about the general performance of the group and about individuals within the group. Graphs are another way to represent visually the distribution of a set of scores. Coordinate graphs add an important visual dimension to the scores. In addition to the scores being arranged in some numerical order, they are also arranged by frequency. A point on a graph tells the reader two things: the raw score and the frequency with which the score appears.

Examine Figures 3-1, 3-2, and 3-3. The data are taken from the three sets of scores discussed in Chapter 2. Though the graphs are labeled similarly, they represent different sets of scores.

WHAT PROPERTY OF A SET OF SCORES IS SHOWN IN THE THREE GRAPHS ON THE HORIZONTAL AXIS? _____

WHAT PROPERTY IS SHOWN ON THE VERTICAL AXIS? _____

By convention, the raw scores are shown on the horizontal axis or X axis, and frequency or percent is shown on the vertical axis or Y axis.

Given either property of a point on the graph, you can determine its other property.

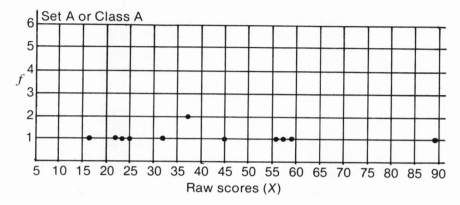

Figure 3-1
Raw scores for Set A by frequency

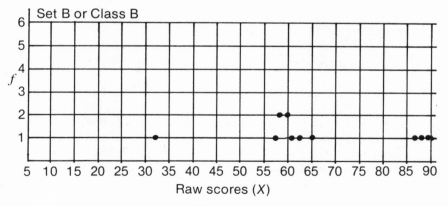

Figure 3-2
Raw scores for Set B by frequency

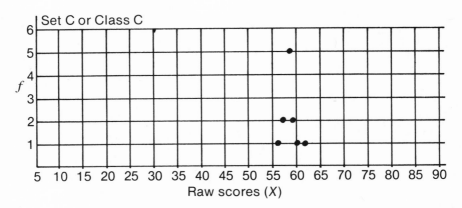

Figure 3-3

Raw scores for Set C by frequency

IN FIGURE 3-1, SET A, WHAT SCORE HAS A GREATER FREQUENCY THAN ONE? $X =$ _____

IN FIGURE 3-2, SET B, WHAT ARE THE PROPERTIES OF THE LOWEST SCORE? $X =$ _____ and $f =$ _____

IN FIGURE 3-3, SET C, HOW FREQUENTLY DOES THE RAW SCORE 58 APPEAR? $f =$ _____

- -

Responses to the above questions should read: $X = 37$; $X = 32$, $f = 1$; and $f = 5$.

Through graphs, large amounts of data are represented in a form that facilitates analysis of the data. Let us say that Figures 3-1, 3-2, and 3-3 show the frequency distribution of scores obtained by the students taking the same test in three different classrooms. The graphs are constructed on the same vertical and horizontal scales, which makes it convenient to compare the performance of the three classes.

LIST THE KINDS OF STATEMENTS THAT CAN BE MADE IN COMPARING PERFORMANCE IN THE THREE CLASSES._____

_____

Your list could include some of the following statements:

1. Class A has the largest range of scores.

2. Except for the extreme scores, students in Class B and Class C performed similarly.

3. Students in Class C performed more like each other than students in either of the other two classes.

4. Students in Class A did not perform, as a whole, as well as students in Class B and Class C.

5. Students in Class B fall into three distinctive achievement groups.

6. Small-group instruction and individual assignments appear appropriate for Class A.

Up to this point we have explored points on a coordinate graph using a small set of data. For a large number of scores, say 30 or more, it is often necessary to group scores in such a way as to reduce the number of scores that are handled. A method for grouping scores to facilitate handling large numbers is discussed next, and then types of graphic representation most commonly used with classroom and system-wide data are explored.

To reduce the number of individual scores in a set of scores, the scores are grouped in *intervals*. As an example, given a range of scores from 40 to 80, an interval size of 3 units is chosen. All scores falling within any interval of that size are grouped together: 40-42, 43-45, . . . 79-81. The numbers of scores within a specific interval are indicated as frequencies rather than as specific scores. The interval now takes the place of the actual scores.

INTERVAL is the distance between two points identified by the lower limit and the upper limit of a designated number of units. When scores are grouped by intervals, the scores falling within the interval are shown as frequencies.

Example: You are given 48 scores ranging from 1 through 80. If the interval size (i) is set as 10 units, the intervals are: 1-10, 11-20, 21-30, 31-40, 41-50, 51-60, 61-70, and 71-80. The scores 23, 25, 25, and 29 are not shown individually, but the interval 21-30 is shown with a frequency of 4.

You do have to pay for the advantage gained in working with a reduced number of scores, and you have to trade off this advantage for a disadvantage in grouping scores in intervals.

WHAT DO YOU SEE AS A POSSIBLE DISADVANTAGE IN GROUP-
ING SCORES IN INTERVALS? _____

_____

_____

An individual score loses some of its identity by becoming a part of an interval; hence there is some loss of information. In the example in the definition box, scores of 23 and of 29 are treated the same way, that is, two scores in the interval 21-30. Many teachers feel the loss is negligible compared to the computational errors that are likely to occur in handling large amounts of data.

Selecting the appropriate interval size (i) is more than guesswork. You will want to consider three things: the amount of information that may be lost; the number of intervals that is most convenient to work with computationally; and the range of the set of scores. The larger the size of the interval, the greater the loss of information. The greater the number of intervals, the more numbers that need to be handled. The larger the range between the highest and lowest score, the greater the need to balance the interval size with the number of intervals in order to accommodate both sources of difficulty—information loss and computational error.

The principals of a midwestern school district were asked to compile data on the number of days parents volunteered their services to their respective schools. Table 3-1 shows a set of 96 scores representing the number of days individual parents assisted in the classroom, lunchroom, library, office, or on field trips in one of the schools. The ninety-six fathers or mothers who volunteered their services made up 40 percent of the families whose children were enrolled in the school.

Table 3-1

Number of days each of ninety-six parents volunteered
in the school during the school year

72	26	15	8	4	2
60	25	15	8	4	2
48	23	14	7	4	2
47	21	13	7	4	2
36	21	13	7	4	2
36	21	12	7	4	1
36	21	12	7	3	1
36	19	11	6	3	1
34	18	10	6	3	1
33	18	10	6	3	1
30	17	10	6	3	1
30	16	10	6	3	1
30	16	9	6	3	1
29	16	9	6	3	1
27	15	9	5	2	1
27	15	9	5	2	1

Table 3-2

Days parents volunteered in school during school year in frequency

Days	Tallies	f	Days	Tallies	f	Days	Tallies	f
72	/	1	25	/	1	11	/	1
60	/	1						
48	/	1						
47	/	1						
36	/ / / /	4						
26	/	1						

COMPLETE TABLE 3-2 BY ARRANGING THE NUMBER OF DAYS
PARENTS VOLUNTEER AS TALLY MARKS AND BY FREQUENCY.
HOW MANY DIFFERENT SCORES ARE SHOWN IN THE FIGURE
YOU HAVE COMPLETED? _____

By arranging the scores according to frequency, the principal has considerably reduced the number of scores to be handled. Only 33 different
scores appear in the frequency table instead of the 96 scores found in
Table 3-1.

The number of scores can be further reduced by grouping the remaining
scores into intervals. The following steps will help you to find the appropriate
interval size.

FINDING THE APPROPRIATE INTERVAL SIZE:
1. Determine the range by subtracting the lowest score from the
highest score.
    Range = (high score – low score), or
$$R = X_{hi} - X_{lo}$$
2. Divide the range by the number of intervals convenient to handle.
This will give the interval size (i).
    interval size = range/number of intervals, or
$$i = R/N$$
3. If the interval size is predetermined, then to find the number of
intervals divide the range by the interval size.
$$N = R/i$$

The principal wants to reduce the number of scores or cases he is handling. He decides to group the scores into intervals.

WHAT INTERVAL SIZE DO YOU SUGGEST THE PRINCIPAL
USE? HOW MANY INTERVALS WILL THIS GIVE HIM TO WORK
WITH? EXPLAIN YOUR REASON FOR THE INTERVAL SIZE. ____

Let us say the principal decided to work with 10 intervals. To determine the interval size he uses the formula:

$$i = R/N \qquad i = (72-1)/10 \qquad i = 71/10, \text{ or}$$
$$i = 7.1$$

The interval size should be rounded off to the nearest whole number, in this case 7. The principal has decided, however, that an interval size of 7 may conceal too much information. He prefers a predetermined interval size of 5 inasmuch as this will display more scores, and grouping scores in intervals of five units immediately feeds back the information in weeks. For every five days, a parent has volunteered one week's service.

From the frequency data in Table 3-2, the principal constructs Table 3-3 which shows the days volunteered in intervals. First he computes the number of intervals:

$$N = (72-1)/5; \quad N = 14.2, \text{ or } 15 \text{ intervals}$$

Table 3-3

Days volunteered by parents in interval frequency

Intervals ($i = 5$)	f
71 - 75	1
66 - 70	0
61 - 65	0
56 - 60	1
51 - 55	0
46 - 50	2
41 - 45	0
36 - 40	4
31 - 35	2
26 - 30	7
21 - 25	6
16 - 20	7
11 - 15	10
6 - 10	21
1 - 5	35
Total number of scores	96

Now the principal is ready to construct a graph showing the number of days volunteered by frequency. To do so he needs to determine the midpoint of the intervals. The midpoint is the halfway point of an interval, and it is the point that represents the interval on the graph. The midpoint of the interval 1–5 is shown below:

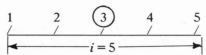

For the interval 1–5, the midpoint is 3. Figure 3-4 presents the graph of the data in Table 3-3. The midpoints of the intervals are connected by a straight line. The resulting figure is called a *frequency polygon* or line graph.

> FREQUENCY POLYGON or LINE GRAPH is a figure illustrating the relationship between scores and frequency (or percent) represented on a coordinate plane. Each point on the graph is connected to the succeeding one, usually with a straight line.

The principal could have used another type of graph for the data in Table 3-3. He could have constructed a *bar graph*, which differs from the frequency polygon along the horizontal axis. In the bar graph the intervals are shown on the horizontal axis rather than the interval midpoints. Figure 3-5 illustrates a bar graph of the days volunteered by parents.

> BAR GRAPH or HISTOGRAM is formed by drawing a vertical bar on a scale representing the limits of an interval and raised to the height of the corresponding frequency.

SHOULD THE PRINCIPAL USE A BAR GRAPH OR A FREQUENCY POLYGON TO REPRESENT THE FREQUENCY DISTRIBUTION OF THE DATA? _____

_____

- -

It is a matter of preference. With interval grouped data, the bar graph saves one step: the midpoint of each interval does not have to be calculated. When scores are not grouped in intervals, then the frequency polygon is the appropriate graph to use to represent the distribution of scores.

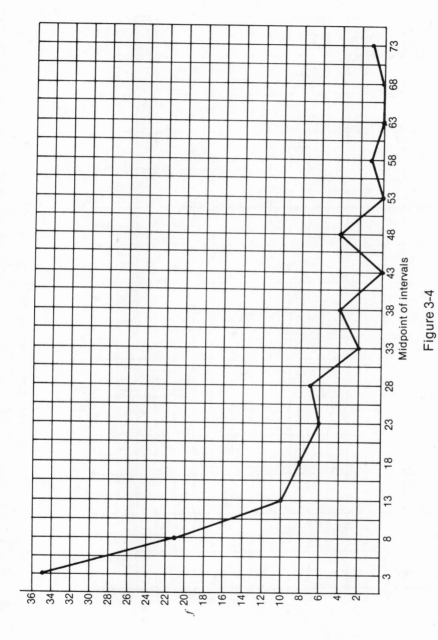

Figure 3-4

Frequency polygon of days volunteered by parents

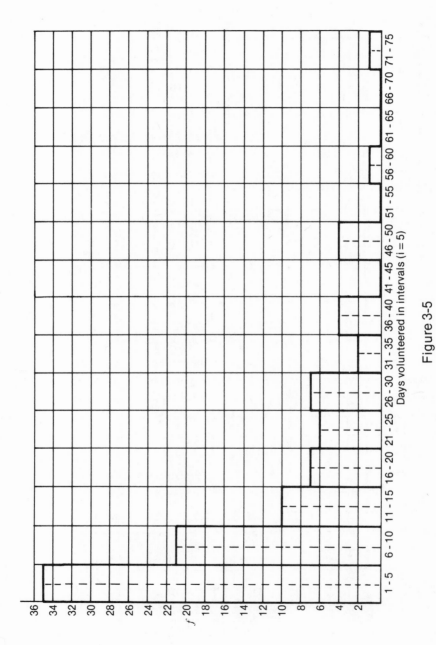

Figure 3-5

Bar graph of days volunteered by parents

Up to this point we have dealt with only one type of scale for quantifying values—an *interval scale.* The interval scale measures continuous values in equivalent units. Each day is of equivalent value and can be measured on a continuous scale. Scores on a test simulate an interval scale if we assume that each additional point represents an additional but equal increment of learning.

INTERVAL SCALE has numerically quantifiable values that are continuous and of equal units of measurement.

Example: The yardstick is an interval scale where each unit of an inch is of equal value to every other unit of an inch.

Two other types of scales are used with classroom and system-wide data: *nominal scales* and *ordinal scales.* The first has mutually excluding categories, while the second implies an order on a continuum. The data are ranked along defined categories that may or may not be of equal units or values.

NOMINAL SCALE is defined by mutually excluding categories or classes.

Examples: sex—male and female; primary colors—red, blue, and yellow; personnel—academic and nonacademic.

ORDINAL SCALE classifies data in a definite order within categories that can be described on a continuum. The categories may or may not be of equal units.

Examples: high, average, and low; always, frequently, sometimes, and never.

The bar graph can be used in imaginative ways to represent visually nominal and ordinal data and to summarize large quantities of data. Figure 3-6 illustrates the results of a district-wide poll of parents concerning their views on starting a hot lunch program. Figure 3-7 summarizes the results of a poll of parents to evaluate an ongoing hot lunch program.

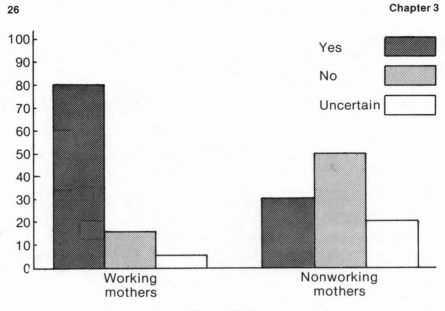

Figure 3-6

Poll of parents on hot lunch program (in percents)

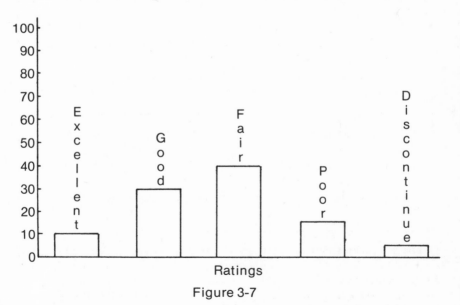

Ratings

Figure 3-7

Parents' evaluation of the hot lunch program (in percents)

EXAMINE FIGURES 3-6 and 3-7. WHICH GRAPH USES A NOMINAL SCALE? _____

ON THE BASIS OF THE GRAPH SHOWN IN FIGURE 3-6, SHOULD THE SUPERINTENDENT MOVE TOWARD A DISTRICT-WIDE HOT LUNCH PROGRAM? _____

_____

_____

_____

_____

WHAT CAN THE SUPERINTENDENT CONCLUDE ABOUT THE HOT LUNCH PROGRAM EVALUATED BY THE PARENTS FROM THE GRAPH IN FIGURE 3-7? _____

_____

_____

_____

_____

_____

The graph shown in Figure 3-6 is based on a nominal scale. The categories are mutually exclusive; the working mother either votes "yes," "no," or "uncertain," as does the other separate group, the nonworking mothers. The superintendent does not have an overwhelming mandate to start a hot lunch program. The working mothers and the nonworking mothers appear to view a hot lunch program differently. There is evidence, at least from the working mothers, that a hot lunch program is desirable. Because they are a separate constituency from the nonworking mothers, the superintendent will have to respond positively to their needs. Half the nonworking mothers voted against the hot lunch program. The superintendent will have to probe further in to the meaning of the negative vote. Are these mothers categorically opposed to a hot lunch program, or are they only indicating that they do not have a need for such a program?

The graph in Figure 3-7 shows that 80 percent of the parents rate the hot lunch program as "fair" or better. On the basis of this evidence, the superintendent can feel that the program has the support of the parents. If, however, the superintendent reads the graph another way, he could conclude that 60 percent of the parents are not very enthusiastic about the program. The graph certainly indicates that there are definite areas for improvement in the program.

A graph is an excellent tool for teachers and administrators to use to order and summarize data. A study of a graphic representation of data can highlight strengths and weaknesses and point up similarities and differences. Of most importance, a graph can suggest further questions that need to be raised in order to ferret out additional information. Nominal and ordinal data as well as interval data can be graphed.

The case studies for Chapter 3 give the teacher additional practice in constructing a graph, analyzing the graphic representations, making instructional or organizational decisions based on the graph, and using nominal and ordinal data.

REFERENCES

Blank, Stanley S. *Descriptive Statistics.* New York: Appleton-Century-Crofts, 1968. Histograms and polygons are developed in a simple programmed learning approach (pp. 31–45).

Downie, N. M., and Heath, R. W. *Basic Statistical Methods,* 2d edition. New York: Harper and Row, 1965. Frequency distributions and graphs are the subject of Chapter 3. Types of curves as represented by skewness and kurtosis are developed.

Klugh, Henry E. *Statistics: The Essentials for Research.* New York: John Wiley and Sons, 1970. Chapter 2 presents graphing distributions and cumulative graphing.

Spence, Janet T., Underwood, Benton J., Duncan, Carl P., and Cotton, John W. *Elementary Statistics,* 2d edition. New York: Appleton-Century-Crofts, 1968. Chapter 3 has a precise discussion of graphic representation.

4.

USE OF STATISTICS IN INTERPRETING RAW SCORES

Up to this point interpretation of raw scores has been based on ordering the scores and noting the position of a single score or cluster of scores in relation to other scores in a set. Graphs assisted in focusing attention on the proximity and distance of scores to one another. Sets of scores were also compared in this manner. Deviant scores as well as representative scores were identified by ordering a set of scores from high to low or by constructing a graph of the data and inspecting the characteristics of the distribution. Although we can obtain information from examining a set of raw scores, the amount of information about the individual in relation to his group or one group to another is limited. Neither graphs nor cursory examination of ordered scores can determine with exactness the differences and similarities among scores and between sets of scores. To obtain further information, the distribution of the scores is examined in terms of its tendency to cluster within a particular area as well as the extent to which scores tend to deviate from the cluster. Thus, this chapter focuses on two concepts: central tendency and deviation.

CENTRAL TENDENCY OF A SET OF SCORES

Three terms are commonly used to describe scores with respect to their relation to a clustering pattern that gives a measure of the central tendency of a distribution. Each term emphasizes a different aspect of the central tendency.

The *mode* is simply an identification of the most frequently observed score in a set of scores. It has limited value in adding information about a set of scores. Some frequency distributions have more than one score that appears with pronounced frequency. Where two scores reoccur frequently in a set of scores the distribution is called bimodal.

MODE is the most frequently occurring score in a set of scores; and a bimodal distribution has two scores that are frequently observed.

Example: Given a set of scores—45, 42, 39, 39, 39, 35, 32, 32, 32, 32, 32, 27, and 18—the mode is 32 for it is the most frequently occurring score in the set. The distribution could be described as bimodal, 39 being the second most frequently occurring score.

The midpoint or halfway position in a distribution is called the *median.* Any score can be described as being above or below the median. The median is directly related to the number of scores in the distribution.

MEDIAN is the midpoint or midposition of a distribution. Mdn is the abbreviation commonly used to denote the median.

Computing the Median (Mdn):
1. Order the raw scores from high to low.
2. Determine the number of scores in the set of scores (N).
3. Divide N by 2 ($N/2$) if N is an even number, or divide ($N + 1$) by 2 ($N + 1)/2$ if N is an odd number.
4. The resulting quotient is used to determine the midpoint by counting down from the top score by the amount of the quotient or up from the bottom score by the same amount.

Examples: a. Given an even number of scores in the set (16, 15, 14, 13, 10, 6, 4, 4, 3, and 1):
1. Order the scores from high to low.
2. $N = 10$
3. $N/2 = 10/2 = 5$
4. Count down five scores from the top. The midpoint of the distribution falls between two scores, $X = 10$ and $X = 6$. To determine the midpoint between the two scores, add the scores and divide by 2: $(10 + 6)/2 = 16/2 = 8$.
The Mdn is 8.

   b. Given an odd number of scores in the set (15, 14, 13, 10, 6, 4, 4, 3, and 1):

1. Order the scores from high to low.
2. $N = 9$
3. Add 1 to N and divide by 2:

$$(N + 1)/2 = (9 + 1)/2 = 5$$

4. Count down five scores from the top score or five scores up from the bottom score.
The Mdn for this distribution is 6.

The *mean* is the combined quantitative value of all raw scores divided by the number of scores in the set. It is the average numerical value that each raw score contributes to the total set of scores.

MEAN is the arithmetic average of a set of scores. $\overline{X}$ (X bar) is the statistical symbol used to designate the mean. Σ (the Greek capital letter sigma) signifies the summation of a set of scores.

Computing the Mean $(\overline{X})$:

1. ΣX Sum up the raw scores (add the scores): 50, 40, 30, 20, and 10,
$50 + 40 + 30 + 20 + 10 = 150$, or,
$\Sigma(50, 40, 30, 20, 10) = 150$.
2. $\overline{X} = (\Sigma X)/N$ Divide the summed scores by the total number of scores (N).

Example: Given a set of 10 raw scores (86, 74, 63, 62, 59, 54, 54, 50, 47, 31):

1. Find the sum of the 10 scores: $\Sigma X = 580$

$$\Sigma(86, 74, 63, 62, 59, 54, 54, 50, 47, 31) = 580, \text{ or}$$

$$86 + 74 + 63 + 62 + 59 + 54 + 54 + 50 + 47 + 31 = 580$$

2. Divide the sum by 10:

$$\Sigma X/N = 580/10 = 58$$

$$\overline{X} = 58$$

By obtaining the mode, the median, and the mean we have increased the amount of information needed to interpret a set of scores or any single score within a set.

The two sets of scores shown in Table 4-1 were obtained from a ninth-grade teacher's quantification of panel discussions. Four components made up each score: presentation of a clearly stated position; willingness to hear out another point of view; framing of a rebuttal; and the ability to summarize an argument. A total of 20 points was possible.

EXAMINE BOTH SETS OF SCORES. DESCRIBE THE PERFORM-
ANCE OF X_7 IN EACH SET.

Set A:_____

Set B: _____

Table 4-1

Scores of students participating in a
ninth-grade panel discussion

Student	Set A	Set B
X_1	16	16
X_2	15	15
X_3	13	13
X_4	13	12
X_5	12	12
X_6	12	12
X_7	12	6
X_8	11	2
X_9	8	1
X_{10}	8	1

Your description should include something about the differences in range between Sets A and B, and in general terms something about the modes, medians, and means, and identification of deviant scores where this is appropriate.

NOW COMPUTE THE MODE, MEDIAN, AND MEAN OF EACH SET.

Central tendency	Set A	Set B
Mode		
Mdn		
$\bar{X}$		

WHAT NEW INFORMATION HAS BEEN ADDED TO EACH SET?

_____

_____

_____

_____

A description of the central tendency is made more explicit by using the information obtained from the mode, median, and mean. For Set A* the mode $= 12$; Mdn $= 12$; and $\bar{X} = 12$. For Set B the mode $= 12$; Mdn $= 12$; and $\bar{X} = 9$.

EXAMINE BOTH SETS OF SCORES AGAIN USING THE ADDED INFORMATION FROM THE CENTRAL TENDENCY STATISTICS.

a. WHAT CAUSED THE MEAN OF SET B TO DIFFER FROM THE MEAN OF SET A? _____

_____

b. IF YOU WERE EXPLAINING SET A SCORES TO THE PARENTS OF X_7, WOULD THE MEAN OR THE MEDIAN GIVE A BETTER PICTURE OF HIS PERFORMANCE?
MEAN_____   MEDIAN_____

c. IF YOU WERE EXPLAINING SET B TO THE PARENTS OF X_7, WOULD THE MEAN OR THE MEDIAN GIVE A BETTER PICTURE OF HIS PERFORMANCE?
MEAN_____   MEDIAN_____

---

*To compute the median and mean of Set A:

$$N/2 \text{ (for even number of scores in a set)}$$
$$10/2 = 5$$

Count five scores down from the top score. The Mdn lies between the fifth and sixth score. Since both scores are 12, the median is 12.

$$\bar{X} = (\Sigma X)/N$$
$$= \Sigma(16, 15, 13, 13, 12, 12, 12, 11, 8, 8)/10$$
$$= 120/10 = 12$$

d. IF YOU WERE EXPLAINING THE PERFORMANCE OF THE TOTAL GROUP IN BOTH SETS A AND B, WHICH WOULD GIVE A BETTER PICTURE OF THE CENTRAL TENDENCY OF THE GROUP, THE MEAN OR THE MEDIAN?
MEAN_____   MEDIAN_____

----

a. Set B has several extremely low scores, which tend to lower the mean of the set.

b., c., and d. The responses to these items can best be answered by the chart below:

Set	Class	Individual
A	$\bar{X}$ or Mdn	$\bar{X}$ or Mdn
B	Mdn	$\bar{X}$ and Mdn

If there are extreme scores (deviant cases) in a set of scores, the median will give a parent a better picture of the performance of the class. The median is less affected by extreme cases than the mean. A clearer picture of performance of an individual is obtained when both statistics are available.

Frequently principals and superintendents report to parents and to the community the results of school- and district-wide testing. It is generally a good rule to report the median rather than the mean, for the latter is sensitive to the deviant scores and may distort somewhat the overall performance of the group. The median can also be misinterpreted by the general public unless the concept itself is fully understood. Many superintendents have been vilified in the press because half the students perform below the median (using district-wide norms). That is, however, the crux of the concept: in every group half of the students perform below the median.

THE DEVIATION OF A SET OF SCORES

From the comparison of the distribution of scores in Sets A and B, it was evident that the range of the scores within a set could affect the mean of the scores. By contrast with the mean (which measures the central tendency of a distribution), the range gives a rough picture of the scatter or variability of the distribution.

There are times when two very different distributions will yield the same means. Consider this situation. A principal is testing several grouping arrangements in the middle grades. In mathematics Class X he has assigned students of the same age and similar ability in the subject. Class Y is designated as a multigrade-multiage intermediate group. The scores of the two classes on a standardized mathematics test at the end of the year show the following distribution characteristics.

Class X: $\bar{X} = 72$
            Mdn $= 70$
            Range $= 25$
Class Y: $\bar{X} = 72$
            Mdn $= 70$
            Range $= 80$

WHAT CONCLUSION CAN YOU DRAW FROM THESE STATIS-
TICS? _____
_____
_____

Although the means and the medians are the same, the range of the classes differ greatly. There is more variability in performance in Class Y than in Class X. The results are highly plausible: the students in Class X have similar ability in mathematics, which is reflected by the narrower range than that found among the students in Class Y, who represent a wider range of ability.

Variability is a key concept in understanding performance. Because all individuals and all groups perform somewhat differently, curriculum and instructional planning as well as designing the school organization must take variability into consideration. To obtain a more accurate measure of the variability of a distribution than that provided by the range, we turn to a statistical concept called the *standard deviation*.

STANDARD DEVIATION is a measure of the variability of a set of scores from the mean. *SD* is the symbol used to denote the standard deviation; other symbols are also used, such as σ or s. The Greek lowercase letter sigma (σ) refers to the standard deviation of a population, and s refers to an unbiased estimate of a population's *SD* based on a sample of the population.

Computing the Standard Deviation:
1. ΣX Compute sum of the scores.
2. $\Sigma X/N$ Calculate the mean.
3. $(X - \bar{X})$ Subtract the mean from each of the raw

	scores. This is called the deviation of the raw scores from the mean.
4. $(X - \bar{X})^2$	Square each of the deviation scores. This is called the squared deviation.
5. $\Sigma(X - \bar{X})^2$	Compute the sum of the squared deviations.
6. $\Sigma(X - \bar{X})^2/N = SD^2$, or σ^2	Divide the sum of the squared deviation scores by N. This gives the average of the squared deviations. SD^2 is called the variance.
7. $\sqrt{\Sigma(X - \bar{X})^2/N} = SD$, or σ	Take the square root of the variance. This is the standard deviation or index of the variability of the distribution.

The formula for computing the standard deviation outlined above is based on scores from a population, such as all third-grade students in the school system, or all boys. Many of the school data, however, are taken from a sample of the total population; one third-grade class from each school in the district. A sample's variance tends to be smaller than that of the total population's variance. A correction is made in the formula by dividing by $(N - 1)$ instead of N (for scores from a sample).

$$SD^2 = \Sigma(X - \bar{X})^2/(N - 1)$$

$$SD = \sqrt{\Sigma(X - \bar{X})^2/(N - 1)}$$

Before computing a standard deviation using actual data, the reader should consult the following pages, which review the arithmetic operations (addition, subtraction, multiplication and division) with positive and negative numbers. If the reader feels the review is unnecessary, he should omit these sections and go on to the subsequent sections.

ADDITION AND SUBTRACTION OF
POSITIVE AND NEGATIVE NUMBERS

All numbers larger than 0 are called positive numbers (+). As a rule we do not use any symbol to designate such a number, although we could show positive 2 as $^+2$. All numbers less than 0 are called negative numbers. We differentiate these from positive numbers with a negative symbol (-) A $^-2$ would be two places below 0. *

---

*It is unfortunate that the negative symbol is the same as that used to indicate the operation of subtraction. To distinguish the operation of subtraction from negative numbers, the negative symbol is shown near the top of the number, while the subtraction symbol is placed in the middle between two numbers. For example, 4 - 2 reads "4 take away 2," but $^-2$ reads "negative 2."

a. *Rules for Adding Positive Numbers*
   1. Add the value of the addends.
   2. The answer is positive.

   Example: $2 + 5 = 7$

b. *Rules for Adding Positive and Negative Numbers*
   1. Subtract the smaller number from the larger number, regardless of the sign of either number.
   2. The answer takes the sign of the larger number.

   Examples: $2 + {}^-5 = {}^-3$; ${}^-2 + 5 = 3$

c. *Rules for Adding Two Negative Numbers*
   1. Add the values of the numbers.
   2. The answer is negative.

   Example: ${}^-2 + {}^-5 = {}^-7$

d. *Rules for Subtraction*
   1. Change the sign of the subtrahend (number to be subtracted).
   2. Change the operation sign from subtraction to addition.
   3. Follow the proper addition rule.

   Examples:

   d.1. To subtract a positive number from a positive number:
   $$4 - 3 = 4 + {}^-3 = 1$$
   $$3 - 4 = 3 + {}^-4 = {}^-1$$

   d.2. To subtract a negative number from a positive number:
   $$4 - {}^-3 = 4 + 3 = 7$$

   d.3. To subtract a negative number from a negative number:
   $${}^-4 - {}^-3 = {}^-4 + 3 = {}^-1$$

   d.4. To subtract a positive number from a negative number:
   $${}^-4 - 3 = {}^-4 + {}^-3 = {}^-7$$

TRY THE TEN PROBLEMS ON THE FOLLOWING PAGE. GIVE THE RULE FOLLOWED FOR COMPUTING THE ANSWER. (The correct responses and rules are shown on the right-hand side of the page.)

		Response	Rule	Correct response	Rule
1.	4 + 6 =			10	a
2.	5 - 7 =			⁻2	d.1
3.	3 + ⁻4 =			⁻1	b
4.	7 - ⁻2 =			9	d.2
5.	4 - 1 =			3	d.1
6.	⁻7 + ⁻3 =			⁻10	c
7.	⁻6 + 2 =			⁻4	b
8.	⁻7 - 3 =			⁻10	d.4
9.	⁻7 - ⁻3 =			⁻4	d.3
10.	7 + ⁻2 =			5	b

MULTIPLICATION AND DIVISION OF POSITIVE AND NEGATIVE NUMBERS

a. *Rules for Multiplying and Dividing Positive Terms*
   1. Multiply or divide the terms as usual.
   2. The product (multiplication answer) and the quotient (division answer) will be positive.

   Examples: $6 \times 7 = 42$; $42/7 = 6$

b. *Rules for Multiplying and Dividing a Positive and a Negative Term*
   1. Multiply or divide the terms as usual.
   2. The answer will always be negative.

   Examples: $^-6 \times 7 = {^-}42$; $^-42/7 = {^-}6$

   $6 \times {^-}7 = {^-}42$; $42/{^-}7 = {^-}6$

c. *Rules for Multiplying and Dividing Negative Terms*
   1. Multiply or divide the terms as usual.
   2. The answer will always be positive.

   Examples: $^-6 \times {^-}7 = 42$; $^-42/{^-}7 = 6$

TRY THE PROBLEMS BELOW FOR PRACTICE AND GIVE THE MULTIPLICATION RULES WHERE APPLICABLE.

	Response	Rule	Correct response	Rule
1. $8^2 = 8 \times 8 =$			64	a
2. $15^2 = 15 \times 15 =$			225	a
3. $21^2 = \quad \times \quad =$			$21 \times 21 = 441$	a
4. $5^2 =$			25	a
5. $5 \times {}^-7 =$			${}^-35$	b
6. ${}^-5 \times 7 =$			${}^-35$	b
7. ${}^-5 \times {}^-7 =$			35	c
8. $5 \times 7 =$			35	a
9. $81/3 =$			27	a
10. ${}^-81/3 =$			${}^-27$	b
11. $81/{}^-3 =$			${}^-27$	b
12. ${}^-81/{}^-3 =$			27	c
13. $7 \times {}^-4 \times {}^-5 =$			140	c
*14. $(4 + 2) \times 3 =$			$6 \times 3 = 18$	
*15. $3 \times (6 + 1) =$			$3 \times 7 = 21$	
*16. $3 + 4 \times 5 =$			$3 + 20 = 23$	

---

*The arithmetic operation indicated within the parentheses is performed first, then the other operations are performed.

Problem 14: $(4 + 2) \times 3 =$
1. add the terms in the parentheses $(4 + 2) = 6$
2. proceed to the next operation $6 \times 3 = 18$

Unless indicated by parentheses, multiplication and division operations precede addition and subtraction operations.

Problem 16: $3 + 4 \times 5 =$
1. multiply the two terms on either side of the multiplication sign $4 \times 5 = 20$
2. proceed to the next operation as indicated $3 + 20 = 23$

COMPUTING A SQUARE ROOT (A table of square roots with a guide to its use is found in the appendix.)

Examples:

 a. $\sqrt{4372}$ b. $\sqrt{2.374}$

1. Mark off in groups of two the numbers to the right and to the left of the decimal point.

 a. $\sqrt{43\ 72.}$ b. $\sqrt{2.37\ 40}$

2. Find the largest number that when squared will go into the first two numbers grouped together.

$$\overset{6}{}$$
 a. $\sqrt{43\ 72.}$ b. $\overset{1}{\sqrt{2.37\ 40}}$

3. Square that number and place it directly under the first group. (This is the only time a term is squared.) Subtract.

 a. $\overset{6}{\sqrt{43\ 72.}}$ b. $\overset{1}{\sqrt{2.37\ 40}}$
    $\underline{36}$ $\underline{1}$
    7 1

4. Bring down the next group of numbers.

 a. $\overset{6}{\sqrt{43\ 72}}$ b. $\overset{1}{\sqrt{2.37\ 40}}$
    $\underline{36}$ $\underline{1}$
    $7\ 72$ $1\ 37$

5. A new division problem is formed by doubling what is now in the quotient, placing it alongside the new dividend. Leave a blank in both quotients to provide a place for the next term.

 a. $\overset{6}{\sqrt{43\ 72}}$ b. $\overset{1}{\sqrt{2.37\ 40}}$
    $\underline{36}$ $\underline{1}$
    $12\ |\ 7\ 72$ $2\ |\ 1\ 37$

6. Estimate what number reading 12? will divide into 772 in example a, and what number reading 2? will divide into 137 in example b.

```
          6 6                                        1. 5
   a. √ 43 72                                 b. √ 2.37 40
          36                                         1
   126 │ 7 72                                  25 │ 1 37
```

7. Multiply the divisor by the new term. Place the answer under the dividend. Subtract.

```
          6 6                                        1. 5
   a. √ 43 72                                 b.√ 2.37 40
          36                                         1
   126 │ 7 72                                  25 │ 1 37
         7 56                                        1 25
          16                                         12
```

8. Go back to the fourth step and repeat through the seventh step. The problem is carried out to as many places as desired. Example a is carried out to the first decimal place, and example b to the second decimal place.

```
          6 6. 1                                     1. 5 4
   a. √ 43 72. 00                             b. √ 2.37 40
          36                                         1
   126 │ 7 72                                  25 │ 1 37
         7 56                                        1 25
  1321 │   16 00                              304 │   12 40
          13 21                                       12 16
           2 79                                        24
   a. √ 4372.00 ≈66.1                         b. √ 2.374 ≈1.54
```

Using the seven steps given previously, we will compute the standard deviation for the scores in Set A: 16, 15, 13, 13, 12, 12, 12, 11, 8, and 8. As each step is described, refer to the work sheet to follow the computations involved.

1. Find the sum of the X's: ($\Sigma X = $). (See column 1 of the work sheet.)

2. Compute the mean: $\bar{X} = (\Sigma X)/N = $. (See column 1 of the work sheet.)

3. Find the deviation of each score from the mean $(X - \bar{X})$. (See column 2 of the work sheet.) Note that from X_8 through X_{10} a negative deviation is obtained. This indicates that the raw score is less than the mean, or it falls below the mean. (You are subtracting a larger number from a smaller number, resulting in a negative remainder.) The sum of column 2 equals zero: $\Sigma(X - \bar{X}) = 0$.

4. Find the square of each deviation $(X - \bar{X})^2$. (See column 3 of the work sheet.) Note that multiplying a ⁻1 by a ⁻1 gives a positive answer. (See the rules for multiplying positive and negative numbers given previously.)

5. Find the sum of the squared deviations: $\Sigma(X - \bar{X})^2 =$ ___ . Add all the numbers in column 3 of the work sheet.

6. Compute the variance: $\Sigma(X - \bar{X})^2/N =$ ___ . The variance is the average sum of the squared deviations.

7. Compute the standard deviation: $SD = \sqrt{\Sigma(X - \bar{X})^2/N} =$ ___ . Since all the scores have been squared, this step converts the quantity to its root. (The square root of a number can be obtained in several ways. To calculate the square root by hand, refer to the examples given previously. An easier method is to use a table of square roots. Such a table is provided in the appendix.)

Work Sheet for Computing Set A SD

Student	Raw score (column 1)	$(X - \bar{X})$ (column 2)	$(X - \bar{X})^2$ (column 3)
X_1	16	$(16-12) = 4$	$4 \times 4 = 16$
X_2	15	$(15-12) = 3$	$3 \times 3 = 9$
X_3	13	$(13-12) = 1$	$1 \times 1 = 1$
X_4	13	$(13-12) = 1$	$1 \times 1 = 1$
X_5	12	$(12-12) = 0$	$0 \times 0 = 0$
X_6	12	$(12-12) = 0$	$0 \times 0 = 0$
X_7	12	$(12-12) = 0$	$0 \times 0 = 0$
X_8	11	$(11-12) = {}^-1$	${}^-1 \times {}^-1 = 1$
X_9	8	$(8-12) = {}^-4$	${}^-4 \times {}^-4 = 16$
X_{10}	8	$(8-12) = {}^-4$	${}^-4 \times {}^-4 = 16$
	$\Sigma X = 120$	$\Sigma(X - \bar{X}) = 0$	$\Sigma(X - \bar{X})^2 = 60$
	$\bar{X} = 120/10$		
	$= 12$		

$SD^2 = \Sigma(X - \bar{X})^2/N$
$SD^2 = 60/10$
$SD^2 = 6$

$SD = \sqrt{\Sigma(X - \bar{X})^2/N}$
$SD = \sqrt{60/10} = \sqrt{6}$
$SD \approx 2.45$*

---

*The square root of 6 approximates 2.45, but does not equal it exactly. The symbol $\approx$ is used to signify an approximation.

USING THE SAME SEVEN STEPS FOR DERIVING THE STAN-
DARD DEVIATION, FIND THE *SD* FOR THE SET B SCORES: 16,
15, 13, 12, 12, 12, 6, 2, 1, and 1.

Work Sheet for Computing Set B *SD*

	Raw score (column 1)	$(X - \bar{X})$ (column 2)	$(X - \bar{X})^2$ (column 3)
X_1	16		
X_2			
X_3			
X_4			
X_5			
X_6			
X_7			
X_8			
X_9			
X_{10}			

$$\Sigma X = \underline{\quad} \qquad \Sigma(X - \bar{X}) = 0 \qquad \Sigma(X - \bar{X})^2 = \underline{\quad}$$
$$\bar{X} = \underline{\quad}$$
$$SD^2 = \Sigma(X - \bar{X})^2/N$$
$$SD^2 = \underline{\quad}$$
$$SD = \sqrt{\Sigma(X - \bar{X})^2/N}$$
$$SD = \underline{\quad}$$

Did your $SD \approx 5.60$? If not, let us backtrack to find the possible error. If
$\bar{X} = 9$, then check the deviation column (column 2) to make sure you subtracted 9 from each of the raw scores. Check the signs: X_7, X_8, X_9, and X_{10}
have negative deviations. The sum of column 2 should equal zero. If you
find no errors to this point, proceed to column 3. Recheck your multiplication. Each deviation is squared. There will be no negative numbers in
column 3. If everything is accurate to this point, the sum of the squared
deviations will be 314. The variance = 314/10. If the variance is correct,
the error is in finding the square root of 31.4. Recheck your hand
computation of the square root or recheck your reading of the table of
square roots. The square root of 31.4 is approximately 5.60.

INTERPRETING STANDARD DEVIATIONS

Once the *SD* is calculated, the distribution can be examined in many ways to help in understanding the performance and in planning for subsequent instruction. In Set A if a raw score deviates from the mean by 1 *SD*, it will lie 2.45 points above the mean or 2.45 points below the mean: $(\bar{X} + 1\ SD)$ or $(\bar{X} - 1\ SD)$. Substituting the values in the formula, scores in Set A that are 1 *SD* above or below the mean are: $(12 + 2.45 = 14.45)$ and $(12 - 2.45 = 9.55)$. In Set A four scores deviate more than 1 *SD* from the mean: X_1, X_2, X_9, and X_{10}. The first two scores are over 1 *SD* above the mean, and the last two scores are over 1 *SD* below the mean.

IN SET B HOW MANY SCORES DEVIATE 1 *SD* ABOVE THE MEAN? 1 *SD* BELOW THE MEAN?

$\bar{X} + 1\ SD = $ _____

$\bar{X} - 1\ SD = $ _____

Substituting the mean in Set B and the *SD* in the formula, you would find that 1 *SD* above the mean is 14.60 (9 + 5.60), and 1 *SD* below the mean is 3.40 (9 - 5.60). Two scores in Set B are greater than 1 *SD* above the mean, and three scores are lower than 1 *SD* below the mean.

Now that we have found the standard deviation of Sets A and B and have located scores that are 1 *SD* above or 1 *SD* below the mean, let us examine the statistic to see how it can be used in interpreting group and individual performance.

REVIEW PREVIOUS ANSWERS TO QUESTIONS ABOUT SETS A AND B. NOW COMPARE SETS A AND B USING THE ADDITIONAL STATISTICAL DATA PROVIDED BY THE STANDARD DEVIATIONS.

WHAT DOES THE STANDARD DEVIATION TELL YOU ABOUT THE PERFORMANCE OF X_5 IN EACH SET?

Set A: _____

Set B: _____

_____

The *SD* is the measure of variability of the scores in relation to the mean. By comparing Sets A and B you should have noted that the scores in Set A varied much less than those in Set B. The range of the scores could have told us this also, but the *SD* gives the exact average quantity by which the scores vary. Although X_5 received the same number of points in both sets, in relation to the specific group, his score was at the mean in Set A and 3 points above the mean in Set B. If his score varied from the mean of each set 1 *SD*, he would require a score of 14.45 in Set A and 14.60 in Set B. To use the *SD* in interpreting his score and comparing his performance across sets of scores, we need to put his raw score into *SD* units.

To compare the extent of the deviation between one score and another in a distribution or between scores in two different distributions, we need to convert the raw scores into standard deviation units. The score is converted into these units by setting up a ratio between the deviation of the score from its mean and the *SD*. We can compare the extent of the deviation of X_5 from the mean in Set A and Set B by setting up such a ratio.

$$X_5 \text{ (Set A): } (X_5 - \bar{X})/SD = 12 - 12/2.45 = 0.00 \; SD \text{ units}$$

$$X_5 \text{ (Set B): } (X_5 - \bar{X})/SD = 12 - \;\; 9/5.60 = 0.54 \; SD \text{ units}$$

The value obtained is the *SD* unit of the raw score or *z score*. The ratio between the deviation of a score from its mean and the standard deviation transforms both raw scores obtained from two different distributions into equivalent units. Now we are able to make comparisons between two different sets of scores by comparing the *z* scores. It is evident from examining the performance of X_5 in Sets A and B that he deviates more than one-half *SD* above the mean on his performance in Set B and his performance in Set A is at the class mean.

---

z SCORE is a value in *SD* units that indicates the extent to which a raw score deviates from the mean.

Computing a z Score:
1. Subtract the mean from the raw score.
2. Divide the difference by the *SD*.

$$z = (X - \bar{X})/SD$$

TEACHER-MADE STATISTIC FOR DERIVING *SD*

Since many teachers avoid using the standard deviation statistic because of their reluctance to get involved in mathematics and because of the time factor, several simpler formulas for deriving the standard deviation have been devised. The following formula for computing the *SD* is practical to use with most classroom data. With a little practice, you will be able to compute the *SD* in a matter of minutes.

TEACHER-MADE STATISTIC FOR DERIVING *SD* *

1. Order the scores from high to low.
2. Find $\frac{1}{6}$ of the total number of scores: ($\frac{1}{6}$ of N).
   a. Given 36 scores in a set of scores ($N = 36$), $\frac{1}{6}$ of 36 would be 6.
   b. Given 20 scores in a set of scores ($N = 20$), $\frac{1}{6}$ of 20 would be $3\frac{1}{3}$.
3. Add $\frac{1}{6}$ of the scores from the top of the set:

$$[\Sigma \frac{1}{6} \text{ of } N \text{ (top scores)}]$$

   a. Since $\frac{1}{6}$ of $36 = 6$, we add the highest six scores.
   b. Since $\frac{1}{6}$ of $20 = 3\frac{1}{3}$, we add the highest three scores plus $\frac{1}{3}$ of the fourth highest score.
4. Add separately, $\frac{1}{6}$ of the scores from the bottom of the set:

$$[\Sigma \frac{1}{6} \text{ of } N \text{ (bottom scores)}]$$

5. Subtract the sum of the bottom $\frac{1}{6}$ of N scores from the sum of the top $\frac{1}{6}$ of N scores.
6. Divide the remainder by $\frac{1}{2}$ of N: when $N = 36$, $\frac{1}{2}N = 18$; when $N = 20$, $\frac{1}{2}N = 10$.

Formula: $SD_{tm} = [\Sigma \frac{1}{6} \text{ of } N \text{ (top)} - \Sigma \frac{1}{6} \text{ of } N \text{ (bottom)}]/\frac{1}{2}N$

---

*"Short-cut Statistics for Teacher-Made Tests," Evaluation and Advisory Service Series, Number 5 (Princeton, N.J.: Educational Testing Services, 1960), 23-24; Harriet Talmage, "Significance Tests of Teacher-Made Formuli for Deriving Standard Deviations," unpublished study, 1967. The formula suggested above differed by three-tenths of a point or less from the formal formula computation of *SD* in 98 percent of the cases compared. The more normally a set of scores are distributed, the less the difference between the answers from the two formulas.

The examples below illustrate the ease in deriving the SD of a set of scores using the teacher-made formula.

Example 1

X		X	X	
76		55	45	
74		55	43	
72	$1/6$ of N	51	42	
70	of	51	41	
68	top	51	40	
66	scores	50	40	
65		50	40	
61		48	35	$1/6$ of N
61		48	32	of
61		48	30	bottom
60		48	29	scores
59		45	26	

$N = 36;$ $1/2 N = 18$

$1/6$ of $36 = 6$

$\Sigma 1/6$ of N (top) $= (76 + 74 + 72 + 70 + 68 + 66) = 426$

$\Sigma 1/6$ of N (bottom) $= (26 + 29 + 30 + 32 + 35 + 40) = 192$

$(426 - 192)/18 = 13.0$

$SD_{tm} = 13.0$

Example 2

X		X	
19	$1/6$ of N	10	
18	of top	10	
16	scores	9	
15	$+$ $1/3$ of 15	9	
15		7	
15		7	
14		6	$1/3$ of 6
13		6	$+$
11		5	$1/6$ of N
11		4	of bottom scores

$N = 20;$ $1/2 N = 10$

$1/6$ of $20 = 3 1/3$

$\Sigma 1/6$ of N (top) $= (19 + 18 + 16 + 5) = 58$

$\Sigma 1/6$ of N (bottom) $= (4 + 5 + 6 + 2) = 17$

$(58 - 17)/10 = 4.1$

$SD_{tm} = 4.1$

Table 4-2 compares the standard deviations obtained from the use of the teacher-made formula to the regular deviation formula rounded off to the nearest tenth.

Table 4-2

Comparison of standard deviations
from teacher-made formula to
regular deviation formula

Examples	SD_{tm}	SD
1	13.0	12.9
2	4.1	4.3

Case studies 7 and 8 involve the reader in the computation of the three
central tendency statistics and variability statistics and their interpretation in
school settings. Some questions may come to mind concerning the value of z
scores and the SD statistics in interpreting performance. Chapter 5 introduces the concept of the normal distribution curve, which will add more
meaning to the use of the standard deviation statistic and the z scores in interpreting system-wide and classroom data.

REFERENCES

Baggaley, Andrew R. *Mathematics for Introductory Statistics: A Programmed
Review.* New York: John Wiley and Sons, 1969. There is a short section reviewing
parentheses and brackets. Chapter 3 takes the reader step by step through the ex-
traction of the square root. Chapter 4 covers the use and laws of summation.

Minium, Edward W. *Statistical Reasoning in Psychology and Education.* New York:
John Wiley and Sons, 1970. Chapter 2 presents a discussion of populations,
samples, and scales.

Spence, Janet T., Underwood, Benton J., Duncan, Carl P., and Cotton, John W. *Elementary Statistics,* 2d edition. New York: Appleton-Century-Crofts, 1968. A
thorough discussion of the concepts of central tendency and variability is given in
Chapters 5 and 6.

Young, Robert K., and Veldman, Donald J. *Introductory Statistics for the
Behavioral Sciences,* 2d edition. New York: Holt, Rinehart and Winston, 1972.
Chapters 4 and 5 discuss the measures of central tendency and variability. Each
discussion is followed by programmed exercises.

Alan A. Kahler
Associate Professo
Agricultural Education

5.

USE OF THE NORMAL DISTRIBUTION CURVE IN INTERPRETING RAW SCORES

DISTRIBUTION CURVES

The reading test scores of the students in four first-level classes are represented on graphs in Figures 5-1a–5-1d. The points on the graph are connected and rounded to simulate a smooth curve. Central tendencies and the standard deviation are indicated.

A teacher assigned to any one of the four classes could learn many things about the performance characteristics of her students from an examination of the four frequency distribution curves. She would also need to modify her initial instructional plans in order to accommodate the differences and similarities within and among the classes.

WHAT RESPONSES TO THE QUESTIONS BELOW CAN A TEACHER INFER FROM THE FREQUENCY DISTRIBUTION CURVES IN FIGURE 5-1?

a. IN WHICH CLASSES ARE THE READING SCORES SYMMETRICALLY DISTRIBUTED?

Class_____   Class_____

b. WHAT CLASS APPEARS TO BE HOMOGENEOUSLY GROUPED?

Class_____

c. WHAT CLASS HAS A FEW EXTREMELY HIGH SCORES?

Class_____

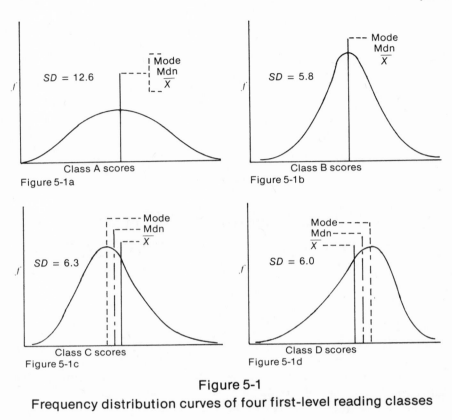

Figure 5-1

Frequency distribution curves of four first-level reading classes

    d. WHAT CLASS HAS A FEW EXTREMELY LOW SCORES?
          Class_____
    e. ALTHOUGH THE STANDARD DEVIATIONS FOR CLASSES B, C, AND D ARE SIMILAR, HOW DO THE DISTRIBUTIONS DIFFER?

_____

    f. WHAT CLASS WOULD YOU PREFER TEACHING AND WHY?

_____

_____

_____

The responses to the above questions will help you to distinguish between symmetrical and asymmetrical curves, the shift in the central tendency statistics depending on the direction of the skewness of the curve, and the inferences you can make about the performance of a class on the basis of the shape of the distribution curves.

a. Class A and Class B. The frequency distributions of Classes A and B are symmetrical, that is, one-half of the curve seems to mirror the other half of the curve.

b. Class B. Students in Class B appear to be homogeneously grouped. Although Classes C and D have *SD*'s not too unlike Class B, they also have a few students at the very low end of the curve (to the left in the case of Class D) and a few at the very high end of the curve (to the right in the case of Class C).

c. Class C. The mean is to the right of (or greater than) the median, which indicates that a few high scores are contributing disproportionately to the size of the mean, although the scores of more than half the class are below the mean.

d. Class D. The mean is to the left of (or less than) the median, which indicates that a few low scores are influencing the size of the mean, although the scores of more than half the class are above the mean.

e. The differences in the distributions of the classes are reflected in the relationship of the mode, median, and mean in each distribution.

f. This, of course, is an individual matter. If one prefers working with the whole class on the same lesson, Class B would be preferable to Classes A, C, or D. If the challenge of a few excellent readers provides the teacher with more instructional options, Class C may be the preference. Many teachers feel that a few students with reading difficulty have much to gain in a group that generally does not have serious reading problems. If such is the case, Class D would be the preference.

Asymmetrical frequency distribution curves are skewed either to the left or to the right. A curve is said to be positively skewed when there are a few extremely high scores; the "tail" of the curve trails off to the right as in Class C. The curve is said to be negatively skewed when the "tail" trails off to the left, as in Class D. In skewed distributions the areas covered under the curve to the left of the mean and to the right of the mean are unequal.

NORMAL DISTRIBUTION CURVES

Symmetrical distribution curves, such as those represented by Classes A and B, have certain characteristics in common. In a perfectly symmetrical curve the mode, median, and mean are represented by the same line, the line that cuts the area under the curve into two equal parts: one-half of the area is a mirror image of the other half. If we drop a perpendicular line from the highest point on the curve to the horizontal axis (X axis), the line cuts the curve in half. The mode, median, and mean are represented on the same perpendicular line; hence the curve is said to be normal, and the trait or set of scores is normally distributed. A curve thus described is called a *normal distribution curve*. Figure 5-2 illustrates the perpendicular line indicating the mode, median, and mean on a normal distribution curve.

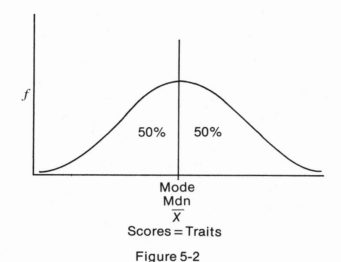

Figure 5-2

The central tendency on a normal distribution curve

NORMAL DISTRIBUTION CURVE is a theoretical frequency distribution whose area under one half of the curve mirrors the area under the other half of the curve. Since the mode, median, and mean are located together, equidistant from the ends of the curve, the curve assumes a bell shape. Any given area under the curve has a definite percent value.

Hypothetically, if the length of every blade of grass in a field were measured, we would find some extremely short blades and some extremely tall blades, but most would be average length. The hypothetical curve describing the frequency distribution of the various lengths of grass would look like Figure 5-3. The tails of the graph, the extremes of tall and short lengths, are shown as approaching zero frequency but never quite reaching these points. There may well be some blade of grass somewhere just a bit longer or shorter than what has been observed thus far.

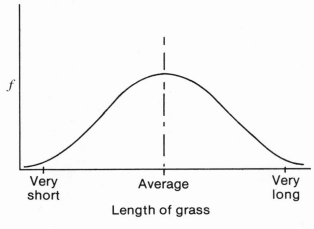

Figure 5-3

Normal distribution curve of the frequency
of the length of grass in a field

RELATIONSHIP BETWEEN STANDARD DEVIATION AND THE AREA UNDER THE·NORMAL DISTRIBUTION CURVE

The normal distribution curve plays an important role in analyzing be-havorial and biological science data. Such a curve adds to the understanding of system-wide and classroom data when the data approximate a normal dis-tribution.

The area under the curve represents 100 percent of the frequency distribu-tion. Since the normal curve is a theoretical model of a hypothetical fre-quency distribution, the area under the curve from the lowest score on the horizontal axis to the mean represents 50 percent of the area. (See Figure 5-2.) If we drop a perpendicular line one standard deviation to the left or to the right of the mean, the percent area covered can be ascertained mathe-matically. The area circumscribed by a perpendicular line dropped from the top of the curve to the point on the horizontal axis representing the mean and extending to a perpendicular line from the top of the curve to a point on the horizontal axis one standard deviation above the mean covers 34.13 percent of the total area under the curve. Figure 5-4 shows the area thus covered. The percent value of any other designated area under the curve can also be obtained. Figure 5-5 shows the percent area covered under the curve corres-ponding to selected *SD* units.

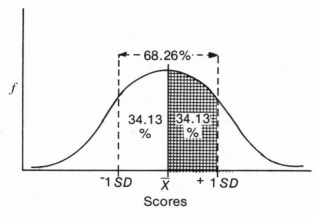

Figure 5-4

The percent area one *SD* above and below the mean
on a normal distribution curve

The percent area is the same as the percent frequency of scores falling within the same area; hence the normal distribution curve can be used to further the understanding of any set of scores that is normally distributed.

IN AN ELEMENTARY SCHOOL GRADUATING CLASS OF ONE HUNDRED, HOW MANY STUDENTS CAN BE EXPECTED TO SCORE BETWEEN 1 *SD* ABOVE AND BELOW THE MEAN ON THE HIGH SCHOOL FRESHMAN ENGLISH EXAMINATION? _____

In Figure 5-4 the area between 1 *SD* above and below the mean covers 68.26 percent of the area under the normal curve. Since the percent area under the curve also describes the percent frequency of a distribution, approximately sixty-eight students will obtain scores within the area of ⁻1 *SD* and ⁺1 *SD*, (100 × 68.26%) or (100 × 0.6826) = 68.26 students or approximately two-thirds of the students.

Two standard deviation values asterisked in Figure 5-5 are of importance in understanding normally distributed measurable traits: first, 95 percent of all measurable traits normally distributed will fall within the area defined by ⁻1.96 *SD* and ⁺1.96 *SD*; and, second, 99 percent of all normally distributed traits will fall within the area defined by ⁻2.58 *SD* and ⁺2.58 *SD*. Figure 5-6 focuses on these areas. The two areas represent important values in *inferential statistics*.

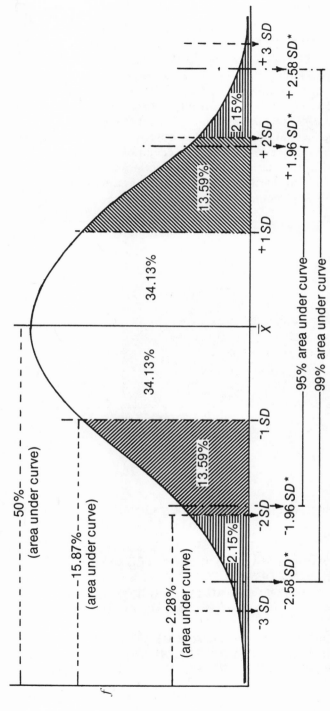

Figure 5-5

Normal distribution curve: Selected *SD* units and areas under the curve

*-1.96 *SD* to +1.96 *SD* and -2.58 *SD* to +2.58 *SD* connote important percent areas under the normal curve. The former covers 95 percent of the area under the curve, the latter 99 percent of the area.

INFERENTIAL STATISTICS refers to that portion of statistics which tests the probability of an event or trait occurring at a given probability level, for example, $\pm 1.96\ SD$ or at the 5 percent probability level; $\pm 2.58\ SD$ or at the 1 percent probability level; or any other designated level. By means of the statistical tests it is possible to determine the level of probability that observed differences are attributable to chance or to a particular condition or treatment. Where an experimental treatment affects the performance of a class beyond that which is ordinarily attributable to chance, we call this a statistically significant change.

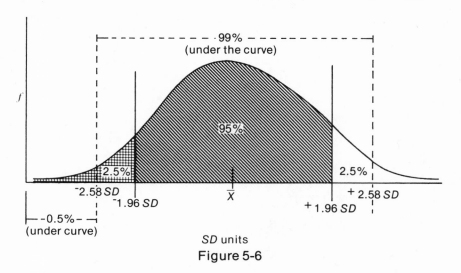

Figure 5-6

Selected areas under the normal curve

STATISTICS FROM NORMALLY DISTRIBUTED SCORES OF THE JUNIOR ENGINEERING DESIGN CLASS ARE: $\bar{X} = 82$; $SD = 10$; $N = 90$. DETERMINE THE FOLLOWING DATA USING INFORMATION ABOUT THE AREA UNDER THE NORMAL DISTRIBUTION CURVE.
    a. WHAT SCORE IS 1 SD ABOVE THE MEAN?_____
    b. WHAT SCORE IS 1 SD BELOW THE MEAN? _____
    c. WHAT PERCENT OF THE SCORES FALL WITHIN $^+$1 SD AND $^-$1 SD?_____

d. HOW MANY OF THE 90 SCORES CAN BE EXPECTED TO FALL BETWEEN ⁻1.96 *SD* AND ⁺1.96 *SD*? (Round off to the larger whole number.)_____

e. WHAT PERCENT OF THE SCORES CAN BE EXPECTED TO FALL ⁺1.96 *SD* ABOVE THE MEAN?_____

Check your responses with the answers shown below:

a. 92. $(\overline{X} + 1\,SD)$, or $(82 + 10) = 92$

b. 72. $(\overline{X} - 1\,SD)$, or $(82 - 10) = 72$

c. 68.26%. This is a given characteristic of the normal distribution curve.

d. 86. Ninety-five percent of the area falls between ⁻1.96 *SD* and ⁺1.96 *SD*; therefore 95 percent of the 90 students will probably obtain scores within this area.

$$95\% = 0.95$$

$$90 \times 95\% = 90 \times 0.95 = 85.50, \text{ or approximately 86 students.}$$

e. 2.5%. (See Figure 5-6.)

RELATIONSHIP AMONG *SD*'s, *z* SCORES, PERCENTILES, AND THE NORMAL DISTRIBUTION CURVE

Since any selected percent area under the normal distribution curve also represents the percent frequency of a normally distributed set of scores, then we can compare the performance of a class, a school, or a school district on a given skill or trait with the expected performance predictable on the theoretical normal distribution curve. In the preceding pages you were able to convert designated *SD* values to percent areas. And you also learned in Chapter 4 how to convert a raw score into *SD* units, which we called *z* scores. Once a raw score is converted to a *z* score, the *z* score can be located on the normal distribution curve, and the percent area above and below the *z* score can also be identified. Since the *z* score is a single point on the horizontal axis of the curve rather than an area under the curve, we use *percentile rank* in place of percent area in discussing *z* scores. The percentile rank is the position of a score in relation to the other scores in a distribution whose value is indicated by the percent of scores falling at or below the given score.

PERCENTILE RANK is the value of a score expressed as the percent of the other scores in the distribution falling on or below the given score.

Example: In a given distribution a score of 150 is at the mean. Since 50 percent of the cases fall below the mean, the score of 150 is at the 50 percentile. If a score of 200 is 1 *SD* above the mean, it is at the 84.13 percentile, that is 50% + 34.13% = 84.13%, or at the 84.13 percentile.

USING THE DATA FROM FIGURES 5-5 and 5-6, CONVERT THE FOLLOWING RAW SCORES INTO z SCORES AND PERCENTILES. THE SCHOOLS IN THE PROBLEMS BELOW ARE FROM A DISTRIBUTION WHOSE $\bar{X}$ = 15 and *SD* =3.

Raw score	z score	Percentile
a. $X_1 = 18$		
b. $X_2 = 15$		
c. $X_3 = 12$		
d. $X_4 = 9$		
e. $X_5 = 16$		

Let us go over each of your computations:

a. $z = 1$; 84.13 percentile. The score of X_1 is 3 points above the mean. To find the z score we subtract the mean from the raw score and divide the difference by the standard deviation:

$$z = (18 - 15)/3 = 3/3 = 1$$

Since the answer is positive, from Figure 5-5 we know that 50 percent of the area is covered from the left end of the curve to the mean. To this is added the percent area covered from the mean to 1 *SD* above the mean, that is 34.13 percent. Hence a z score of 1 is at the 84.13 percentile.

b. $z = 0$; 50 percentile. Substituting the values in the z score transtormation formula:

$$z = (15 - 15)/3 = 0/3 = 0$$

A z score of 0 is at the mean, hence at the point that cuts the curve in half. A z score of 0 is at the 50 percentile.

   c. $z = {}^-1$; 15.87 percentile. Substituting values:

$$z = (12 - 15)/3 = {}^-3/3 = {}^-1$$

A negative z score falls below the mean, which indicates that the score will fall below the 50 percentile. Subtract the percent area covered between $^-1$ SD and the $\bar{X}$ from 50%; thus 50% – 34.13% = 15.87%, or a score of 12 is at the 15.87 percentile or approximately at the 16 percentile.

   d. $z = {}^-2$; 2.28 percentile. Substituting values:

$$z = (9 - 15)/3 = {}^-6/3 = {}^-2$$

Referring to Figure 5-5, $^-2$ SD or $z = {}^-2$ covers an area of 2.28 percent, that is, 50% – (34.13% + 13.59%) = 2.28%. A score of 9 points ranks at the 2.28 percentile.

   e. $z = 0.33$; percentile unknown. Again, substituting the values:

$$z = (16 - 15)/3 = 1/3 = 0.33$$

Finding the percentile presents another problem. The information is not available from Figures 5-5 or 5-6.

Finding percentile values is difficult unless the exact mathematical equivalents of the percent area under the curve are available. It is fortunate that a table of values has been worked out so that every z score can be located on the normal distribution curve and its percentile equivalent obtained. One conversion table is reproduced in Table 5-1.

EXPLANATION FOR USING THE NORMAL DISTRIBUTION CURVE TABLE OF AREAS

There are two types of columns in the table: $(X - \bar{X})/SD$ stands for the standard deviation unit or z score; and the percent area column represents the proportionate percent area under the curve from the mean to the corresponding z score.

Given a z score of 0.60, to find the percent area from the mean to $z = 0.60$, you should read down the z column until you locate 0.60. The corresponding proportionate percent area is directly to the right. It is 22.57 percent. Since z is positive, it is to the right of the $\bar{X}$; therefore we add 50 percent to 22.57 percent for 72.57 percent, or a $z = 0.60$ is at the 72.57 percentile. (See Figure 5-7.)

Table 5-1

Percent of area under the normal curve[a] (in *SD* units)

$(X - \bar{X})/SD$	Percent of area	$(X - \bar{X})/SD$	Percent of area	$(X - \bar{X})/SD$	Percent of area	$(X - \bar{X})/SD$	Percent of area
.00	00.00						
.01	00.40	.41	15.91	.81	29.10	1.21	38.69
.02	00.80	.42	16.28	.82	29.39	1.22	38.88
.03	01.20	.43	16.64	.83	29.67	1.23	39.07
.04	01.60	.44	17.00	.84	29.95	1.24	39.25
.05	01.99	.45	17.36	.85	30.23	1.25	39.44
.06	02.39	.46	17.72	.86	30.51	1.26	39.62
.07	02.79	.47	18.08	.87	30.78	1.27	39.80
.08	03.19	.48	18.44	.88	31.06	1.28	39.97
.09	03.59	.49	18.79	.89	31.33	1.29	40.15
.10	03.98	.50	19.15	.90	31.59	1.30	40.32
.11	04.38	.51	19.50	.91	31.86	1.31	40.49
.12	04.78	.52	19.85	.92	32.12	1.32	40.66
.13	05.17	.53	20.19	.93	32.38	1.33	40.82
.14	05.57	.54	20.54	.94	32.64	1.34	40.99
.15	05.96	.55	20.88	.95	32.89	1.35	41.15
.16	06.36	.56	21.23	.96	33.15	1.36	41.31
.17	06.75	.57	21.57	.97	33.40	1.37	41.47
.18	07.14	.58	21.90	.98	33.65	1.38	41.62
.19	07.53	.59	22.24	.99	33.89	1.39	41.77
2.0	07.93	.60	22.57	1.00	34.13	1.40	41.92
.21	08.32	.61	22.91	1.01	34.38	1.41	42.07
.22	08.71	.62	23.24	1.02	34.61	1.42	42.22
.23	09.10	.63	23.57	1.03	34.85	1.43	42.36
.24	09.48	.64	23.89	1.04	35.08	1.44	42.51
.25	09.87	.65	24.22	1.05	35.31	1.45	42.65
.26	10.26	.66	24.54	1.06	35.54	1.46	42.79
.27	10.64	.67	24.86	1.07	35.77	1.47	42.92
.28	11.03	.68	25.17	1.08	35.99	1.48	43.06
.29	11.41	.69	25.49	1.09	36.21	1.49	43.19
.30	11.79	.70	25.80	1.10	36.43	1.50	43.32
.31	12.17	.71	26.11	1.11	36.65	1.51	43.45
.32	12.55	.72	26.42	1.12	36.86	1.52	43.57
.33	12.93	.73	26.73	1.13	37.08	1.53	43.70
.34	13.31	.74	27.04	1.14	37.29	1.54	43.82
.35	13.68	.75	27.34	1.15	37.49	1.55	43.94
.36	14.06	.76	27.64	1.16	37.70	1.56	44.06
.37	14.43	.77	27.94	1.17	37.90	1.57	44.18
.38	14.80	.78	28.23	1.18	38.10	1.58	44.29
.39	15.17	.79	28.52	1.19	38.30	1.59	44.41
.40	15.54	.80	28.81	1.20	38.49	1.60	44.52

[a]Condensed from Table 1 of *Biometrika Tables for Statisticians,* ed. E. S. Pearson and H. O. Hartley, 3d edition (London: Cambridge University Press, 1965), I. Reprinted by permission of Biometrika Trustees.

Table 5-1 (*continued*)

$(X - \bar{X})/SD$	Percent of area	$(X - \bar{X})/SD$	Percent of area	$(X - \bar{X})/SD$	Percent of area	$(X - \bar{X})/SD$	Percent of area
1.61	44.63	2.01	47.78	2.41	49.20	2.81	49.75
1.62	44.74	2.02	47.83	2.42	49.22	2.82	49.76
1.63	44.84	2.03	47.88	2.43	49.25	2.83	49.77
1.64	44.95	2.04	47.93	2.44	49.27	2.84	49.77
1.65	45.05	2.05	47.98	2.45	49.29	2.85	49.78
1.66	45.15	2.06	48.03	2.46	49.31	2.86	49.79
1.67	45.25	2.07	48.08	2.47	49.32	2.87	49.79
1.68	45.35	2.08	48.12	2.48	49.34	2.88	49.80
1.69	45.45	2.09	48.17	2.49	49.36	2.89	49.81
1.70	45.54	2.10	48.21	2.50	49.38	2.90	49.81
1.71	45.64	2.11	48.26	2.51	49.40	2.91	49.82
1.72	45.73	2.12	48.30	2.52	49.41	2.92	49.82
1.73	45.82	2.13	48.34	2.53	49.43	2.93	49.83
1.74	45.91	2.14	48.38	2.54	49.45	2.94	49.84
1.75	45.99	2.15	48.42	2.55	49.46	2.95	49.84
1.76	46.08	2.16	48.46	2.56	49.48	2.96	49.85
1.77	46.16	2.17	48.50	2.57	49.49	2.97	49.85
1.78	46.25	2.18	48.54	2.58	49.51	2.98	49.86
1.79	46.33	2.19	48.57	2.59	49.52	2.99	49.86
1.80	46.41	2.20	48.61	2.60	49.53	3.00	49.87
1.81	46.49	2.21	48.64	2.61	49.55	3.02	49.87
1.82	46.56	2.22	48.68	2.62	49.56	3.04	49.88
1.83	46.64	2.23	48.71	2.63	49.57	3.06	49.89
1.84	46.71	2.24	48.75	2.64	49.59	3.08	49.90
1.85	46.78	2.25	48.78	2.65	49.60	3.10	49.90
1.86	46.86	2.26	48.81	2.66	49.61	3.20	49.93
1.87	46.93	2.27	48.84	2.67	49.62	3.30	49.95
1.88	46.99	2.28	48.87	2.68	49.63	3.40	49.97
1.89	47.06	2.29	48.90	2.69	49.64	3.50	49.98
1.90	47.13	2.30	48.93	2.70	49.65	3.60	49.98
1.91	47.19	2.31	48.96	2.71	49.66	3.70	49.99
1.92	47.26	2.32	48.98	2.72	49.67		
1.93	47.32	2.33	49.01	2.73	49.68		
1.94	47.38	2.34	49.04	2.74	49.69		
1.95	47.44	2.35	49.06	2.75	49.70		
1.96	47.50	2.36	49.09	2.76	49.71		
1.97	47.56	2.37	49.11	2.77	49.72		
1.98	47.61	2.38	49.13	2.78	49.73		
1.99	47.67	2.39	49.16	2.79	49.74		
2.00	47.72	2.40	49.18	2.80	49.74		

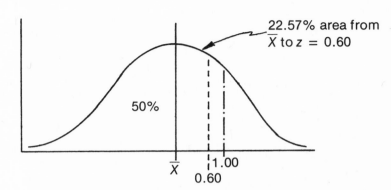

Figure 5-7

Area under the curve when $z = 0.60$

With the information from Table 5-1, three steps need to be performed in order to convert a z score to a percentile.

1. Select the z score.

2. Find the corresponding percent area in the table. The percent area is from the mean to the z score.

3. If the z score is greater than zero, add the percent area found in the second step to 50 percent; or, if the z score is less than zero, that is, if it is a negative number, subtract the percent area obtained in the table from 50 percent.

With this additional information, return to problem e to find the percentile for a z score of 0.33. First locate 0.33 under the z column in the table. The corresponding column shows the percent area to be 12.93. Since z is positive, add 50 percent to 12.93 percent. The equivalent percentile is 62.93.

TRY THESE PROBLEMS:

1.

	z score	Percent of area under curve	Percentile
a.	1.25		
b.	.50		
c.	2.00		
d.	⁻.25		
e.	⁻1.25		

2. GIVEN THE FOLLOWING INFORMATION, $\bar{X} = 25$, $SD = 10$, and SELECTED RAW SCORES, FIND THE z SCORES AND PERCENTILES.

	Raw score	z score	Percentile
a.	25		
b.	10		
c.	15		
d.	35		

Correct responses to the above problems:

1.	Percent of area under curve	Percentile
a.	39.44%	50% + 39.44% = 89.44
b.	19.15%	50% + 19.15% = 69.15
c.	47.72%	50% + 47.72% = 97.72
d.	9.87%	50% - 9.87% = 40.13
e.	39.44%	50% - 39.44% = 10.56

2.	z score	Percentile
a.	0.0	50% + 0.00% = 50
b.	‑1.5	50% - 43.32% = 6.68
c.	‑1.0	50% - 34.13% = 15.87
d.	1.0	50% + 34.13% = 84.13

Converting Percentiles to z Scores

If you have the percentile and want the z score equivalent, the table is again useful. The steps are:

1. When the percentile is greater than 50 percent of the area, subtract 50 percent from the percentile; or when the percentile is less than 50 percent of the area, subtract the percentile from 50 percent. Thus,

$$84.13 \text{ percentile} \text{ ------> } 84.13 - 50 = 34.13\%$$

$$15.87 \text{ percentile} \text{ -------> } 50 - 15.87 = 34.13\%$$

2. Look under the area column for the percent of the area obtained in the first step. The z score is in the corresponding column. If the percentile was greater than 50, the z score is positive; if the percentile was less than 50, the z score is negative.

FIND THE z SCORES FOR THE FOLLOWING:

1. 90.32 percentile z = _____

2. 9.68 percentile z = _____

3. 72.57 percentile $z =$ _____
4. 27.43 percentile $z =$ _____
5. 88.10 percentile $z =$ _____
6. 11.90 percentile $z =$ _____

Correct responses to the above problems:
1. $z = 1.30$

    $90.32 - 50 = 40.32\%$

    Look up 40.32% in the percent area column of Table 5-1: $z = 1.30$. Since the percentile was greater than 50, z is positive.
2. $z = ^-1.30$.

    $50 - 9.68 = 40.32\%$

    Look up 40.32% in the percent area column of Table 5-1: the value is 1.30. Since the percentile is less than 50, z is negative.
3. $z = 0.60$
4. $z = ^-0.60$
5. $z = 1.18$
6. $z = ^-1.18$

Converting z Scores to Raw Scores

To convert a z score back to its equivalent raw score, we need to solve for X in the following equation:

$$z = (X - \bar{X})/SD$$

HOW WOULD YOU CONVERT A z SCORE BACK TO A RAW SCORE? (Do not work too long on this one.)

Did you reverse the procedures? It involves solving for an unknown in a simple algebraic equation. Use the following steps.
1. The original equation:

$$z = (X - \bar{X})/SD$$

2. Multiply both sides of the equation by SD:

$$(SD)(z) = SD(X - \bar{X})/SD$$

The *SD* in the numerator on the right-hand side of the equation cancels the *SD* in the denominator.

$$(SD)(z) = \cancel{SD}(X - \bar{X})/\cancel{SD}$$

3. Add $\bar{X}$ to both sides of the equation:

$$(SD)(z) + \bar{X} = X - \bar{X} + \bar{X}$$

A positive $\bar{X}$ and a negative $\bar{X}$ are equal to zero; therefore, the equation now reads:

$$(SD)(z) + \bar{X} = X, \text{ or } X = (SD)(z) + \bar{X}$$

RETURN TO YOUR ANSWERS TO THE SECOND PROBLEM ON PAGE 62: $\bar{X} = 25$ AND $SD = 10$. USING THE ABOVE FORMULA, FIND THE RAW SCORES WHEN THE z SCORES ARE 0, 1.0, AND ⁻1.5.

$z = 0;\quad X = \underline{\hspace{2cm}}$

$z = 1.0;\quad X = \underline{\hspace{2cm}}$

$z = {}^-1.5;\quad X = \underline{\hspace{2cm}}$

The formula to use is:

$$X = (SD)(z) + \bar{X}$$

When $z = 0$, then $\quad X = 10(0) + 25$

$\qquad\qquad\qquad X = 0 + 25$

$\qquad\qquad\qquad X = 25$

When $z = 1.0$, then $X = (10)(1.0) + 25$

$\qquad\qquad\qquad X = 10 + 25$

$\qquad\qquad\qquad X = 35$

When $z = {}^-1.5$; then $X = (10)({}^-1.5) + 25$

$\qquad\qquad\qquad X = {}^-15 + 25$

$\qquad\qquad\qquad X = 10$

The answers should check with the raw score values given in problems 2a., 2d., and 2b., on page 63.

OTHER DERIVED NORMATIVE SCORES

The z score transformed the raw score into *SD* units and made the score interpretable on the normal distribution curve. There are other derived scores that are also used to interpret raw score data on the normal curve. Two types of scores widely used in reporting standardized tests are T scores and stanines. The T score transforms a distribution so that its $\bar{X}$ is 50 and its SD 10*; the stanine transforms the distribution so that its $\bar{X}$ is 5 and its SD 2. T scores range from 0 to 100; stanines range from 1 through 9.

A stanine differs from the other derived scores we have discussed. It represents a band along the horizontal axis on the normal distribution curve. As an example, stanine 5 covers an area of 20 percent. Stanine 1 covers an area of 4 percent; hence any score in the fourth percentile or lower is reported as one stanine. Scores in stanine 5 are scores whose percentiles range from 40 to 60. Once a score is reported as a stanine, the actual raw score is lost. Figure 5-8 illustrates the relationship among the various derived scores on the normal distribution curve. Table 5-2 shows stanine and percentile equivalents.

Table 5–2

Stanine and percentile equivalents

Stanine	Percentile
1	4 and below
2	11–4
3	23–11
4	40–23
5	60–40
6	77–60
7	89–77
8	96–89
9	100–96

Try the problems shown below for practice.

GIVEN A NORMALLY DISTRIBUTED SET OF SCORES WITH $\bar{X} =$ 15 AND $SD = 7.60$, FIND THE EQUIVALENTS OF THE RAW SCORES:

Raw score	z score	Percentile	Stanine
1. $X_1 = 15$			
2. $X_2 = 35$			
3. $X_3 = 2$			

(Round the z scores to the nearest hundredth. You will need to refer to Tables 5-1 and 5-2 and Figure 5-8.)

---

*Formula for transforming a z score to a T score:

$T = 10(z) + 50$, or $(10)\,[(X - \bar{X})/SD] + 50$

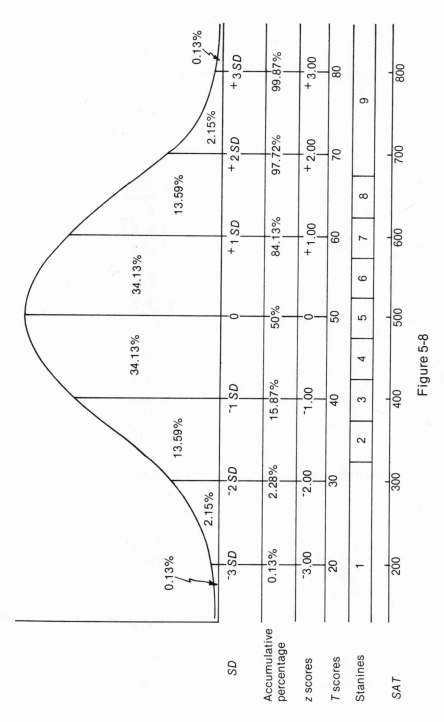

Figure 5-8

Relationship among derived scores to the normal distribution curve

----

Before you obtained the percentile and stanine equivalents of a raw score, you had to derive the z score.

1. $z = (X - \bar{X})/SD$

$z = (15 - 15)/7.60 = 0/7.60 = 0$

Thus, when $X_1 = 15$, $z = 0$.

From Table 5-1, the percent area under the curve when $z = 0$ is 0%. Subtract 0% from 50%, and the answer is 50%. Thus when $z = 0$, the score of 15 is at the 50 percentile. From Figure 5-8, 50% of the area under the curve lies in the stanine 5 band. Thus, when $X_1 = 15$, the stanine score is 5.

2. $z = (35 - 15)/7.60 = 20/7.60 = 2.63$

Thus, when $X_2 = 35$, then $z = 2.63$.

50% + 49.57% = 99.57%, or 99.57 percentile. From Figure 5-8, 99.57% area falls in the stanine 9 band.

3. $z = (2 - 15)/7.60 = {}^-13/7.60 = {}^-1.71$

Thus, when $X_3 = 2$, then $z = {}^-1.71$.

Since the z score is negative, we subtract the percent area from 50%. Thus, 50% - 45.64% = 4.36% or 4.36 percentile. Thus, when $z = {}^-1.71$, X_3 is at the 4.36 percentile. The 4.36 percentile falls in stanine 2.

INTERPRETATION OF CONVERTED RAW SCORES

For many types of school performance, departmental and system-wide data can be used to set up performance norms if the scores are normally distributed. Total class performance and individual performance are compared to the performance of the norming group. The work of students in this year's class can be compared to previous classes. The performance of individuals or groups can also be compared on two different tests or traits if the raw scores are transformed to z scores, percentiles, T scores, or stanines.

To establish norm-referenced data from departmental, school, and system-wide performance, a *random sample* of students is frequently used as the norming group. It is important that the sample used is randomly chosen so that the sample replicates the measured characteristics of the whole population. If only students with scores in the eightieth percentile or higher are selected, the sample will not reflect the population, hence it will be unsuitable as a sample. Class and individual performance is then compared to the school system's own norming group.

RANDOM SAMPLE. To obtain a random sample of a measured trait from a total population, each individual in the population must be given an equal opportunity to be selected for the sample. A table of random numbers or the "old hat" is used to ensure that each individual has an equal opportunity of being chosen.

Example: There are 1,200 freshmen entering a high school. All do not have to be tested to determine the distribution of scores on a mathematics test measuring computational skills. Two hundred students are randomly selected by placing all 1,200 names in the hat, shaking the contents, and drawing the first name from the hat. The hat is reshaken to give the remaining 1,199 names an equal chance to be selected. The process is repeated until the names of 200 students are selected. The administration can plan the number of sections of fast-paced, average-paced, slow-paced, and remedial mathematics classes for the incoming freshman class on the basis of the 200 scores. (A table of random numbers is frequently used to make random selections. Many elementary statistics books include such a table.)

Converting raw scores to derived scores does not give us all the information needed to evaluate the performance of an individual or a class. As educators we have the responsibility of understanding the larger instructional context. The following problem serves as an example of the limitations of the statistical data studied to this point.

X_2 HAS A RAW SCORE OF 15, $z = 1.07$. HIS PERFORMANCE IS AT THE 85.77 PERCENTILE. HOW DO WE EVALUATE A PERFORMANCE RANKING AT THE 85.77 PERCENTILE? _____

At this point in the interpretation of performance or product of performance, the teacher must ask the following questions.
1. With what group is the student being compared:
   a. a fast group?
   b. a slow group?
   c. his age and/or grade peers?
2. With what areas of the student's own performance is he being compared:

a. past performance?

b. expected level of performance?

c. study habits?

d. strengths and weaknesses in other cognitive areas?

3. How reliable is the raw score that quantified the student's performance?

4. How valid is the performance or product of a performance as a measure of the trait you have quantified?

Only on the basis of answers to these questions can we further interpret the 85.77 percentile rank of X_2. The first question must always be explicated before any score can be meaningfully interpreted. Aspects of the second, third, and fourth questions are taken up in Part II, Chapters 6, 7, and 8.

We must be careful not to overuse the normal distribution curve to interpret classroom performance. The number of students in a classroom is usually too small for a measured performance to replicate a normal distribution. Teachers do, however, need to understand the concept of normal distribution in order to compare their students' performance with norming groups whose performance is predicated on the normal distribution curve. Criterion-referenced data are based on a fixed standard of performance; hence the concept of normal distribution does not pertain. (See Chapter 2.)

The two cases studies for this chapter (Cases 9 and 10) will give you further practice in transforming raw scores to derived scores and in interpreting scores using norm-referenced data.

REFERENCES

Downie, N. M., and Heath, R. W. *Basic Statistical Methods,* 2d edition. New York: Harper and Row, 1965. Chapter 6 on standard scores and the normal curve gives a mathematical analysis of areas under the normal curve.

McCollough, Celeste, and Van Atta, Loche. *Statistical Concepts: A Program for Self-Instruction.* New York: McGraw-Hill, 1963. Lesson 10 compares percentiles and standard scores in a programmed format.

Mehrens, William A., and Lehmann, Irwin J. *Standardized Tests in Education.* New York: Holt, Rinehart and Winston, 1969. The transformation of raw scores to types of scores interpretable on the normal distribution curve is discussed on pages 52–61.

Spence, Janet T., Underwood, Benton J., Duncan, Carl P., and Cotton, John W. *Elementary Statistics,* 2d edition. New York: Appleton-Century-Crofts, 1968. Chapter 7, on normal distribution curve, contains a good discussion of probability of occurrence of an event based on the distribution theory of the frequency of occurrence as defined by the normal distribution curve.

Part II
Correlation, Reliability, and Validity: Concepts and Related Statistics for Evaluating Performance Data

Part II introduces concepts in measurement and evaluation that open the raw score to further examination. We need to subject the raw score to such questions as: How is it related to scores on other performances or products of performance? How accurately does the score represent the true performance? How valid is the score in representing a skill, understanding, or trait?

The concept of correlation is introduced in Chapter 6. It provides the foundation for subsequent discussions in Chapters 7 and 8 on reliability and validity, two fundamental concepts in measurement theory and evaluation. These concepts are the bases for establishing standards for constructing and evaluating measurement instruments and for ascertaining the confidence teachers and administrators can place in the raw score as an accurate and valid measure of performance.

At the conclusion of Part II the reader should be able to:

1. Define the concept of correlation in terms of its two variables: a predictor and a criterion.

2. Construct a scattergram using the scores from predictor and criterion variables.

3. Interpret the spread of the plotted points on a scattergram to determine the type of correlation: positive or negative.

4. Given a scattergram, estimate the degree of correlation between the predictor and criterion variables.

5. Discuss the regression line on a scattergram in terms of the "best-fitting" straight line.

6. Explain the meaning of a given value of a correlation coefficient.

7. Compute a Pearson Product-Moment Correlation coefficient.

8. Compute a correlation coefficient from rank order data.

9. Define the concept of reliability in terms of error.

10. Define the concept of reliability in terms of internal consistency.

11. Identify the sources of error in a score related to the instrument, the object, event, or trait, and the administration and scoring.

12. Contrast the three concepts used in discussing reliability: stability, equivalence, and internal consistency.

13. Indicate, through examples, the relationship between the true score, the observed score, and the error component.

14. Compute the reliability of an instrument: test-retest; split-half or odd-even; equivalency; teacher-made formula for internal consistency.

15. Use the Spearman-Brown Formula to adjust the reliability coefficient derived from split-half or odd-even reliabilities.

16. Interpret a raw score in terms of the reliability coefficient and the standard error of measurement.

17. Determine the confidence limits for interpreting a raw score.

18. Discuss other measurement factors that affect the reliability of an instrument.

19. Define the concept of validity in terms of content, criterion-related, and construct validities.

20. Explain the role of instructional objectives in ascertaining content validity.

21. Explain the role of prediction in criterion-related validity.

22. Explain the role of psychological theory in construct validity.

23. Interpret the validity coefficient for determining the confidence a test user can place in the predictive ability of an instrument.

*24. Predict a score on the criterion from a score on a predictor, and predict a score on the predictor from a score on a criterion.

---

*For readers who studied pages 119–122.

6.
CORRELATION: MEANING AND RELATED STATISTICS

The first five chapters examined a single trait (defined by scores assigned to a performance or its product) in order to compare individuals and groups. The information was used to make instructional and organizational decisions. In education, the type of performance on one task (or variable) is frequently found to be correlated with that of another task. As an example, educational research has documented over and over a *correlation* between performance on a pretest, such as in reading, and subsequent reading achievement. We continuously seek information about the relatedness between school performance generally and verbal ability; between students' performance in science classes and mathematics classes; between high school class rank and subsequent college performance; between teachers' *National Teacher Examinations* scores and later effectiveness in the classroom. Teachers and administrators can add to their decision-making data base by studying the correlations between different sets of performances. The following illustration points up the use of correlated data.

> CORRELATION is an association or interrelation between two or more performances. To determine the degree of correlation we observe the extent to which the performance of one task varies with the performance on a second task.

A concerned parent group criticized the grouping practices in a school. Scores on the *Scholastic Ability Test* were used to assign students to advanced, regular, or remedial sections of the mathematics classes. The parent group felt that the test discriminated against many students because of its heavy emphasis on verbal ability; thus students who might have profited from instruction in advanced mathematics were systematically excluded from such classes because of their verbal ability and usually ended up assigned to remedial sections.

At the last meeting of the community-school council, a committee of parents and teachers was formed to devise alternative methods for assigning students to the various mathematics classes.

AS A MEMBER OF THE COMMITTEE, WHAT WOULD YOU SUGGEST AS A BASIS FOR GROUPING MATHEMATICS STUDENTS OTHER THAN SCORES ON THE *SCHOLASTIC ABILITY TEST?* ___

Any number of suggestions may be worth testing: interests of students, study habits, grades on previous report cards, teachers' recommendations, personality, creativity, self-selection, or some other test to determine ability in mathematics.

After discussing the merits and negative aspects of each suggestion, the committee could not come to a consensus on any one method of assignment. On the principal's recommendation, the committee agreed to pilot test the three methods having the most support: the present ability test, a study skill test, and a personality measure.

It was decided to assign randomly three groups of fifteen students to three especially formed advanced mathematics classes for a twelve-week instructional period. At the start of the instructional pilot period, Group A was administered the *Scholastic Ability Test;* Group B was given the *Study Skills Inventory;* and Group C responded to the *General Personality Profile Schedule.* The instruments were to serve as *predictors* of achievement in mathematics. At the end of the twelve-week instructional period achievement was again measured using a standardized mathematics test (the *criterion*) that was administered to all three groups. The problem was to determine, through the pilot test, the extent of a correlation between each of the predictor variables and the criterion variable.

PREDICTOR is the variable used to predict future performance on the basis of a given personal characteristic, ability, or other measurable trait.

CRITERION is the variable used as the standard for measuring a performance after a period of instruction or treatment.

ON THE BASIS OF YOUR OWN EXPERIENCE, WHICH OF THE THREE PREDICTORS WILL CORRELATE HIGHEST WITH ACHIEVEMENT IN MATHEMATICS? _____

_____

_____

Before discussing your response, let us explore ways of deriving an empirical answer, after which we can recheck your response.

Table 6-1

Raw scores of the predictor and criterion variables of Class A

Student	Scholastic Ability Test	Standardized mathematics achievement test
Mary J.	162	50
Kim R	154	48
Juan G.	145	50
Bryant L.	140	35
Terrence B.	137	42
Clifford D.	136	36
Gwen C.	125	38
Imogene E.	120	38
Stewart P.	119	38
John T.	117	47
Roberta S.	110	24
Morgan N.	105	37
Hilliard R.	97	21
Maynard V.	90	20
Vernon M.	88	16

SCATTERGRAMS

One way to determine the relatedness between the two sets of quantitative data on each of the fifteen students is to plot the data on a coordinate graph. First, scores on the *Scholastic Ability Test* and on the standardized mathematics achievement test are plotted for Group A. The scores of the fifteen students on the two variables are shown in Table 6-1, and the plotted scores are shown in Figure 6-1. The predictor score is shown on the *X* axis, and the criterion score on the *Y* axis. The plotted points form a graph we call a scattergram. The points shown in this fashion may or may not assume a pattern of a straight line. The more nearly the points approach a straight line, the greater the degree of correlation between the variables. By studying the pattern formed by the plotted points (that is, the extent to which the points scatter away from a hypothetical straight line or tend to cluster around a straight line), we can make an educated guess about the correlation. By examining Figure 6-1 we can say that the scores tend to lie near the straight line; hence the predictor and criterion scores are highly correlated.

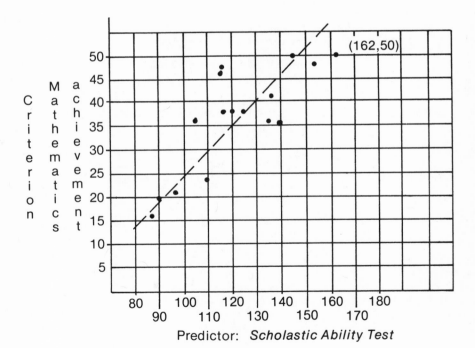

Figure 6-1

Scattergram of Class A

The scores on the *Study Skills Inventory,* used to predict the achievement in mathematics of Class B, are plotted as shown in Figure 6-2.

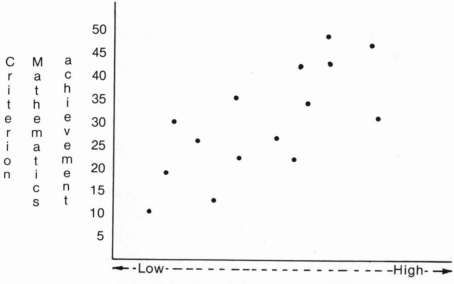

Predictor: *Study Skills Inventory* scores

Figure 6-2

Scattergram of Class B

HOW WOULD YOU DESCRIBE THE CORRELATION BETWEEN *STUDY SKILLS INVENTORY* SCORES AND MATHEMATICS ACHIEVEMENT SCORES FROM THE SCATTERGRAM IN FIGURE 6-2? _____

_____

_____

_____

_____

The scattergram in Figure 6-2 is a little more difficult to interpret. There seems to be a tendency for the scores to move upward from the lower left-hand corner of the graph toward the upper right-hand corner. Although the correlation is not clearly defined as in Figure 6-1, we can say that higher *Study Skills Inventory* scores tend to correlate somewhat with higher mathematics achievement test scores.

The scattergram of the scores of Class C, which used the *General Personality Profile Schedule* to predict scores on the standardized mathematics achievement test, is shown in Figure 6-3.

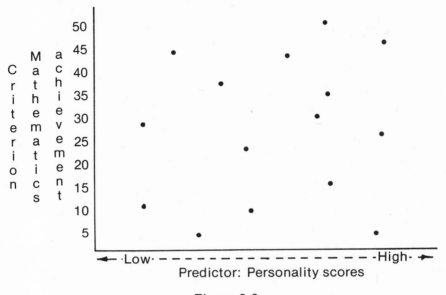

Figure 6-3

Scattergram of Class C

HOW WOULD YOU DESCRIBE THE CORRELATION ILLUSTRATED IN FIGURE 6-3?_____

_____

_____

_____

Since it is almost impossible to sketch a straight line around which the scores appear to cluster, we can say there is little or no correlation between personality and mathematics achievement.

When the direction of the points tend to go from the lower left-hand corner of the scattergram toward the upper right-hand corner, we say the correlation is positive. As the measure of one variable rises, the measure of the other variable also increases. Conversely, when the measure of one variable falls, the measure of the other variable decreases. When the plotted points tend to go from the upper left-hand corner to the lower right-hand corner, we say the correlation is negative. In a negative correlation, as one variable increases the other variable decreases.

A negative correlation is illustrated by the scattergram in Figure 6-4. The points represent data on two variables: parental interest in school as the predictor variable, and absenteeism as the criterion.

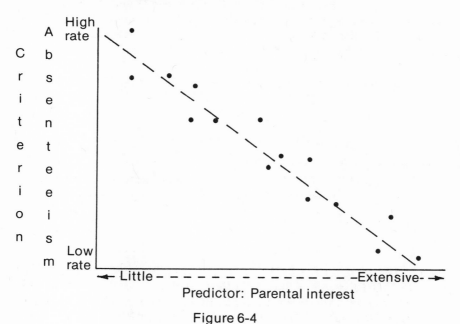

Figure 6-4

Scattergram of parental interest and absenteeism

WHAT DOES FIGURE 6-4 INDICATE ABOUT THE RELATEDNESS BETWEEN PARENTAL INTEREST IN SCHOOLING AND THE RATE OF ABSENTEEISM? _____

_____

_____

_____

- -

There appears to be a strong negative correlation between parental interest in schooling and the rate of absenteeism. The greater the interest in

schooling the lower the absentee rate. The points tend to cluster around a
hypothetical line extending from the upper left-hand corner of the scattergram to the lower right-hand corner.

Correlations are assigned a quantitative value ranging from ⁺1 (a perfect
positive correlation) to ⁻1 (a perfect negative correlation). The value, which
indicates the degree of correlation, is called a *correlation coefficient*. All correlation coefficients have a value somewhere between ⁺1 and ⁻1 on a continuum. Perfect correlations are only hypothetical. The more the coefficient
approaches 1, either ⁺1 or ⁻1, the greater the degree of correlation. Figure 6-5
illustrates a number of correlation coefficient values on a continuum.

⁻1   ⁻0.75   ⁻0.50   ⁻0.25   0   ⁺0.25   ⁺0.50   ⁺0.75   ⁺1

Figure 6-5

Correlation coefficients on a continuum

CORRELATION COEFFICIENT is a quantitative value ranging
from ⁺1 to ⁻1 assigned to the degree of correlation between two or
more variables.

ASSIGN A QUANTITATIVE VALUE (COEFFICIENT) TO EACH OF
THE THREE SCATTERGRAMS IN FIGURE 6-2 THROUGH FIGURE
6-4 AND EXPLAIN WHY YOU SELECTED THE SPECIFIC COEFFI-
CIENT TO REPRESENT THE DEGREE OF CORRELATION.

	Coefficient	Explanation
Figure 6-1	0.80	Points tend to fall around the line in a positive direction.
Figure 6-2		
Figure 6-3		
Figure 6-4		

The responses can, at best, only be educated guesses. For the scattergram
in Figure 6-2, a straight line best fitting the plotted points could be drawn;
the points would not, however, lie as close to the line as the points do in

Figure 6-1. On this basis a positive coefficient of around 0.60 may be a satisfactory estimate of the correlation. The plotted points in Figure 6-3 assume a random pattern; hence a coefficient near 0 should be the assigned value. The scattergram in Figure 6-4 takes on a negative direction with the plotted points clustered nearer to a hypothetical straight line than the plotted points in Figure 6-1. A coefficient of ⁻0.90 is a reasonable estimate of the correlation.

The committee of parents and teachers was faced with the task of explaining the results of the pilot test. Personality measures used for selecting students for mathematics classes grouped according to ability were no better than assigning students by chance. Though study habits did show some positive correlation with achievement in mathematics, it was certainly not a sufficient basis for assigning students to particular classes. The committee was back to the *Scholastic Ability Test*. Since prior ability in mathematics was the best predictor of future achievement, the committee recommended the selection of a different ability test, one less dependent on verbal skills than the test presently in use, with additional input on the students' study habits.

REREAD YOUR RESPONSE TO THE QUESTIONS ON PAGE 71. ON THE BASIS OF YOUR OWN EXPERIENCE, WOULD YOU GO ALONG WITH THE COMMITTEE'S REPORT? _____

_____

_____

_____

- -

If you are uncertain, the succeeding section may provide you with a better basis for making a decision.

There are a number of statistical procedures available for determining with greater accuracy the correlation between two variables than the educated guesses we have used to this point. Two statistical tests are described in the following section. Both are predicated on the existence of a linear relationship between the variables. The first statistical test to be described utilizes interval scale data; the second ordinal scale date. (See Chapter 3.)

PEARSON PRODUCT-MOMENT CORRELATION

The *Pearson Product-Moment Correlation* is a statistical procedure for deriving a correlation coefficient. It assumes that a linear rather than a nonlinear relationship exists between the variables and that the data are normally distributed. In deriving the coefficient, we make use of two concepts we have encountered previously: the mean and the standard deviation.

PEARSON PRODUCT-MOMENT CORRELATION is a statistical procedure for deriving a coefficient that defines numerically the correlation between two variables, if: both variables are linearly related, and both variables are normally distributed. The lowercase letter r is the statistical symbol used to represent a correlation. The coefficient is a numerical value describing the correlation.

Formula:

$$r = \frac{\Sigma(X - \bar{X})(Y - \bar{Y})}{N(SD_X)(SD_Y)}$$

where
X = one variable
Y = a second variable
$(X - \bar{X})$ = deviation score of the first variable
$(Y - \bar{Y})$ = deviation score of the second variable
$\Sigma(X - \bar{X})(Y - \bar{Y})$ = the sum of the cross products of each deviation score
N = number of paired scores
SD_X = standard deviation of the X variable
SD_Y = standard deviation of the Y variable

Using the two sets of data from Table 6-1, let us compute the exact correlation between the *Scholastic Ability Test* scores and the standardized mathematics achievement test scores.

NOTE THAT THE SCORES ON THE ACHIEVEMENT TEST ARE NOT ORDERED FROM HIGH TO LOW. WHY NOT? _____

_____

_____

We are correlating the scores of the same student on both variables. Bryant L.'s score is fourth from the top on the *Scholastic Ability Test,* but his score is eleventh from the highest score on the standardized mathematics achievement test. The concept of correlation is destroyed if we confuse one person's score on one variable with another person's score on a second variable.

Six steps for deriving a coefficient using the data in Table 6-1 are developed.

1. Obtain the mean of each set of scores.

$$\Sigma X = 1845 \qquad\qquad \Sigma Y = 540$$
$$\Sigma X/N = 1845/15 \qquad\qquad \Sigma Y/N = 540/15$$
$$\bar{X} = 123 \qquad\qquad \bar{Y} = 36$$

2. Find the deviation scores for each set of scores.

	Predictor				Criterion		
Student	X	$(X - \bar{X})$	x (see box below)	Student	Y	$(Y - \bar{Y})$	y (see box below)
X_1	162	162–123	39	Y_1	50	50–36	14
X_2	154	154–123	31	Y_2	48	48–36	12
X_3	145	145–123	22	Y_3	50	50–36	14
X_4	140	140–123	17	Y_4	35	35–36	⁻1
X_5	137	137–123	14	Y_5	42	42–36	6
X_6	136	136–123	13	Y_6	36	36–36	0
X_7	125	125–123	2	Y_7	38	38–36	2
X_8	120	120–123	⁻3	Y_8	38	38–36	2
X_9	119	119–123	⁻4	Y_9	38	38–36	2
X_{10}	117	117–123	⁻6	Y_{10}	47	47–36	11
X_{11}	110	110–123	⁻13	Y_{11}	24	24–36	⁻12
X_{12}	105	105–123	⁻18	Y_{12}	37	37–36	1
X_{13}	97	97–123	⁻26	Y_{13}	21	21–36	⁻15
X_{14}	90	90–123	⁻33	Y_{14}	20	20–36	⁻16
X_{15}	88	88–123	⁻35	Y_{15}	16	16–36	⁻20

The lowercase letter x is the statistical shorthand symbol for the deviation score.

Example: $(X - \bar{X}) = x$
   $(Y - \bar{Y}) = y$

$(x \cdot y)$ is the statistical shorthand symbol indicating multiplication of the X variable deviation scores and the Y variable deviation scores, called the cross products.

---

3. Multiply each deviation score on the one variable by the corresponding deviation score on the other variable.

$(X - \bar{X}) \cdot (Y - \bar{Y})$		$=$	$(X - \bar{X})(Y - \bar{Y}) = (x \cdot y)$
39	14		546
31	12		372
22	14		308
17	⁻1		⁻17
14	6		84
13	0		0
2	2		4
⁻3	2		⁻6
⁻4	2		⁻8
⁻6	11		⁻66
⁻13	⁻12		156
⁻18	1		⁻18
⁻26	⁻15		390
⁻33	⁻16		528
⁻35	⁻20		700

4. Find the sum of the cross products (add the right-hand column in the third step):

$$\Sigma(X - \bar{X})(Y - \bar{Y}), \text{ or } \Sigma(x \cdot y)$$

a. Add the positive cross products.
b. Add the negative cross products.
c. Subtract the smaller term from the larger term. The answer carries the sign of the larger term. (Refer to the rules in Chapter 4 for adding positive and negative terms.)

$$3088 + {}^-115 = 3088 - {}^+115 = 2973$$
$$\Sigma(X - \bar{X})(Y - \bar{Y}) = 2973$$

5. Compute the standard deviation of each variable:

$$SD_X = \sqrt{\Sigma(X - \bar{X})^2/N} \qquad SD_Y = \sqrt{\Sigma(Y - \bar{Y})^2/N}$$

$$SD_X = 21.86 \qquad\qquad SD_Y = 10.75$$

6. Insert the computed terms into the product-moment correlation formula:

$$r = \frac{\Sigma(X - \bar{X}(Y - \bar{Y})}{N(SD_X)(SD_Y)}$$

$N = 15$ (the number of pairs of scores)

$SD_X = 21.86$

$SD_Y = 10.75$

$\Sigma(X - \bar{X})(Y - \bar{Y}) = 2973$ (from the fourth step)

$$r = \frac{2973}{(15)(21.86)(10.75)} = 0.84$$

The estimated correlation coefficient for the scattergram in Figure 6-1 was 0.80; the computed correlation coefficient is $r = 0.84$.

INTERPRETATION OF THE CORRELATION COEFFICIENT

What does $r = 0.84$ mean? We know it is a positive correlation and that it is closer to $^+1$ than to 0 on the continuum. In this case it indicates that the *Scholastic Ability Test* may be a fairly effective method to use for selecting students who could succeed in an advanced mathematics class; that is, the ability test may be able to predict with some degree of accuracy the successful future performance of students in an advanced mathematics class. It is unfortunate that, even with a correlation as high as 0.84, there will be students incorrectly placed. Some students who do not belong in an advanced class will be assigned to the class, and others will be excluded who could succeed if given the opportunity. The greater the magnitude of the coefficient, either as a positive or negative value, the more the error of selection is reduced. But error is never totally eliminated. A correlation coefficient is merely a guide. Teachers and administrators must add their own professional understanding of the instructional context to the correlation data when they are making decisions.

Although the committee of parents and teachers recommended another type of mathematics ability test as a predictor of subsequent achievement in the field, one less dependent on verbal ability, they decided to pursue the question of what constitutes an adequate coefficient in order to avoid excess errors in placement. The question the committee asked was: How many students will be incorrectly placed given $r = 0.84$?

Before the committee could respond to the question, they had to draw on their understanding of the students' performance in mathematics. Basing their decision on the past performance of students in the advanced mathematics class, the committee determined that after instruction students needed to obtain a score of 36 points or better on the standardized mathematics achievement test to meet the standards of the mathematics department. A score of 118 points on the *Scholastic Ability Test* was used as a placement cutoff score. Students earning scores of 118 or better demonstrated that they had the requisite skills to succeed in the advanced class. Given these conditions the committee was ready to study the placement errors.

The committee examined carefully the information depicted in Figure 6-1 and noted the position of the plotted points in relation to the hypothetical straight line. The line, called the *regression line* or predictor line, best fits all the plotted points.

REGRESSION LINE is the straight line that best fits the plotted scores on a scattergram. It predicts performance on the criterion from the predictor scores.

LOCATE GWEN C.'S SCORES ON THE SCATTERGRAM (PREDICTOR: $X = 125$; CRITERION: $Y = 38$). HOW ACCURATE IS THE PREDICTION OF GWEN'S SUBSEQUENT PERFORMANCE? _____

LOCATE JOHN T.'S SCORES ON THE SCATTERGRAM (PREDICTOR: $X = 117$; CRITERION: $Y = 47$). HOW ACCURATE IS THE PREDICTION OF JOHN'S SUBSEQUENT PERFORMANCE? _____

IS CLIFFORD D.'S POSITION ON THE SCATTERGRAM IN RELATION TO THE REGRESSION LINE ENOUGH TO PREDICT SUCCESSFUL PERFORMANCE IN THE ADVANCED MATHEMATICS CLASS ($X = 136$; $Y = 36$)? _____

Gwen's scores fall right on the regression line. On the basis of this information, we can assume that, with a score of 136 on the *Scholastic Ability Test,* Gwenn should have done satisfactorily in the advanced mathematics class. On the other hand, John's plotted scores lie a distance from the regression line. It would appear that on the basis of his score on the *Scholastic Ability Test,* we could expect that he would not perform adequately in the advanced class. His performance on the criterion measure does not, however, bear this out. Just by observing Clifford's scores in relation to the regression line it is difficult to tell how accurately the *Scholastic Ability Test* can predict his subsequent performance. Given the criterion cutoff point, Clifford just comes up to the mathematics department's standard.

If fifteen students were randomly assigned to the advanced mathematics class, without having their selection based on any predictor measure, we could expect that by chance alone 50 percent of the students would be properly placed, while 50 percent would be incorrectly placed.

WITH $r = 0.84$ AND USING THE CUTOFF POINTS ESTABLISHED BY THE COMMITTEE, HOW MANY STUDENTS WERE IM- PROPERLY INCLUDED AND EXCLUDED FROM THE ADVANCED MATHEMATICS CLASS?

Improperly included_____   Improperly excluded _____

- -

Bryant L. was improperly included in the advanced class. His score on the predictor measure was well over the cutoff point, but his actual perform- ance did not come up to criterion. Two students were improperly excluded from the advanced class: John T. and Morgan N. Their performance on the criterion measure indicated satisfactory performance. John's perform- ance was, in fact, in the upper 20 percent of the class.

If a correlation between the predictor and criterion variables were below $r = 0.84$, the vertical distance between the plotted points and the regression line would be greater, which makes it more difficult to predict performance accurately. In addition to a high value for r, it is necessary to select the proper cutoff point for making placement decisions.

WHAT PREDICTOR CUTOFF POINT WOULD LEAD TO LESS ERROR IN SELECTION THAN THE 118 POINTS USED BY THE SELECTION COMMITTEE (RETAINING THE CRITERION OF 36 POINTS), AND WHY? _____

_____

_____

- -

If the committee had placed the cutoff point of the predictor at 110 points, only one student would have been improperly excluded and one student improperly included. Thus, this would have been a better cutoff point.

RANK ORDER CORRELATION

Many of the school data are ordinal scale data, such as class standing, performance ratings, the rank of schools within the school system, and the like. The product-moment correlation procedure for ascertaining the co- efficient is generally used with rank order data because we cannot assume that such data are normally distributed, an assumption of the product-moment correlation. A *rank order correlation* is based on the difference between any two sets of ranked data.

RANK ORDER CORRELATION is a statistical procedure for deriving a coefficient that defines the numerical relationship between two variables on the basis of the rank order of the data. The Greek letter rho (ϱ) is the statistical symbol used to represent a rank order correlation.

Formula

$$\varrho = 1 - \frac{6\Sigma d^2}{N(N^2 - 1)}$$

where   1 and 6 = constants

d = difference between a pair of ranks

d^2 = square of each difference

Σd^2 = sum of the squared difference of each pair

N = number of paired cases

N^2 = square of N

Table 6-2

Illustration of calculations for rank order correlation coefficient

Prospective teachers	Group X (column 1)	Group Y (column 2)	$d = (X - Y)$ (column 3)	$d^2 = (X - Y)^2$ (column 4)
A	1	3	⁻2	4
B	2	1	1	1
C	3	2	1	1
D	4	7	⁻3	9
E	5	4	1	1
F	6	5.5 } --tie	0.5	0.25
G	7	5.5	1.5	2.25
H	8	9	⁻1	1
I	9	8	1	1
J	10	10	0	0
				$\Sigma d^2 = 20.50$

The faculty of a school district was asked to participate in interviewing and selecting prospective teachers for two available positions. Since this was the first time teachers were involved in the selection process, the superintendent had two groups of teachers submit a rank order list that each group had agreed upon independently of the other. The superintendent intended to correlate the rank order lists to determine the feasibility of involving teachers in the selection process in the future. Table 6-2 shows the two ranked lists. The calculations for obtaining the rank order correlation coefficient are also shown in the table.

The steps for obtaining the rank order correlation coefficient follow.

1. Order the ranks on both measures. (In case of a tie in ranking, the position occupied by two or more ranks are averaged and the tied ranks assigned the average. Group Y assigned the same rank to prospective Teachers F and G. Because they are in the fifth and sixth ordered positions, they are assigned the rank of 5.5. Prospective Teacher D follows; he is assigned the seventh position.)

2. Obtain the difference between the two ranks for each pair (column 3):

$$d = (X - Y)$$

3. Square the difference of each ranked pair (column 4):

$$d^2 = (X - Y)^2$$

4. Obtain the sum of the squared differences (bottom of column 4):

$$\Sigma d^2 = \Sigma(X - Y)^2$$

5. Substitute values in the formula.

$$\varrho = 1 - \frac{6\Sigma d^2}{N(N^2 - 1)} \quad \varrho = 1 - \frac{6(20.5)}{10(10^2 - 1)} = 1 - \frac{123}{990} =$$

$$\varrho = 1 - 0.124, \text{ or } \varrho = 0.88$$

Interpreting a correlation coefficient depends on the educational context. In the case above, the superintendent felt the value of rho was sufficiently high to continue involving teachers in the selection process. He could accept with confidence the ratings by different groups of teachers as providing consistent information.

If we need a broad view of a student, data from different variables are more useful if they are not highly correlated. Reading achievement and manual dexterity are not highly correlated. Data on a student from these two variables would provide a broader picture than data from two highly correlated variables, such as verbal ability and reading achievement.

The best rule to follow, however, in obtaining a predictor for selection or rejection purposes is to choose one that correlates with a criterion as close to $+1$ or -1 as possible. Since this is an ideal and not often obtainable in education, educators must always be alert to the errors in selecting or rejecting students. The correlation coefficient merely serves as a guide; we must always be aware of the error factor regardless of how high the correlation coefficient. We cannot hide behind a statistic to escape the responsibility of professional judgment. The key word is "caution" in accepting or rejecting on the basis of the correlation between a predictor and a criterion.

There is one additional precaution about using correlations. A correlation does not describe a causal relationship. We cannot say that high scholastic scores caused the students to be successful in an advanced mathematics class any more than we can say personality was not the cause of success in that class. We can say that the size of one's hat is positively correlated with the size of one's head, but we cannot say the large hat size is the cause of a large head.

Case studies 11 and 12 provide activities for applying the concepts related to correlations to everyday school problems.

REFERENCES

Koosis, Donald J. *Statistics*. New York: John Wiley and Sons, 1972. For additional exercises, Chapter 7, pages 182–190, includes material to familiarize the reader with constructing and interpreting scattergrams.

McCollough, Celeste, and Van Atta, Loche. *Statistical Concepts: A Program For Self-Instruction*. New York: McGraw-Hill, 1963. Lesson 18 develops the concept of linear regression from a simple mathematical approach and relates it to the concept of correlation.

Wesman, Alexander G. "The Three-Legged Coefficient (the meaning of correlations)." *Test Service Bulletin*. Number 40. New York: The Psychological Corporation (304 East 45th Street, New York, N.Y., 10017), December 1950. This publication stresses the importance of exerting professional judgment in reading meaning into a correlation coefficient. It is available from the above address, free upon request.

Young, Robert K., and Veldman, Donald J. *Introductory Statistics*, 2d edition. New York: Holt, Rinehart and Winston, 1972. Chapter 16 provides a readable discussion of the concept of correlations and includes programmed material based on the discussion in pages 395–430.

7.
RELIABILITY: MEANING AND
RELATED STATISTICS

In Chapter 2 we examined Ronald's raw score of 58 points on an assignment and interpreted it descriptively. His score could have also been interpreted using statistics such as the mode, median, mean, standard deviation, and standard scores. Regardless of the data base used to discuss Ronald's score, we have not questioned the accuracy of the 58 points as a measure of Ronald's performance. Any number of circumstances could contribute to the 58 points, many of which have little to do with his "true" score.

LIST SEVERAL FACTORS THAT COULD AFFECT RONALD'S PER-
FORMANCE AND THEREBY MAKE THE 58 POINTS AN INACCU-
RATE REPRESENTATION OF HIS PERFORMANCE. _____

_____

_____

_____

_____

_____

As you examine your list, you may observe that the inaccuracies come from one of three sources: the assignment as an instrument measuring Ronald's performance; inconsistencies in performance related to Ronald himself; and error or inconsistencies in the administration and scoring of the assignment.

SOURCES OF INCONSISTENCY
The Instrument

One source of inconsistency is related to the measurement instrument. Accurate instruments used in measuring distance, weight, or volume, such as a yardstick, scale, or graduate, yield more consistent results than instruments used to measure achievement or other behavioral characteristics. For the latter type of instruments, inconsistencies come from ambiguous test items, inaccurate data supplied in tests for use in responding to an item, miskeyed item responses, items not appropriate for the grade or competency level, or information contained in an item that inadvertently assists only a few students in responding to the item. We need to ask: is the instrument so constructed that students with similar characteristics, or the same student at another time, will obtain the same or similar scores?

The Object, Event, or Trait

The second source of inconsistency or inaccuracy relates to variations in the object being measured. A fixed object, such as a table, varies little from one measurement of its length to the next. There may be slight changes owing to humidity or temperature, but, for the purpose of measuring a table in centimeters, the differences in its length attributable to these factors are too minute to be detected by such an ordinary instrument as a meter stick. Human performance and products of performance, however, are very susceptible to internal and external environments. Even with accurate instruments, scores will differ because of the variations in the individual's performance from one time to the next. Room temperature, humidity, a headache, irritation with the teacher, lack of motivation at one time and not the next—all these and other factors produce differences in the measured performance. This means we need to ask whether Ronald's observed score of 58 points is a "true" measure of his performance. Variations owing to chance elements, such as those mentioned above, will produce scores that reflect errors of measurement, thus reducing the reliability of the instrument.

The Administration and Scoring

The third source of inconsistency relates to administration and scoring procedures. Poorly stated directions, directions that vary from one administration of the instrument to the next, variation in the amount of completion time provided different students, and differences in the physical arrangement of the room from one administration of the test to another cause inconsistencies in performance.

The scoring of an instrument should not vary from one time to the next; nor should the scores given a single performance differ from scorer to scorer.

Inconsistencies in scoring are, however, easily introduced through errors in summing up the subscores and in transcribing the scores. Essays and open-ended responses tend to produce greater variations in scoring then objective responses.

WAYS OF CONCEPTUALIZING RELIABILITY

The sources of inconsistency in measurement alert the user of a measurement instrument to the nature of errors associated with the instrument. To use an instrument wisely, we need information about its freedom from error. Taking the sources of inconsistency into consideration, measurement specialists talk about an instrument's reliability, or freedom from error, in terms of stability, equivalence, and internal consistency.

Stability

A stable instrument consistently yields the same or similar measurements from time to time and from scorer to scorer. We must ask: Is the instrument, in this case the assignment, consistent in its measurement of Ronald's performance from one time to another, all other sources of possible inconsistencies remaining constant? As an example, if Ronald weighs 108 pounds on the nurse's scale at 10:35 a.m., we would expect him to weigh 108 pounds on the same scale at 10:40 a.m. the same day. A measurement instrument that consistently yields similar results when measuring the same object, event, or trait is said to be a reliable instrument because it has *stability*.

> STABILITY. The reliability of an instrument is dependent on its stability, that is, on the degree to which the instrument measures an object, event, or trait with consistent results, all other sources of inconsistency held constant.

Equivalence

An instrument's reliability can also be determined by comparing Ronald's weight on one scale with his weight on another scale (*equivalence*). The extent to which both scales yield similar results is another way of representing the concept of reliability.

> EQUIVALENCE. Two instruments are said to be equivalent when the measurement of an object, event, or trait on one instrument is the same or similar to the measurement of the same object, event, or trait on a similar instrument.

Internal Consistency

Instruments such as tests, checklists, and questionnaires are reliable to the extent they are internally consistent. Each question in a test or item in a checklist should contribute to the measurement of the object, event, or trait in a way that provides for intratest consistency. For example, in a 50-item achievement test in the social studies, each item should contribute to the measurement of the student's achievement of the social studies' curriculum objectives. We say the instrument has *internal consistency* to the extent the items contribute to the total measurement. The greater the internal consistency of the instrument, the higher its reliability.

> INTERNAL CONSISTENCY. The degree to which each item contributes to the measurement of some aspect of an object, event, or trait being measured determines the internal consistency reliability of the instrument.

Observed Score and True Score

Theoretically we can discuss reliability as the extent to which a score is free from error. The "true" score can be viewed as the sum of two components: the raw score component and the error component. This is shown in the equation:

$$X_{true} = X_{obs} + X_e$$

where X_{true} = the true score
X_{obs} = the observed score or measured score
X_e = the error component

As the observed score varies less and less from the true score, the error component of a score gets smaller and smaller. When $X_e = 0$, or there is no error in the measurement, then the observed score is equal to the true score:

$$X_{true} = X_{obs} + 0, \text{ or}$$
$$X_{true} = X_{obs}$$

Ronald's score of 58 points may or may not be his true score. If we could test Ronald innumerable times, the average of the scores would approach his true score. Once the reliability of an instrument can be determined, whether it is conceptualized as stability, equivalency, or internal consistency, we can obtain an estimate of the amount of error of measurement in an observed score.

Before we proceed to the statistics associated with reliability, the exercise below may help you to summarize the concepts discussed in the above sections.

TWO SCIENCE TEACHERS WERE ASKED TO JUDGE PROJECTS IN A SCIENCE FAIR. THEY WERE GIVEN A CHECKLIST FOR SCORING THE PROJECTS.

1. What is the measurement instrument? _____
2. What are the objects being measured? _____
3. Who are the scorers? _____
4. What are the possible sources of inconsistency? _____

_____

_____

_____

5. What concept of reliability is involved: stability, equivalency, or internal consistency? _____

The answers to the first three questions are specific:
1. The checklist is the instrument.
2. The science projects are the objects to be measured.
3. The two science teachers are the scorers or raters.

There is more leeway in the responses to the fourth and fifth questions:
4. Possible errors in measurement are due to all three of the sources of error that create inconsistency in the measurements: the checklist, the students who constructed the projects, and the teachers who rated the projects.
5. When both teachers score or rate the same project, they are obtaining repeated measurements; hence the concept of stability of measurement is involved. If two similar checklists had been used, then we would need to consider equivalency. If we examine each item on the checklist for its interitem correlation, then we are talking about internal consistency.

DETERMINING STATISTICALLY THE RELIABILITY OF AN INSTRUMENT

Several statistical procedures are used to determine the reliability of an instrument. Reliability, viewed as stability of measurement, requires a statistical procedure that repeatedly measures the object, event, or trait. Reliability based on equivalency of measurement uses the results obtained from one instrument along with the results obtained from measuring the same objects, events, or traits using a similar instrument. Although the data used for determining the stability and equivalency reliability are different, the general procedures are the same.

WHAT STATISTIC INTRODUCED PREVIOUSLY COULD BE USED TO DETERMINE STABILITY AND EQUIVALENCY RELIABILITY?

A correlation coefficient is computed using the scores obtained on one occasion and the scores on the same object, event, or trait on a second occasion, whether the same instrument is used or two similar instruments are used.

Several statistical procedures are used for determining internal consistency reliability. One method requires splitting the test in half and correlating the two halves. A number of procedures require analysis of variance. (You will recall that the variance is the average of the deviation scores in a distribution.)

Computing Reliability as Stability of Measurement

A correlation statistic is used to compute the reliability coefficient of an instrument to determine its consistency in measuring an object, event, or trait under similar conditions. The product-moment correlation for deriving the coefficient of stability is used. A test-retest condition is set up. The instrument is used to collect data on a first occasion. The measurement is repeated on a second occasion. The two sets of scores are then correlated.

The formula is the same as that shown in Chapter 6. Changing the subscripts of the symbols helps one keep clearly in mind what measurements are being correlated.

$$r_{12} = \frac{\Sigma(X_1 - \bar{X}_1)(X_2 - \bar{X}_2)}{N(SD_1)(SD_2)}$$

where r_{12} = correlation coefficient resulting from measurements obtained on the first occasion with measurements of the same object, event, or trait on the second occasion

X_1 and $\bar{X}_1$ = raw score and mean on the first measurement
X_2 and $\bar{X}_2$ = raw score and mean on the second measurement
SD_1 and SD_2 = standard deviations of the first and second set of scores
N = number of paired scores

THINK THROUGH THE TEST-RETEST METHOD IN THE LIGHT OF YOUR EXPERIENCES IN THE CLASSROOM. WHAT CAUTIONS COME TO MIND IN USING THIS METHOD OF DETERMINING RELIABILITY OF STABILITY? _____

_____

_____

_____

Assuming that there are no changes in the administration and scoring of the instrument, we still need to consider changes in the students. They may learn from the test itself on the first occasion and use the knowledge on the second occasion. Or the students could be continuing to learn from instruction between the time of the first and second testing. From one test to the next the students tend to become more testwise. Problems owing to stomach aches, indisposition, and other physical and emotional conditions tend to be evenly represented from test to test; however, if Alfred felt fine at the time of the first test but poor at the time of the second, this could adversely affect the correlation coefficient.

Statistics for Computing Reliability as Equivalency Measurement

Two similar instruments are used to measure the same set of objects, events, or traits to determine consistency of measurement. The student is administered two similar forms of the same test. Form A can be administered first, followed in a short time (several days or a week) by the administration of the parallel test, Form B. In this way repeated measurements are obtained. Applying the product-moment correlation procedure, a coefficient of the equivalency of the instruments is computed. This is shown in the formula below. By changing the subscripts, it may help you to understand how the data are used in the formula.

$$r_{ab} = \frac{\Sigma(X_a - \bar{X}_a)(X_b - \bar{X}_b)}{N(SD_a)(SD_b)}$$

where r_{ab} = correlation between Form A and Form B

X_a and $\bar{X}_a$ = the raw score and mean of Form A

X_b and $\bar{X}_b$ = the raw score and mean of Form B

SD_a and SD_b = standard deviation of Form A and Form B

N = number of paired scores

WHAT WEAKNESS DO YOU FIND IN THE ABOVE METHOD? ____

____

____

There is always the danger of a certain amount of learning from one form
of the test that the student brings to the equivalent form.

To compensate for this, the test may be given to two different groups of
students. During the first week Form A is administered to Group 1 and Form
B to Group 2. During the second week Group 1 takes Form B and Group 2
Form A. All the scores from Form A are combined, and all the scores from
Form B are combined. Any advantage Group 1 may have had by taking
Form B after Form A is compensated by the advantage Group 2 had by
taking Form A after Form B. Table 7-1 illustrates the point.

Table 7-1

Administration of Forms A and B to two groups of students

Form	First week	Second week	Total for correlation
A	Group 1	Group 2	Groups 1 + 2
B	Group 2	Group 1	Groups 1 + 2

Computing Reliability as Internal Consistency of a Measurement Instrument

A reliability coefficient for determining the internal consistency of an
instrument can be obtained from several statistical procedures. Four of these
are discussed: split-half reliability, Kudar-Richardson Formula 20, Hoyt's
analysis of variance procedure, and a teacher-made formula based on Kudar-
Richardson Formula 20. The last gives a reasonable estimate of internal consistency reliability for classroom purposes.

Split-Half Reliability

The items in a single instrument are used, and either the first half of the
items are correlated with the last half of the items or the odd-numbered items
are correlated with the even-numbered items using the product-moment
correlation statistic. With the split-half procedure, separate scores from, let
us say, the first 50 items in a 100-item test and separate scores from the last
50 items are obtained. The scores are then correlated.

WHAT PROBLEMS DO YOU SEE ARISING WITH THIS METHOD?

One problem is the slow-working student who is likely to complete the first half of the test but not the second half. In addition, many constructors of tests include easier items in the beginning section of the test and increase the difficulty of the items in later portions of the test. Split-half correlation coefficients, in this case, do not give a good index of the reliability of the test.

To compensate for these difficulties in the split-half reliability, the odd-even reliability correlates the sum of the quantitative value assigned to all the odd-numbered items and the sum of the quantitative value assigned to all the even-numbered items. A student who may be indisposed will perform equally poorly on both odd items and even items, slow students will complete as many odd items as even items, and the students will encounter as many easy items as difficult items. The subscripts for split-half and odd-even reliabilities using the Pearson Product-Moment Correlation formula are shown below.

$$r_{\frac{1}{2}\frac{1}{2}} = \frac{\Sigma(X_1 - \bar{X}_1)(X_2 - \bar{X}_2)}{N(SD_1)(SD_2)}$$

where

$$r_{\frac{1}{2}\frac{1}{2}} = \text{split-half reliability}$$

$$r_{oe} = \frac{\Sigma(X_O - \bar{X}_O)(X_e - \bar{X}_e)}{N(SD_O)(SD_e)}$$

where

$$r_{oe} = \text{odd-even reliability}$$

The size of the reliability coefficient is dependent on the number of items in an instrument. The larger the number of items, the greater the coefficient. The split-half and odd-even reliabilities represent two tests with half the number of items in each test as in the original test. Hence the coefficients tend to be smaller than one might obtain if a reliability coefficient is computed for the total test. If the *Spearman-Brown Formula* is applied to the split-half reliability, it gives an estimate of the instrument's reliability based on the total number of items in the instrument.

SPEARMAN-BROWN FORMULA is a formula for estimating the reliability of an instrument based on its original number of items from a split-half or odd-even reliability coefficient.

Formula:

$$r_{tt} = \frac{2r_{\frac{1}{2}\frac{1}{2}}}{1 + r_{\frac{1}{2}\frac{1}{2}}}$$

where r_{tt} = reliability of total test

Example: Given a total test length of 100 items, $r_{\frac{1}{2}\frac{1}{2}}$ = 0.78 (based on 50 items):

$$r_{tt} = \frac{2(0.78)}{1 + 0.78} = \frac{1.56}{1.78} = 0.88$$

Split-half reliability has several advantages over test-retest and parallel test reliabilities.

WHAT ARE SOME OF THE ADVANTAGES? ⎯⎯⎯⎯⎯⎯⎯

One big advantage relates to the number of correlated scores. With split-half reliability there are two sets of scores to be correlated for each student. With test-retest or parallel tests, some students present during the first round may be absent at the time of the second administration of the test; these scores cannot, therefore, figure in the calculations. In addition, the problem of transfer of learning from test to retest is eliminated, and all other conditions are similar.

Kudar-Richardson Formula 20

Kudar and Richardson have developed many formulas to determine the internal consistency of an instrument. K-R Formula 20 obtains interitem agreement from, first, the proportion of a group obtaining the correct and incorrect answers to each item; second, the number of items in the instrument; and, third, the observed total score variance (SD squared). The formula is shown below:

$$r = (\frac{N}{N-1})(\frac{SD^2 - \Sigma pq}{SD^2})$$

where r = estimate of internal consistency reliability
            N = number of items in the test
            SD^2 = variance or standard deviation squared
            p = percent of students passing a given item
            q = percent of students failing the same item

One restriction needs to be followed in using Formula 20. The items contributing to the total score can have only a weight of one point. If there are 40 items measuring a single factor, the total possible score would be 40 points.

Hoyt's Analysis of Variance Reliability

Hoyt's procedure for estimating the internal consistency reliability is a more advanced concept than we can handle at this level. Many standardized tests today report the instrument's internal reliability using Hoyt's analysis of variance procedure or some similar statistical procedure. The coefficient of reliability obtained from Hoyt's formula is comparable to the Kudar-Richardson Formula 20.

Teacher-Made Formula*

Several short-cut formulas are available that yield comparable coefficients to the K-R Formula 20. School personnel need not hesitate to use the teacher-made formula (r_{tm}) for computing the internal consistency reliability of their own instruments. One such formula is shown below:

$$r_{tm} = 1 - \left[\frac{\bar{X}(N - \bar{X})}{N(SD^2)} \right]$$

where r_{tm} = estimate of teacher-made reliability

           $\bar{X}$ = mean of the test

           N = number of items in the test

           SD^2 = variance

The formula can be used with ease and does not involve any statistics we have not encountered previously. The same restrictions on the weight of the items hold, however, as in the case of K-R Formula 20.

---

* "Short-cut Statistics for Teacher-Made Tests." Evaluation and Advisory Service Series, Number 5, Princeton, N.J.: Educational Testing Services, 1960.

CALCULATE THE INTERNAL CONSISTENCY RELIABILITY OF A
60-ITEM TEACHER-MADE SCIENCE TEST USING THE TEACHER-
MADE FORMULA WITH $\bar{X} = 35$ AND $SD = 7$.

$$r_{tm} = 1 - \left[\frac{\bar{X}(N - \bar{X})}{N(SD^2)} \right]$$

$$r_{tm} = \underline{\hspace{2cm}}$$

The information necessary for computing the formula follows:

$N = 60$; $\bar{X} = 35$; $SD = 7$; $SD^2 = 49$

These figures are substituted in the formula:

$$r_{tm} = 1 - \left[\frac{35(60-35)}{(60)(49)} \right]$$

$$r_{tm} = 1 - \left[\frac{875}{2940} \right] = 1 - 0.298$$

$$r_{tm} = \quad 0.702 \text{ or } 0.70$$

INTERPRETATION OF A RELIABILITY COEFFICIENT

The beginning of the chapter presented various sources of error that oper-
ate to reduce the consistency of a raw score. Reliability was discussed theoretically in terms of true scores and observed scores. Then we explored
several concepts of reliability in terms of stability, equivalence, and internal
consistency. The statistics applicable for deriving the reliabilities were discussed. Now we are ready to interpret the resulting reliability coefficients.

A reliability coefficient has a range similar to the correlation coefficient
with one distinction. The value of the reliability coefficient is always positive,
ranging from 0 to $^+1$. Negative reliability coefficients are meaningless.

IN THE EXERCISE ABOVE, WE OBTAINED A RELIABILITY OF
0.70. WHAT DOES THIS TELL US ABOUT THE MEASUREMENT
INSTRUMENT AND ABOUT THE RAW SCORES OBTAINED? ____

A rule of thumb can be applied: the closer the coefficient approaches 1, the more reliable the instrument. We shall, therefore, look for an instrument with a high coefficient. In addition to the rule of thumb, we need to answer the above question with a question: for what purpose is the measurement to be used? The answer to the question will aid in interpreting the reliability coefficient. First, it will help determine the acceptable quantitative value of the coefficient for your purpose. Second, it will guide you in interpreting an individual raw score on the basis of the instrument's approximation of the true score.

If an instrument is to be used for making decisions with regard to placement, such as tracking students in ability-grouped classes, admission to professional or trade schools, or other decisions where an individual's future is being decided, then we must insist on very high reliability coefficients. Even with a coefficient as high as 0.95, placement errors will be made. For a teacher-made test, reliability coefficients are usually very low. Just knowing how low it is will make teachers and administrators more cautious in using the raw score as an absolute measure of the performance of a student or a class on the basis of the score alone. In addition, knowing the reliability coefficient of teacher-made instruments will help teachers develop better measurement instruments.

There is another way to interpret raw scores when one knows the reliability coefficient. Let us assume the reliability of the teacher-made science test is 0.70. It is far from a perfect measurement instrument. With a reliability of less than 1, we know the obtained raw scores are not the true scores; knowing the reliability, however, we can estimate the extent of variability of the obtained scores around the true scores. This estimate is called the *standard error of measurement*. Theoretically it represents the standard deviation of a distribution obtained from a series of measurements of the same student on the same instrument. The standard error of measurement can be calculated from the standard deviation and the reliability without repeatedly measuring the same student.

The concept of standard error of measurement is an important tool for obtaining further information about the raw score. The standard error of measurement gives us the range of the raw scores that covers the true score. The higher the reliability coefficient of the instrument, the smaller the standard error of measurement or the variability of the observed score around the true score.

STANDARD ERROR OF MEASUREMENT is the variability of the observed scores around the true score. It represents the standard deviation of the distribution of errors of measurement. SE_{meas} is its statistical symbol.

Formula:

$$SE_{meas} = SD \sqrt{(1 - r)}$$

where $\qquad$ SD = the standard deviation
$\qquad\qquad$ r = the reliability

USING THE FORMULA FOR COMPUTING THE STANDARD ERROR OF MEASUREMENT, FIND SE_{meas}, GIVEN THE $SD = 7$ AND $r = 0.70$.

$$SE_{meas} = SD\sqrt{(1 - r)}$$

$$SE_{meas} = \underline{\qquad\qquad}$$

- -

Substitute the values in the formula:

$$SD_{meas} = 7\sqrt{(1 - 0.70)}$$
$$SD_{meas} = 7\sqrt{0.30} = 7(0.55)\,*$$
$$SD_{meas} = 3.85$$

Table 7-2 illustrates the different values for the standard error of measurement corresponding to selected reliability coefficients. From the table we read that if an instrument has a reliability of 0.70 and a standard deviation of 7, the true score will lie somewhere within ±3.85 points of the observed score.

WHAT HAPPENS TO THE SE_{meas} AS THE RELIABILITY COEFFICIENT APPROACHES 1.00? $\underline{\qquad\qquad\qquad\qquad\qquad}$

$\underline{\qquad\qquad\qquad\qquad\qquad\qquad\qquad\qquad\qquad\qquad\qquad\qquad\qquad\qquad\qquad}$

- -

---

*The square root of 0.30 rounded off to the nearest hundredth is 0.55.

As the reliability coefficient approaches 1.00, the SE_{meas} gets smaller, thereby reducing the range of values within which the true score may fall.

Table 7-2

Values of reliability coefficients and corresponding standard errors of measurement

r	SD	SE_{meas}
0.00	7	7.00
0.50	7	4.97
0.70	7	3.85
0.80	7	3.15
0.90	7	2.24
0.95	7	1.54
1.00	7	0.00

One more piece of information is needed in order to use the standard error of measurement in interpreting the raw score. The standard error of measurement (in the case above 3.85) is the standard deviation of a distribution of errors of measurement. It can be interpreted on the normal distribution curve as illustrated in Figure 7-1. We can assume that, given a score of 58

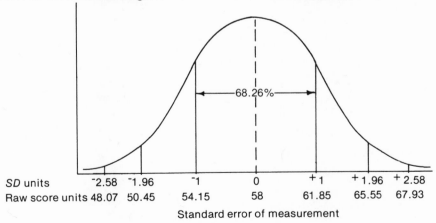

SD units	⁻2.58	⁻1.96	⁻1	0	⁺1	⁺1.96	⁺2.58
Raw score units	48.07	50.45	54.15	58	61.85	65.55	67.93

Standard error of measurement

Figure 7-1

SE_{meas} and raw scores on the normal curve

points (from a distribution having a standard deviation of 7 points and with an instrument whose reliability coefficient is 0.70), the interval covering the true score has a range of ±3.85 points around the true score. This means scores between 54.15 and 61.85 are observed approximately two-thirds of the time or exactly 68.26 percent of the time within the interval covering the true score. In interpreting the 58 points, we will get a better estimate of the performance if we think in terms of the range of 54.15 and 61.85 points rather than in terms of the specific score. The higher the reliability the more we narrow the range for interpreting the raw score.

If we want to build greater confidence into the interpretation, we can calculate the value of 1.96 SE_{meas} and 2.58 SD_{meas}. In this case, we can estimate the interval covering the true score around which the observed score may lie 95 and 99 percent of the time. To compute the range of observed scores in which the true score can fall in a given area under the normal distribution curve, the following formula is used:

$$X \pm (SD \text{ unit}) (SE_{meas})$$

Table 7-3 shows the computations and resulting ranges for three designated areas under the normal curve: ± 1SD, ± 1.96 SD, and ± 2.58 SD, which represent, respectively, 68.26 percent, 95 percent, and 99 percent of the area under the normal curve.

Table 7-3

Computing confidence levels of standard errors of measurement

Calculations	$X \pm SE_{meas}$	Range	Confidence level (in percents)
58 ± (1 SD) (3.85)	58 + 3.85 and 58 − 3.85	61.85–54.15	68.26
58 ± (1.96 SD) (3.85)	58 + 7.55 and 58 − 7.55	65.55–50.45	95
58 ± (2.58 SD) (3.85)	58 + 9.93 and 58 − 9.93	67.93–48.07	99

The question below indicates how the table can be used in interpreting the raw score.

YOU WANT TO INTERPRET A PERFORMANCE REPRESENTED BY A RAW SCORE OF 58 POINTS. WHAT CONFIDENCE HAVE YOU THAT THE INTERVAL 65.55 AND 50.45 COVERS THE TRUE SCORE? _____

You can estimate that 95 percent of the time the true score of the student who obtained a raw score of 58 points will be included in the interval 65.55 and 50.45 points.

OTHER FACTORS AFFECTING RELIABILITY

Other factors also play a part in affecting the reliability of a measurement instrument. These must be taken into consideration when one is interpreting a score or evaluating the measurement instrument.

1. The number of items in the instrument affect its reliability. The greater the number of items, the more likelihood of a higher reliability coefficient.

2. The greater the homogeneity of the items, the more likely a high reliability coefficient. Internal consistency reliability is greatly affected by the homogeneity of the items. If care is not taken in constructing the test items, the items may be too similar and measure the same thing over and over without adding any new information about the performance or its product.

3. The level of difficulty of the items affect the reliability. Chapter 9 discusses item difficulty in detail. For optimum reliability, an average item difficulty of 50 percent is advised. The level of difficulty is dependent, however, on the purpose of a test. For criterion-referenced tests, the desired average item difficulty may be set at 70 percent, 80 percent, 85 percent, or any other prespecified value. We need to consider, therefore, the purpose of the instrument when we interpret the reliability coefficient.

4. The larger the variability of the group, the greater the likelihood of a higher reliability. A measurement instrument can more readily detect large differences than it can small differences within the group.

Cases 13 and 14 extend the reader's understanding of reliability, standard error of measurement, and computation of the teacher-made reliability coefficient through their application in practical school situations.

REFERENCES

Brown, Frederick G. *Principles of Educational and Psychological Testing.* Hinsdale, Ill.: Dryden Press, 1970. Chapters 3 and 4 focus on several aspects of reliability: consistency, homogeneity, and errors in scores.

Davis, Frederick B., Chairman. *Standards for Educational and Psychological Tests.* Washington, D.C.: American Psychological Association, Inc., 1974. The seventy-six-page booklet is a joint statement by the American Psychological Association, the American Educational Research Association, and the National Council on Measurement in Education on standards for tests and manuals. Discussion of reliability affirms the importance of the concept for establishing the worth of an instrument for measurement. The role of the standard error of measurement in interpreting the reliability coefficient is emphasized.

Hoyt, Cyril J. "Reliability." In *Encyclopedia of Educational Measurement,* 3d edition. Ed. Chester W. Harris. New York: Macmillan, 1960. The work includes (pp. 1144–1147) a folksy example of sampling error as well as a readable discussion of the true score as a theoretical concept.

Stanley, Julian C. "Reliability." In *Educational Measurement,* 2d edition. Ed. Robert L. Thorndike. Washington, D.C.: American Council on Education, 1971. This is a thorough discussion of the theoretical concepts associated with reliability.

8.
VALIDITY: MEANING AND RELATED STATISTICS

The previous chapter discussed the question of confidence teachers and administrators can place in a score obtained from a measurement instrument. The nurse's scale used to measure Ronald was determined to be a reliable instrument for it yielded consistent measurements under the same conditions, and the readings were about the same when checked with similar scales. In the same office there were several other instruments: a pharmaceutical scale, a stopwatch, and a vertical rod marked off in centimeters and meters. Each of these instruments was found to have high reliability.

---

1. FOR WHAT PURPOSE WOULD THE NURSE USE THE INSTRUMENTS?
    a. PHARMACEUTICAL SCALE: _____
    b. STOP WATCH: _____
    c. VERTICAL MEASURING ROD: _____
2. WHY DID THE NURSE USE THE NURSE'S SCALE TO WEIGH RONALD RATHER THAN ANY OF THE OTHER RELIABLE INSTRUMENTS? _____
_____

Although it is essential to know the reliability of an instrument before using the obtained score to interpret the skill, knowledge, or trait represented by the score, there is another measurement concept that requires our examination. It focuses on the question of purpose. Each of the instruments in the nurse's office is valid for a specific purpose. Regardless of how reliable the instrument is, the measurements it yields are valid only for the purpose for which it was designed.

Validity, as a basic concept in measurement, focuses on two types of questions related to the purpose of an instrument or the obtained scores.

1. What does the measurement represent? Does the instrument measure the skills, understandings, or traits it purports to measure? How well does the score represent the behavior the instrument was designed to measure?

2. What does the measurement predict? What other skills, understandings, or traits can be predicted from the performance on the instrument? What can be inferred about other behaviors from the obtained score?

To establish the validity of an instrument we need to know what type of inferences we plan to draw from the scores. In Chapter 6 the teachers were drawing inferences about the students' ability to succeed in an advanced mathematics class from a test of ability administered prior to assignment to the class.

WHY DID PARENTS AND TEACHERS QUESTION THE *SCHOLASTIC ABILITY TEST?* _____

_____

_____

_____

_____

Parents and teachers raised two types of questions concerning validity. They questioned the validity of the instrument as a measure of performance in mathematics because of its heavy reliance on verbal proficiency. They questioned, in addition, its ability to predict future performance in advanced mathematics classes from the obtained scores on the *Scholastic Ability Test*. There was no question of the test's reliability, although this is also necessary to establish.

Although the questions asked to establish the validity of an instrument are interrelated, for clarity, validity is classified by the inferences to be drawn. By convention* the terms content validity, criterion-related validity, and con-

---

*From *Standards for Educational and Psychological Tests* (Washington, D.C.: American Psychological Association, Inc., 1974).

struct validity are used to describe the methods of validation. Establishing the validity of an instrument can become a highly research-oriented and technical study. Teachers and administrators will not, in most cases, conduct the research studies required to carry out validation studies. As consumers of standardized tests and developers of classroom and school evaluation instruments, however, they must have an awareness of the various types of validities and an understanding of the means used to establish validity in order to make inferences cautiously and intelligently.

CONTENT VALIDITY

Teachers are most directly concerned with ascertaining the content validity of an instrument. In developing their own classroom tests, they are bound by many of the guidelines that developers of standardized tests follow. The items constructed for the instrument should represent a sample of the behavior the instrument purports to measure. This holds for achievement tests to measure acquired skills and knowledge, for checklists, rating scales, and observation inventories to obtain data about the classroom environment, overt behavior, attitudes, and interests, as well as teacher-made instruments to collect data about many other facets of the instructional program.

A JOURNALISM CLASS WAS STUDYING EDITORIAL WRITING. THE TEACHER HAD THE CLASS CONTRAST EDITORIALS ON SIMILAR TOPICS THAT APPEARED IN NEWSPAPERS AND MAGAZINES OF DIFFERING POLITICAL PERSUASIONS. NEAR THE CONCLUSION OF THE UNIT, THE TEACHER PREPARED A TEST. WHAT TYPE OF ITEMS SHOULD BE INCLUDED IN THE TEST? _____

The items will depend on the objectives of the unit. Do the objectives concentrate only on identifying a newspaper's political orientation from its editorials? Do the objectives include an understanding of different editorial styles: satire, sarcasm, polemics? Do the objectives cover fallacious argumentation? Do the objectives work toward developing skills in writing editorials? Or, do the objectives focus on understanding the political positions from their historic antecedents?

The items making up such a test will differ greatly depending upon the objectives of the unit. The objectives identify the behaviors the test items intend to measure. Responses to the test items should elicit responses that indicate the extent to which the instructional objectives have been achieved. Content validity is situation-specific as well as population-specific. What may be an effective set of items for measuring fallacious arguments found in editorials (situation-specific) may not be suitable for measuring editorial styles. And what might be an appropriate set of items for a twelfth-grade class may well be inappropriate for a sixth-grade or intermediate class (population-specific).

Standardized tests in mathematics, English grammar, or science build the test around items that reflect the learning behaviors most commonly identified in current textbooks, teachers' manuals, and curriculum guides. Hence, a standardized test has validity to the extent the items are representative samples of the curriculum of a school, the school district, or general consensus of what constitutes the objectives for a given subject at a specific level.

Content validity of an instrument is also dependent on the representativeness of the items. The items included should measure all facets of the intended behavior. A test measuring the four arithmetic operations, as an example, must include items covering addition, subtraction, multiplication, and division. The items should cover a range of difficulty using all four operations and should contain a representative sample of skills and understandings that will indicate achievement at a given level of performance.

CONTENT VALIDITY is concerned with the representativeness of items in an instrument to elicit or to describe specified behavior in a defined content area for a given population.

CRITERION-RELATED VALIDITY

Chapter 6 introduced the reader to the terms "predictor variables" and "criterion variables" and their relationship. As its label implies, *criterion-related validity* is based on the relationship between a predictor and a criterion. Criterion-related validity applies to inferences that can be made from the scores on an instrument about performance on some other variable. A distinction is made between two types of criterion-related validities based on time interval. When future performance is inferred, on the basis of present performance, we term this predictive validity. Concurrent validity, the second type of criterion-related validity, is not used generally to predict subsequent performance after a time interval. In effect, concurrent validity indicates whether one type of measurement can be substituted for another in order to make similar inferences. This substitution may occur for such reasons as convenience of administration, cost, or availability of materials and personnel.

CRITERION-RELATED VALIDITY permits inferences to be made about one variable (the criterion) from scores obtained on another variable (the predictor).

Predictive Validity

Predictive validity is concerned with inferring future performance from present performance. High scores on instruments with established predictive validity should lead to high scores on future performance measured on a criterion variable. The predictive validity of one instrument is used as a guide for making many of the classroom and school district instructional and curriculum decisions about future behavior.

Such questions as setting prerequisites are predicated on prediction. For example, in the elementary social studies curriculum should the local community be studied before society at the national or international level? Should students master concepts concerning whole numbers before learning decimals? Should we drill students on the notes of a scale before teaching them a song? To determine prerequisites we need to know what knowledge, skills, or personal attributes are necessary for successful performance in a future learning situation. Will students with high scores on a test that measures understanding of whole numbers have an advantage in comprehending decimals over students who score low on the same test?

Accepting or rejecting students for specific programs is predicated on an instrument's predictive validity. Students with low verbal ability usually fare poorly in college-oriented curricula. Students with poor manual dexterity and low levels of responsibility tend to be a hazard in shop courses. By measuring verbal ability we can predict future success in college-oriented curricula, and by measuring manual dexterity and maturity we can predict future success in shop courses. Verbal ability, manual dexterity, and maturity are the predictor variables, and subsequent performance in college-oriented courses or shop courses are the criterion variables.

Selecting the appropriate criterion and predictor variables requires the exercise of professional judgment on the part of teachers and administrators. It calls for an understanding of the criterion and a rationale for choosing the predictor. Criterion-related validation of the predictor should lead to better decisions than are possible without the predictor. The problem presented below requires professional judgment.

AT A PARTICULAR HIGH SCHOOL, GIRLS WERE EXCLUDED IN THE PAST FROM AUTO MECHANICS COURSES. THE COURTS RULED THIS TO CONSTITUTE A SEX BIAS; HENCE, ALL AUTO

MECHANICS CLASSES HAD TO BE OPEN TO FEMALE STU-
DENTS. THE SCHOOL WAS NOT PREPARED TO ACCEPT THE
NUMBERS OF STUDENTS WHO WANTED TO ENROLL IN THESE
CLASSES.

1. What admissions criterion is relevant?_____

2. What predictor has potential for predicting criterion performance?

_____

_____

Your responses will vary. Regardless of the criterion and predictor you
selected, there must be an educationally justifiable reason for the criterion, and the predictor should hold potential for making better selections than without the aid of the predictor.

1. The criterion selected in the above case represents the desired behavioral outcomes upon completion of the auto mechanics course. One
criterion could be the employability of the students in top-rated auto
shops. Or, the criterion could be a demonstration of mastery of advanced
tasks of auto maintenance, such as tuning the engine, changing a water
pump, replacing brake linings, and so forth. Or, the criterion could
simply be the ability to perform such standard tasks as changing the oil,
tires, and filters. The curriculum objectives will help determine the
criterion.

2. The predictor differs in each of the criterion examples cited above.
Certainly for the first two criteria, the ability to read charts, diagrams,
and tables is an entrance skill that can be part of the predictor measure.
Skill in mathematics, at least through fractions and decimals, is another
entrance skill. For the third example of a criterion, interest or need to
know how to do one's own auto maintenance are reasonable entrance
skills that can be used as predictors.

One additional example is cited to emphasize the relationship between the
predictor and the criterion for establishing the validity of the predictor.

A HIGH SCHOOL WOULD LIKE TO FACILITATE EARLY PLACE-
MENT OF THE ENTERING FRESHMEN IN THE VARIOUS ENG-
LISH CLASSES IN ORDER TO PLAN FOR THE TYPE OF SECTIONS
AND THE DEPLOYMENT OF FACULTY. PLACEMENT IN A SPECI-
FIC SECTION IS CONTINGENT ON ACHIEVEMENT IN ENGLISH
GRAMMAR. THE HIGH SCHOOL NEEDED SOME WAY OF PRE-

DICTING PROPER PLACEMENT. WOULD YOU SUGGEST USING THE SCORES FROM A STANDARDIZED GRAMMAR TEST ADMINISTERED TO ALL THE EIGHTH-GRADE CLASSES AT THE END OF THE FIRST SEMESTER OR THE REPORT CARD GRADES ASSIGNED AT THE END OF THE FIRST SEMESTER? EXPLAIN.

Your choice would depend upon which of the two predictors correlates higher with future performance in the freshmen English classes. Let us say the report card marks proved a better predictor of performance than the grammar test. This does not diminish the possible validity of the grammar test for predicting some other criterion performance. *Predictive validity* is not something inherent in a measurement instrument. The predictive validity of a test depends on its relation to a specified criterion.

> PREDICTIVE VALIDITY is predicated on the extent to which an instrument or entering performance will predict future success on a criterion measure.

Concurrent Validity

Teachers and administrators frequently make decisions that require concurrent validation. As an example, a primary teacher lacks the time to listen to each child read orally in order to determine specific reading problems. Can she make inferences about her students' reading problems if she substitutes for the oral reading a silent reading exercise followed by responses to oral questions? To the extent that the teacher can make similar inferences about her students' reading behavior, the silent reading exercise has *concurrent validity*. In effect, concurrent validity permits a choice of a number of measures for making inferences about behavior.

> CONCURRENT VALIDITY establishes the equivalence of two instruments that are used to infer similar behavior, all other factors being equal.

An index of concurrent validity is derived from correlating the scores on the two instruments and obtaining the correlation coefficient. Students scoring highest on an oral reading exercise should be expected to obtain a high score on the silent reading exercise. Students scoring low on the one would be expected to score low on the other. The correlation coefficient would establish the concurrent validity of the instrument. If the two measures do not correlate highly, then the teacher should not substitute one for the other to make inferences about the students' reading problems. If a low correlation coefficient is obtained, it could mean the two measures are tapping different skills associated with reading.

THREE STANDARDIZED TESTS ARE ALL SHOWN TO CORRELATE HIGHLY WITH EACH OTHER. WHAT CRITERIA WOULD YOU USE TO SELECT FROM AMONG THE TESTS? _____

_____

_____

_____

The following criteria should guide you in making your selection: high reliability coefficient; content validity; initial cost; time and training needed to understand the design of the tests; ease of administration; extent of disruption of the ongoing instructional program; scoring problems; information the producer of the test supplies to interpret test results; extent of dependence on outside consultants to interpret results; length of test; replacement costs. Other criteria can include interesting test items and clarity of directions for responding to the items and the statement of the items. Where interest and clarity have not affected the reliability of the instrument, they do serve as selection criteria. In most instances, however, these factors would have affected the test's reliability. What about the length of the test? A short test whose items are a representative sample of the behaviors intended for measurement is just as effective as a test twice the length. It is preferable, in fact, to the longer test in terms of cost and time.

CONSTRUCT VALIDITY

We commonly assign verbal labels to traits that are not directly observable but are inferred from patterns of overt behavior. Such traits as sociability, creativity, aggressiveness, or reading readiness represent constructs. Developing out of psychological theory, constructs are valid to the extent that the theory can predict the behavior patterns associated with the construct. A theory of social behavior underlies the construct of sociability. If valid, the test scores obtained from an instrument developed to measure sociability should differentiate between persons who display high and low sociability behavior as predicted by the theory.

Instruction in large measure is predicated on a theory supporting the construct of readiness. Teachers are expected either to sense intuitively when students are ready for a new level of instruction or are guided by a list of behaviors that describe readiness characteristics. To the extent that the students can succeed at a new task when they display the requisite readiness characteristics, the construct is valid.

THE PRIMARY TEACHERS IN A SCHOOL DISTRICT PLAN TO INDIVIDUALIZE THE READING PROGRAM. THEY ASSUME THAT READING READINESS SCORES WILL HELP MAKE DECISIONS ABOUT WHERE EACH STUDENT SHOULD ENTER INTO THE READING PROGRAM. WHAT TYPES OF CONSTRUCT VALIDITY DATA SHOULD THE TEACHERS LOOK FOR IN SELECTING A READING READINESS TEST? _____

_____

_____

- -

The publisher of the test should state the assumptions about reading readiness upon which the test is predicated. Studies such as those cited below should be presented in support of the assumptions and theory. First, studies that show children with high scores on the reading readiness test learn to read sooner than children with low scores on the same test. Second, studies that show a positive correlation between readiness tasks in the test and reading skills taught in beginning reading classes. Third, comparative studies of reading readiness scores of children with different characteristics, such as socioeconomic background, sex, and maturity. Fourth, studies showing a relationship between reading readiness scores and scores on tests measuring other characteristics associated with readiness for normal instruction.

Awareness of the types of evidence that establish *construct validity* is essential for the intelligent use of tests measuring psychological constructs. Awareness of evidence may not, however, always be sufficient. A new theory may demand a new set of validity criteria.

CONSTRUCT VALIDITY is determined by the degree to which theoretical bases for a psychological or mental trait are supported by correlating evidence.

METHODS FOR DETERMINING VALIDITY

The type of validity under discussion determines the methods used in establishing an instrument's validity. Several methods for gathering data to ascertain the validity of an instrument are used. Content, criterion-related, and construct validities use one or more of these approaches: correlation, experimental, and logical.

Content Validity

There are no simple statistical tests for determining the content validity of an instrument. The user does need to ask the right questions before selecting or developing the appropriate instrument. Before selecting a standardized test, teachers and administrators must know what the test purports to measure. The test manual should be explicit in identifying the purpose of the test and the skills and understandings covered by the test items. The test manual should also identify the specific test items related to each separate skill and understanding as well as the population for which the test is intended.

A STANDARDIZED PRIMARY READING TEST PURPORTS TO MEASURE READING ACHIEVEMENT. WHAT SKILLS AND UNDERSTANDINGS WOULD YOU EXPECT TO BE COVERED? (In this case primary reading teachers are much better judges of content validity than are other readers.) _____

_____

_____

_____

_____

Before responding to the above question, you should have noted that the population is specified. Primary reading achievement is measured by two major components: comprehension and vocabulary. Each component has a number of subcomponents.

Tests constructed with a particular reading program in mind or a specific approach to learning science or mathematics should be expected to include items that measure the unique characteristics of the program.

In constructing teacher-made tests, the objectives must be spelled out and the items built around the objectives. Behaviorally stated instructional objectives specify in advance the intended learning behaviors and thus make it easier to develop items that elicit the relevant behaviors. A subsequent chapter discusses teacher-made tests in detail.

The best method for determining content validity is to return to the first set of questions raised at the beginning of the chapter and use the questions as guides: What does the measurement represent? Does the instrument measure the skills, understandings, or traits it purports to measure? How well does the score represent the behavior the instrument was designed to measure?

Criterion-Related Validities

The reader will readily recognize the similarity between criterion-related validities and the concept of correlation introduced in Chapter 6. The Pearson Product-Moment Correlation coefficient (r) is widely used in predictive and concurrent validity studies. It may be well for the reader to review the assumptions for using the Pearson correlation and the examples correlating predictor and criterion variables. The resulting r statistic is the validity coefficient. You will recall the formula for finding a product-moment correlation coefficient (with only the subscripts changed) as:

$$r_{xy} = \frac{\Sigma(X - \bar{X})(Y - \bar{Y})}{N(SD_x)(SD_y)}$$

where r_{xy} = correlation
      X = predictor
      $\bar{X}$ = mean of predictor
      Y = criterion
      $\bar{Y}$ = mean of criterion
      N = number of paired scores
    SD = standard deviation

Once the validity coefficient of an instrument has been determined, we can use the information to predict a score on the criterion from the predictor score, or a predictor score from the criterion. For the mathematically oriented reader, the following discussion is included for determining the equation for a regression line. The regression line equation is used to predict the scores on the criterion. Other readers can proceed directly to the section following this discussion.

REGRESSION LINE EQUATION FOR PREDICTING PREDICTOR AND CRITERION SCORES

Given a score on a predictor instrument, let us say a standardized test measuring English grammar, we can ascertain the report card grade if we know the equation of the regression line. The regression line is the line best-fitting the sets of scores plotted on a scattergram. (See Chapter 6.) The reader with some background in mathematics will recognize the equation shown below as that of a straight line.

$$\hat{Y} = a + (b_{yx})(X)$$

where X = predictor score (standardized grammar test score)

   Y = criterion score (grade on report card)

   a = the Y intercept

   b_{yx} = the slope of the regression line of Y on X

Three mathematical steps are needed to obtain the necessary information for deriving the report card grade from a given standardized grammar test score.

1. Find the slope of the regression line.

$$b_{yx} = r_{xy} \left[\frac{SD_y}{SD_x} \right]$$

where b_{yx} = slope

   r_{xy} = validity coefficient

   SD_x = standard deviation of predictor

   SD_y = standard deviation of criterion

2. Find the Y intercept.

$$a = \bar{Y} - \left[b_{yx}(\bar{X}) \right]$$

where a = Y intercept

   $\bar{X}$ = mean of predictor scores

   $\bar{Y}$ = mean of criterion scores

   b_{yx} = slope of the regression line from the first step

3. Substitute values in the straight line equation.

$$\hat{Y} = a + \left[(b_{yx})(X) \right]$$

a. Substitute in the equation the value of b_{yx} from the first step.

b. Substitute in the equation the value of a from the second step.

c. Multiply b_{yx} and the predictor score (X

d. Add the value of a to the product of step 3.c.

Let us predict a student's report card grade ($\hat{Y}$) from his score on the standardized grammar test (X). The following information is needed:

Given	Criterion (grades converted into quantitative values)
$X = 30$	A $= 4.0$
$\bar{X} = 27$	B+ $= 3.5$
$\bar{Y} = 2$	B $= 3.0$
$r_{xy} = 0.41$	C+ $= 2.5$
$SD_x = 8$	C $= 2.0$
$SD_y = 1.50$	D+ $= 1.5$
	D $= 1.0$

To predict the grade ($\hat{Y}$) from the score of 30 on the standardized grammar test, we use the above information in the regression equation following the three steps.

$$\hat{Y} = a + \left[(b_{yx})\,(X) \right]$$

1. Find the slope of the regression line.

$$b_{yx} = 0.41\,(1.5/8)$$
$$= 0.077$$

2. Find the Y intercept.

$$a = 2 - \left[(0.077)\,(27) \right]$$
$$= 2 - 2.079$$
$$= ^{-}0.079$$

3. Substitute b_{yx} and a in the regression equation.

$$\hat{Y} = ^{-}0.079 + (0.077)\,(30)$$
$$= ^{-}0.079 + 2.310$$
$$\hat{Y} = 2.231$$

A $\hat{Y} = 2.231$ falls between a grade of C and C+ on the criterion. On the basis of the correlation between the standardized grammar test and the grades in English, we have found that a score of 30 points on the grammar test predicts a grade of C to C+.

To predict the same student's score on the standardized grammar test from his report card grade, we reverse the procedure. The equation now reads:

$$\hat{X} = a + \quad [\,(b_{xy})\,(Y)\,]$$

$$b_{xy} = r_{xy} \quad \left[\frac{SD_x}{SD_y}\right]$$

$$a = \bar{X} - \quad [\,b_{xy}\,(\bar{Y})\,]$$

where $\hat{X}$ = predicted X score

b_{xy} = the slope of the regression line of X on Y

a = the X intercept

r_{xy} = correlation coefficient

$\bar{X}$ and $\bar{Y}$ = the predictor and criterion means

SD_x and SD_y = the predictor and criterion standard deviations

There is one important caution in using the prediction equation: *the obtained score is only as accurate (valid) as the value of the correlation coefficient.*

Interpretation of the Criterion-Related Validity Coefficient

How high must a validity coefficient be for teachers and administrators to accept an obtained score as an adequate predictor of some subsequent performance? The answer is contingent on the use made of the data obtained from the instrument. Where scores are used for admission, placement, employment, or other decisions concerning acceptance and rejection, we need assurance of the instrument's validity as indicated by a high correlation coefficient. If we are given a validity coefficient of $r_{xy} = 0.41$, how much confidence can we have that the obtained score is a valid predictor of the criterion behavior?

A table of values is available to determine the confidence we can place in the validity coefficient. Table 8-1 shows sample listings from such a table. The $p = 0.05$ and $p = 0.01$ columns indicate the levels of significance that are predicated on the percent area under the normal distribution curve. The number of paired scores is shown under the column N. The r values shown under the columns of the levels of significance vary according to the number of correlated scores.

A probability of 0.01 (or 1 percent level of significance) means that in 1 case out of 100 the observed correlation is attributable to chance factors. Therefore we can accept a validity coefficient that is larger than the table reading with 99 percent confidence that the observed correlation was not due to chance. If $p = 0.05$, we can accept with 95 percent confidence that a high score on the predictor and a high score on the criterion (where the coefficient is positive) are not due to chance. Where the coefficient is negative, high scores on one variable predict low scores on the other. It also cautions us that in 5 percent of the cases the correlation between the predictor and the criterion may be due to chance.

Table 8-1

Values of *r* for different levels of significance

N[a]	(df)	$p = 0.05$	$p = 0.01$
10	8	0.632	0.765
11	9	0.602	0.735
21	19	0.433	0.549
31	29	0.355	0.456
52	50	0.273	0.354

[a]The standard *r* tables used in statistics list the degrees of freedom (*df*) and not the number of paired scores (*N*). The degrees of freedom are obtained by subtracting 2 from *N*: $df = N - 2$.

To read the table, first locate the number of paired scores (*N*) in the correlation. Let us say $N = 31$. Second, move horizontally across the table to locate the *r* values under the probability listings. If the observed validity coefficient is greater than the table reading (*r*), select the lowest probability to determine the confidence with which you can interpret the validity coefficient.

FOR $r = 0.41$ AND 31 PAIRED SCORES, WHAT IS THE LOWEST PROBABILITY THAT CHANCE FACTORS INFLUENCED THE OBTAINED VALIDITY COEFFICIENT? $p = $_____AT WHAT CONFIDENCE LEVEL CAN YOU ACCEPT THE VALIDITY COEFFICIENT? _____%

The probability is 0.05 ($p = .05$) that chance factors influenced the validity coefficient, and we can with 95 percent confidence accept the obtained validity coefficient.

The greater the *N*, the lower the validity coefficient required for the same level of significance. Conversely, the fewer the number of paired scores, the greater the validity coefficient must be to accept it with the same level of confidence. As an example, with an $N = 21$ we must obtain a validity coefficient of $r_{xy} = 0.433$ and $r_{xy} = 0.549$ to accept with 95 and 99 percent confidence, respectively, that the obtained coefficient was not due to chance.

As intelligent users of standardized tests, teachers and administrators must demand that constructors of tests provide evidence of validity and an interpretation of the validity data.

Construct Validity

Determining construct validity necessitates amassing correlational, experimental, and logical evidence. Data on how well the construct correlates with a criterion that is known to have some relationship to the construct and how well the construct correlates with other factors that give additional meaning to the construct should be obtained. Evidence from experimental studies helps to determine whether certain behavior or changes in behavior take place in the direction anticipated by the construct and under what conditions. Construct validity is an ongoing process of confirming or disconfirming the psychological construct and revising the instrument accordingly.

A raw score has value only to the extent that it is a valid measure of a skill, understanding, or trait for a given purpose and it is free from error. As stated in *Standards for Educational and Psychological Tests* (p. 31) *"No test is valid for all purposes or in all situations or for all groups of individuals."* Validity and reliability serve as reminders to educators of the caution that must be taken in interpreting raw scores as well as the need to be aware of sources of invalidity and errors of measurement.

Case studies 15 and 16 provide the reader with additional activities in distinguishing types of validity, in computing a validity coefficient, and in interpreting the obtained coefficient.

REFERENCES

Brown, Frederick G. *Principles of Educational and Psychological Testing.* Hinsdale, Ill.: Dryden Press, 1970. Chapters 5 and 6 define the different types of validity and present in detail methods for determining the validity of tests.

Cronbach, Lee. "Validity." In *Encyclopedia of Educational Measurement,* 3d edition. Ed. Chester W. Harris. New York: Macmillan, 1960. On pages 1551–1555 is a clear discussion of the concepts associated with validity.

Davis, Frederick B., Chairman. *Standards for Educational and Psychological Tests.* Washington, D.C.: American Psychological Association, Inc., 1974. Discussion of the types of validity serves as a guideline for test constructors and consumers. *Standards* sets the criteria for acceptable test validation.

Selected *Test Service Bulletins,* especially "Better Than Chance," Number 45; "Expectancy Tables—A Way of Interpreting Test Validity," Number 38. New York: The Psychological Corporation (304 East 45th Street, New York, N.Y., 10017). These bulletins are available free upon request from the address given.

Part III
Application of Statistics to
Procedures Used in Evaluation

The concepts of reliability and validity discussed in Part II provide criteria for determining the confidence we can place in instruments of measurement. Part III examines the types of instruments most commonly used in the classroom and the school system. The concepts of reliability and validity are applied to teacher-made tests, standardized tests, and observation procedures. Included in Part III are suggestions for developing data-collecting instruments and cautions in using the data to evaluate student, class, and school performance as well as other aspects of schooling.

The statistics introduced in Part I are employed as tools for the further study of instruments and in the analysis of the data obtained.

At the conclusion of Part III the reader should be able to:

1. Discuss the sources of error in a teacher-made test.
2. Determine the reliability of a teacher-made test in terms of stability, equivalency, or internal consistency.
3. Discuss the relationship between the reliability of a measurement instrument and the standard error of measurement.
4. Determine the validity of a teacher-made instrument.
5. Construct a test matrix by item and content.
6. Construct a test matrix by objective and content.
7. Analyze a test in terms of its item "goodness."
8. Calculate item difficulty and item discrimination.
9. Set item difficulty levels and item discrimination indexes in terms of criterion-referenced and normative-referenced tests.
10. Use the short-cut method for determining item difficulty and item discrimination.
11. Prepare an individual item matrix.
12. Select the item or items that need to be changed on the basis of the item difficulty and item discrimination data.

13. Show how to apply reliability and validity to essay tests.

14. Read a standardized test manual and identify: the purpose of a test; the rationale of a test; the content of the test.

15. Determine the usefulness of a standardized test for your purpose.

16. Use the norming data supplied in a test manual to interpret a score.

17. Prepare an individual profile based on a standardized test battery.

18. Find references about a standardized test in O.K. Buros, *Mental Measurements Yearbooks.*

19. Use the statistical data supplied by the test developer to interpret a score.

20. Use a standardized test score for evaluating performance and plan subsequent instruction.

21. Compare the advantages and disadvantages of the checklist, frequency checklist, and rating scale.

22. Select the appropriate observation procedure for obtaining the desired data.

23. Quantify a checklist or rating scale.

24. Discuss the validity of observations.

25. Discuss the sources of error in observation procedures.

26. Reduce the degree of instability in an individual observation.

27. Strengthen observer agreement between two observers.

28. Use the data obtained from observations to evaluate performance.

29. Explain the difference in interpreting observation data for criterion-referenced and normative-referenced performance.

30. Construct an observation instrument suitable for obtaining data related to some aspect of schooling.

9.

USE OF STATISTICS IN EVALUATION
OF TEACHER-MADE TESTS

In the past number of years the focus of teacher-made tests has shifted from using the test results solely for the purpose of assigning grades to that of obtaining maximum information about the students' achievement in order to make appropriate instructional decisions.

WHAT TYPE OF DECISIONS CAN STUDENTS' PERFORMANCE ON A TEACHER-MADE TEST HELP YOU MAKE? _____

The performance of the class as a whole is a stop-proceed signal. It will indicate whether the class has achieved the intended objectives. If so, the next steps are implemented with modifications suggested by the test results. If not, a decision about how to proceed is in order: to repeat, to reinforce, to use other types of activities, to select other instructional materials, or to move forward at the same time correcting the learning difficulty. Instructional decisions about individuals can also be made as well as grouping students for instruction.

For teacher-made tests to be of value in making instructional decisions, they must provide the information upon which decisions are based. The tests should be able to identify the aspects of the intended learning that the students are achieving and aspects of intended learning that are not being achieved. And the test should give clues as to why the students are or are not achieving the objectives.

Any decisions based on the results obtained from teacher-made tests can only be made after we have assurance the test itself is a reliable and valid instrument. Meaningful interpretation of the performance of individual students and of the class is dependent on the ability of the measurement instrument to obtain accurate measurements and to sample effectively the instructional objectives.

The chapter examines teacher-made tests for reliability; introduces a method for constructing tests for content validity; studies the test items for "goodness," difficulty, and discrimination; applies measurement concepts to essay tests; and utilizes statistical procedures developed in Part I to interpret the test results.

RELIABILITY APPLIED TO TEACHER-MADE TESTS

The following is an example of this concept.

A HEALTH CLASS COMPLETED A UNIT ON FIRST AID. THE TEACHER PREPARED A 50-ITEM MULTIPLE-CHOICE TEST COVERING THE UNIT. OF THE THREE WAYS DISCUSSED IN CHAPTER 7 FOR CONCEPTUALIZING RELIABILITY, WHICH WOULD YOU SUGGEST THE TEACHER APPLY TO HIS TEST FOR DETERMINING THE RELIABILITY OF THE INSTRUMENT, AND WHY? _____

_____

_____

----

1. Stability. He could determine the reliability of his test by repeatedly measuring the students. If the test consistently yielded the same or similar raw scores for each student, the test would be reliable. The correlation coefficient derived from test-retest responses will also give an index of stability.

2. Equivalency. The teacher could have developed two similar tests covering the same general areas of content with the same difficulty. Reliability would then have been determined by ascertaining the equivalency of the two parallel tests. Or he could have split the test in half and determined the equivalency of the two halves. (But this assumes that the test was developed to provide for parallel halves.)

3. Internal consistency. He could use the teacher-made formula for deriving the internal consistency reliability of the test.

There are, however, some disadvantages in all of the above types of reliability. The split-half and the teacher-made internal consistency reliability have certain advantages that outweigh the disadvantages in the above case. It would be instructionally unsound to test and retest the students continuously to obtain a reliability based on the stability of measurement, to say nothing of risking the transfer of learning from the first test to the second. Developing two 50-item equivalent tests is too time consuming for a single teacher. If, however, the tests were used district-wide, over a period of time, two or even three equivalent forms could have value. The odd-even form splits a test in half and yields, it is to be hoped, equivalent tests with 25 items on each, although the reliability coefficient will be somewhat lower than for a reliability on the total test. The Spearman-Brown Prophecy Formula applied to the odd-even reliability can be used in this case. (See Chapter 7.) To obtain an internal consistency reliability coefficient, each item can only be assigned a weight of one. If there are 50 items on the test, the highest possible score is 50 points. There is another caution in using internal consistency reliability. If the test is measuring more than one independent factor, separate internal consistency reliability coefficients for each factor should be obtained.

How high must the reliability coefficient be before the teacher can use his own test with some degree of confidence? There is no agreement among measurement specialists. Some, wishing to remain noncommittal, say as high as possible. Others have ventured the opinion that a reliability coefficient below 0.60 for a teacher-made test indicates a worthless instrument. Several have suggested more stringent requirements, that is, coefficients in the 0.70s.

All teachers and administrators must realize the need to obtain a high reliability to ensure accurate interpretation of a raw score. But a very high reliability coefficient may not always indicate a reliable instrument.

WHAT CAN CAUSE A RELIABILITY COEFFICIENT TO BE ARTIFICIALLY INFLATED?

First, if the test is too easy, it inflates the reliability coefficient. Second, if the group or class differs widely in ability or achievement, the instrument will appear to have a higher reliability than if it is administered to a more homogeneous class.

Regardless of the reliability coefficient, we must always interpret the raw scores with caution. The standard error of measurement provides us with some safeguards.

VALIDITY APPLIED TO TEACHER-MADE TESTS

Once the teacher establishes the reliability of the instrument, he determines its validity. A decision about which type of validity to use is not too difficult to make; content validity is the most appropriate type of validity for achievement tests.

HOW WOULD YOU SUGGEST THAT THE TEACHER DETERMINE THE CONTENT VALIDITY OF THE FIRST AID TEST? _____

_____

_____

_____

If he plans the unit systematically, he could develop instructional objectives and explicitly state the intended learning as behavioral outcomes. The instructional objectives are the framework for constructing the test items. The content validity of the test is determined by the degree to which his test items reflect the instructional objectives.

The teacher was a meticulous planner. His instructional objectives were concerned with both the content and the learning process, which he stated as behavioral outcomes. The matrix he used for planning the test items ensured its content validity. Table 9-1 illustrates the test content matrix.

The first aid unit covered five topics. The class was introduced to the purpose of first aid and to cautions in applying the information without adequate training. The students then learned about two types of frequent injuries and the techniques to apply immediately in cases of burns and fractures. Water safety was another topic covered in the unit, with special emphasis on rescue techniques. As a final topic, the students identified symptoms of shock and techniques of prevention and remediation. The teacher took special care in constructing the test items to include items in each of the five topics.

In addition to measuring the topics, the teacher was also measuring the types and levels of learning. He wanted to measure the three domains of learning: cognitive, psychomotor, and affective. Cognitive learning under the five topics was measured at three levels: knowledge, application of knowledge, and, on a higher cognitive level, integration of knowledge, that is, the ability to analyze, synthesize, and evaluate a first aid situation.

Table 9-1

Content matrix for first aid test

| Content topics | Learning processes | | | | Psychomotor (to be demonstrated) | Affective |
| | Cognitive[a] | | | | | |
	Knowledge of knowledge	Application of knowledge	Integration	Subtotal		
Purpose of first aid	4	4	0	8	—	2
Burns	5	4	1	10	Treating a burn	2
Fractures	6	3	1	10	Applying a splint	2
Water safety	7	3	1	11	Casting a lifeline	2
Shock	7	3	1	11	Preventing shock	2
Subtotal of items by level	29	17	4	50		10

[a]Classification of the levels of learning subsumed under "Cognitive domain" vary. Whatever classification system a teacher uses, he must be aware of the need to test several levels of learning. It will vary according to the purpose of the test. See the list of references at the end of the chapter for further information.

In the psychomotor domain the student was to show that he was able to carry out specific first aid procedures. On the affective level, the teacher was interested in ascertaining the extent to which the student liked the unit and the instructional approach.

As illustrated in Table 9-1, across the top of the matrix the three domains of learning and sublevels within the cognitive domain are listed. The five content topics covered in the unit are shown along the left side of the matrix. The numbers in the body of the matrix refer to the number of test items in each matrix cell.

The discussion will focus on the 50-item cognitive test. The teacher felt that for this unit a written test was not appropriate to measure psychomotor learning. He therefore had no test items covering this domain; instead, the students demonstrated their ability to carry out the first aid procedures, and he prepared a rating scale to measure their achievement in psychomotor skills. The responses to the affective items were not scored right or wrong, but were used later to help the teacher in planning other units.

HOW CAN THE TEACHER USE THE SUBTOTALS, BOTH HORI-ZONTAL AND VERTICAL, TO GIVE HIM IMPORTANT INFORMA-TION ABOUT THE FIRST AID TEST? _____

_____

_____

_____

- -

A study of the subtotals shows: how well the test is balanced for questions in each topic in the unit; if the number of items in each vertical subtotal reflects the emphasis placed on the topic as indicated in the instructional objective; if the test gives adequate coverage to many cognitive levels; and if the emphasis is on lower or higher cognitive levels of learning.

Many teachers prefer to list the test item number in the matrix cells rather than merely the number of items. An example of this arrangement is illustrated in Table 9-2.

For a more thorough analysis of test items, the matrix cells can also show the number of the instructional objective alongside the item number. In this case the numbers in the cell indicate the test item, and, in the parentheses following the item number, the number of the instructional objective. This is illustrated for two of the topics in Table 9-3.

To determine whether the instructional objectives are being measured, the teacher needs only to prepare a summary table similar to Table 9-4.

Table 9-2

Content matrix by item number

| Content topics | Cognitive domain | | | |
	Knowledge	Application of knowledge	Integration of knowledge	Number of items
Purpose of first aid	3, 8, 19, 46	4, 5, 18, 24		(8)
Burns	1, 11, 14, 43, 49	30, 31, 32, 47	6	(10)
Fractures	2, 7, 10, 20, 21, 36	25, 26, 27	28	(10)
Water safety	12, 17, 22, 23, 29, 42, 50	37, 44, 45	34	(11)
Shock	9, 15, 33, 35, 38, 40, 41	13, 48, 39	16	(11)
Total number of items	(29)	(17)	(4)	(50)

Table 9-3

Content matrix with objectives

| Content topics | Cognitive domain | | | |
	Knowledge	Application of knowledge	Integration of knowledge	Number of items
Purpose	3 (1), 8 (1), 19 (2), 46 (2)	4 (1), 5 (2), 18 (1), 24 (2)		8
Burns	1 (3), 11 (4), 14 (3), 43 (3), 49 (4)	30 (4), 31 (4), 32 (4), 47 (5)	6 (5)	10

Thus far in this section we have only examined content validity. The teacher might also be concerned with the predictive validity of his test instrument. He would determine how well his test correlated with another first aid

Table 9-4

Summary of items under objectives

Instructional objectives	Test items	Number of items
Number 1, Purpose	3, 4, 8, 18	4
Number 2, Purpose	5, 19, 24, 46	4
Number 3, Burns	1, 14, 43	3
Number 4, Burns	11, 30, 31, 32, 49	5
Number 5, Burns	6, 47	2
Number 6, Fractures	2, 7, 10, 25	4
Number 7, Fractures	20, 26	2
Number 8, Fractures	21, 27	2
Number 9, Fractures	28, 36	2
.	.	.
.	.	.
.	.	.
Number 15, Shock	13, 16, 40	3

test, or he might correlate his students' performance on his test with their future behavior in situations involving first aid. Since his test was not being used for any purpose other than to measure achievement of the instructional objectives, he did not pursue the predictive validity of the test.

ITEM ANALYSIS APPLIED TO TEACHER-MADE TESTS

Once the validity and the reliability of the teacher-made tests are established, the next step is to study the test items one by one. There are three ways of analyzing test items: their "goodness," their difficulty, and their ability to discriminate between high and low scorers on the test.

"Goodness" of Test Items

A careful analysis of the items demonstrates some of the reasons for the low reliability or lack of content validity.

ON THE BASIS OF YOUR OWN EXPERIENCES AS A TEST TAKER AND TEST WRITER, LIST SEVERAL THINGS ABOUT THE ITEMS THAT MAY CONTRIBUTE TO LOWERING THE RELIABILITY?____

_____

_____

_____

Everyone has been faced with ambiguous test items: What does the question mean? What does the teacher want? Poor directions for responding to an item are a sure cause of confusion. Incorrect keying of the answers will necessarily make the test unreliable. Poor diagrams used in the test, incorrect spelling, typographical errors, and poor or awkward sentence structure are all factors that tend to lower the reliability of a test.

We need to be aware of the sources contributing to the lack of *item "goodness."* By improving the items, we reduce the number of factors that cloud the true performance of an individual. Heeding these cautions will improve the reliability of the test.

> ITEM "GOODNESS" is concerned with factors other than those the student brings to the test which affect the student's score. These factors are related to the test and to the individual test items.

Item Difficulty

Item difficulty is a ratio, usually expressed in percent, between the number of students answering an item correctly and the number of students responding to the item. It is obvious that an "easy" test is composed of test items that are easy to answer. It will not be difficult for most students to respond correctly to these items. The two examples below show how item difficulty is computed.

1. Determine the number of students taking the test: N_t. Determine the number of students who obtained the correct answer: NR. Set up a ratio between N_t and NR.

$$NR/N_t = \text{item difficulty}$$

Given the following data, $N_t = 30$ and $NR = 10$, the item difficulty is calculated as:

$$\text{diff} = 10/30 = 0.333 = 33^1/_3\%$$

2. Given: $N_t = 30$ and $NR = 24$

$$\text{diff} = 24/30 = 0.80 = 80\%$$

As you will note from the two examples, the greater the *item difficulty* index shown in percent, the larger the number of students getting the answer correct. Although this may appear confusing at first, it is the conventional way to report item difficulty. Thus, high percent = easy item; low percent = difficult item.

ITEM DIFFICULTY is represented by the percent of students in a class who respond correctly to an item in relation to the total class.

Formula:

$$\text{diff} = NR/N_t$$

where NR = number of students responding correctly

N_t = total number of students in the group

TO THE RIGHT OF THE INDEX OF ITEM DIFFICULTY IN PERCENT, INDICATE HOW DIFFICULT EACH PERCENT IS USING THE FOLLOWING RESPONSE SYMBOLS: a. A DIFFICULT ITEM; b. AN ITEM OF AVERAGE DIFFICULTY; c. AN EASY ITEM.

1. diff = 90% __   3. diff = 50% __   5. diff = 0% __   7. diff = 40% __
2. diff = 20% __   4. diff = 95% __   6. diff = 25% __   8. diff = 60% __

---

1. c   3. b   5. a   7. b
2. a   4. c   6. a   8. b

AN ITEM DIFFICULTY IS 35%. WHAT PERCENT OF THE STUDENTS ANSWERED THE ITEM CORRECTLY?___ WHAT PERCENT INCORRECTLY?___

Given an item difficulty of 35%, 35% of the students obtained the correct answer, and 65% obtained the incorrect answer.

What is an acceptable difficulty level for a test item? Once again we are faced with a question whose answer is dependent on the purpose of the test. If a teacher or the district staff prepares a diagnostic test, it is designed to obtain as much information as possible about the students' achievement: their weaknesses, strengths, misconceptions, levels of learning, and so on. The information is used for instructional planning and curriculum decisions. We obtain the maximum amount of information about students as a class if a test has an average difficulty level of 50 percent. It does not mean all items must be at the 50 percent level. It means that when the difficulty levels of the items are averaged, 50 percent provides optimum diagnostic information. It permits a high ceiling (some very difficult items) and a low floor (a few very easy items). Thus all students can perform in some capacity. Some test developers recommend that the test's item difficulty range from 40 to 60 percent. Others suggest a range for teacher-made tests from 30 to 70 percent. Educational Testing Services suggests a difficulty range from 30 to 80 percent.

On the other hand, if the purpose of the test is to ascertain mastery of the instructional objectives (a criterion-referenced test), then a mastery test is used to determine whether the students have reached criterion learning. As an example, a third-grade mathematics teacher plans to introduce the operations of multiplication and division. She wants to determine whether her class can perform the operations of addition and subtraction with sufficient mastery to proceed to the operation of multiplication and division. From experience she knows that the students who cannot respond correctly to 90 percent of the addition and subtraction problems have difficulty with multiplication and division. The selection of a mastery level, in this case 90 percent, is not guesswork. It is based on experience and on evidence presented by instructional and learning specialists. Her expectations are that out of twenty addition and subtraction problems the students should answer eighteen problems correctly.

The test items for mastery tests are selected for the purpose of measuring mastery regardless of their difficulty. Though some aspects of addition may be very easy, the easy items should be retained if they measure aspects of addition not covered by other items.

There is always the possibility of manipulating the item difficulty in order to guarantee that a large number of students obtain the correct answers for 90 percent of the items. One needs only to make the item difficulty index high enough. The items may then, however, be poor measures of the skill or understanding associated with mastery.

The following questions provide the reader with some practice in interpreting the difficulty index of given tests.

A DIAGNOSTIC ACHIEVEMENT TEST HAS AN OVERALL DIFFICULTY LEVEL OF 90%.

1. DOES IT SEPARATE THE FAST STUDENTS FROM THE AVERAGE STUDENTS?_____

2. DOES IT SEPARATE MOST STUDENTS FROM THE SLOW STUDENTS?_____

CONVERSELY, A DIAGNOSTIC TEST HAS AN OVERALL DIFFICULTY LEVEL OF 30%.

3. DOES IT SEPARATE THE FAST STUDENTS FROM THE AVERAGE STUDENTS?_____
4. DOES IT DISTINGUISH MOST STUDENTS FROM THE SLOW STUDENTS?_____

The responses to the first and second questions are no and yes, respectively. A test with an item difficulty of 90 percent can only separate the very low scorers from the rest of the class. The responses to the third and fourth questions are yes and no, respectively. A test with an item difficulty of 30 percent separates the high scorers from the balance of the class. Medical school entrance examinations have a low item difficulty index. The purpose of the test is to eliminate all but the high scorers.

WHAT CAN YOU CONCLUDE ABOUT THE STUDENTS' PERFORMANCE FROM THE DIFFICULTY LEVEL OF A DIAGNOSTIC TEST?_____
_____
_____

A diagnostic test's average item difficulty level either tells you the test is too hard or too easy for the group taking it. If a teacher is certain her test samples typical performance, and her class finds the test easy, it could indicate an advanced class. If the group finds the test more difficult than what is expected of a grade level or an age group, the class may be having difficulties.

HOW DOES A TEACHER SELECT THE PROPER DIFFICULTY LEVEL FOR A TEST? _____
_____

A teacher bases her selection of the difficulty level on the type of test (such as diagnostic, mastery, or power) and the kind of information she is seeking about the performance of the class.

WHEN DO YOU FIND OUT IF YOUR TEST HAS THE DIFFICULTY LEVEL YOU HOPED TO OBTAIN? _____
_____
_____

It is only after you measure the students' performance using the teacher-made test that you can determine its level of difficulty. From the students' responses you can determine whether the average item difficulty level met your intended index of item difficulty. The item difficulty index on standardized tests is obtained from a specified norming group. The same test item given to different norming groups can yield different indexes of difficulty.

Item Discrimination

Item Discrimination is a correlation between the performance of the high and low scorers on each test item. The students taking the test are divided into two groups: the upper half of the scorers represent the top group and the lower half the bottom group. A number of statistical procedures are used to determine item discrimination. Each procedure is dependent on the type of scores (nominal, ordinal, or interval). There are also different ways of differentiating the top and bottom scorers. The general pattern, regardless of procedure, is to:

1. determine the number in the top group of scorers who answer a particular item correctly;
2. determine the number in the bottom group of scorers who answer the same item correctly;
3. subtract the number in the lower group obtaining the correct answer from the number in the top group obtaining the correct answer; and
4. divide by the number of scores in either the top or the bottom group. (This will be the same number regardless of which group is used.)

ITEM DISCRIMINATION is a correlation of the performance of high scorers and low scorers. The index of discrimination indicates the degree to which an item can differentiate between the two groups.

Formula:

$$r_{disc} = \frac{NR_{hi} - NR_{lo}}{N_{hi}}$$

where r_{disc} = index of discrimination

NR_{hi} = number right (responding correctly) in the high group

NR_{lo} = number right in the low group

N_t = number of students in both groups: $N_t = N_{hi} + N_{lo}$

Example: N_t = 40

N_{hi} = 20 NR_{hi} = 15

N_{lo} = 20 NR_{lo} = 10

$$r_{disc} = \frac{15 - 10}{20} = 0.25$$

An index of item discrimination ranges from $^-1$ to $^+1$. The higher the positive discrimination, the more an item favors the high scorers. Put another way, the higher the positive or negative discrimination index, the greater the ability of the test item to discriminate between high scorers and low scorers.

WHAT DOES A NEGATIVE INDEX OF ITEM DISCRIMINATION SIGNIFY?

An item with a negative index of discrimination indicates that more low scorers obtained the correct answer than high scorers. It is a poor item and should either be revised or eliminated from the test. In most cases, on second reading of the item you would find that it is ambiguously worded, that it is keyed incorrectly, or that some other factors are operating to affect its "goodness."

WHAT WOULD AN INDEX OF 0 SIGNIFY (r_{disc} = 0)?

The test item is incapable of distinguishing the performances of the high scorers from the low scorers.

In order to determine what an acceptable discrimination index is, we must, again, know the purpose of the test. For a diagnostic achievement test, a number of factors must be taken into consideration.

First, many measurement specialists hold that discrimination indexes of less than 0.20 do not tell enough about the differences in performance between high and low scorers to add any information. They recommend not retaining items with indexes of discrimination below 0.20.

Second, discrimination indexes too much above 0.80 on teacher-made tests indicate the test item is too hard for the low scorers and too easy for the high scorers.

Third, for teacher-made tests, the recommended average index of discrimination falls between 0.30 and 0.70, with individual items as low as 0.20 and as high as 0.80.

Fourth, all agree that items with negative discrimination indexes should be discarded.

For mastery tests, the item should be able to discriminate between those who have mastered the understanding or skill and those who have not. The group that has mastered the understanding or skill should be able to respond correctly to most of the items. The criterion or standard for mastery is predetermined. The learner must be able to master successfully most of or all the subparts before the skill itself is mastered. The items will have low discrimination indexes between high and low scorers in classes where most of the students have achieved mastery of the skill being measured. The same items will have high discrimination indexes in classes where most of the students have not achieved mastery of the skill.

Both item difficulty and item discrimination affect the reliability of a test. To improve the reliability, the items should be rewritten to raise the discrimination index, but caution must be exercised so as not to lose too much information by having an index of discrimination that is too high. The reliability of a test can be raised by making the test too easy. There is a point, however, at which we can make the test so easy that we ensure high reliability, but sacrifice the value of the test. Making the test too easy may also weaken the validity of the instrument.

SHORT-CUT METHODS FOR DETERMINING ITEM DIFFICULTY AND DISCRIMINATION AND ANALYZING ITEM "GOODNESS"

A teacher with forty students in a class would find the task of item analysis overwhelming unless some short-cut methods are available. The methods illustrated in the following section have been shown to give accurate estimates of item difficulty and item discrimination.

Given are a diagnostic multiple-choice test in which each item has four options; the test has forty items; the number of students taking the test is N_t = 40.

1. a. The class papers are ordered from high scores to low scores.
   b. The top 25 percent of the papers are selected to represent the high scorers: 25% of 40 = 10; N_{hi} = 10.
   c. The bottom 25 percent of the papers are selected to represent the low scorers: 25% of 40 = 10; N_{lo} = 10.
   d. In case two or more members of the class have the same score as the tenth score from the top or bottom, one of the papers should be selected randomly. As an example:

$$X_{10} = 24$$
$$X_{11} = 24$$
$$X_{12} = 24$$

Thus, the three papers are tied for tenth position. Shuffle the three papers. Select one. In this way each of the tied scores has an equal chance of being selected. The same procedure would be followed for tied scores in the tenth from the bottom position.

    e. You now have two dichotomized groups with ten papers representing the high group and ten papers the low group.

2. a. Prepare a matrix of the responses of the ten high and ten low scorers for each of the test items. Table 9-5 illustrates a cutaway portion of such a matrix. (Responses to items 11 through 30 are not shown in the table, although they would ordinarily be included.)

    b. Across the top of the table, the item number and the correct response are shown.

    c. The first column on the left indicates the students in the high- and low-scoring groups ($X_1, X_2, \ldots X_{10}$ and $X_{31}, X_{32}, \ldots X_{40}$).

    d. In each cell, record the incorrect response for each student and for each item.

    e. A cell left empty indicates the item was correctly answered.

    f. If an item is left unanswered, a dash is entered in the appropriate cell.

    g. To analyze the matrix, item 3 serves as an example. The correct response was "D." This is indicated above the item number. Four high scorers chose an incorrect option; six low scorers chose incorrect options or did not respond. An examination of item 3 indicates that the incorrect option "A" was the choice of six out of ten students who responded incorrectly and was a more attractive option to the high scorers than to the low scorers.

WHAT DO THE RESPONSES TO ITEM 32 (TABLE 9-5) INDICATE?

Something is definitely wrong. The first thing to check is the key. There might be an error in recording the correct response. The item analysis test matrix gives a fast overall picture of how the items are functioning. In item 32 it permits us to recognize discrepancies and other weaknesses in the item.

Table 9-5

Item analysis test matrix

Items →	A 1	C 2	D 3	C 4	A 5	A 6	B 7	B 8	D 9	C 10	11 … 30	D 31	D 32	A 33	A 34	B 35	C 36	B 37	A 38	A 39	C 40	Total score
High scorers																						
X1						B				-			C									
X2		A				B				-			C						B		A	
X3			A			B				A			B	B								
X4					C			A		D			C									
X5		A				B				B			C					C			A	
X6			A							B			C					C				
X7										-			C						C		-	
X8			A			B		C		A			C	B	C				D			
X9			A							A			B					D				
X10		D			C					A			C									
Low scorers																						
X31		A	B							B			C	C	A			-	-		A	
X32	B	A	-							A			B					A				
X33		B	A		C			C		B			C		A			C	D		A	
X34	D									B			C	C		A						
X35	D			D	B					B			C		A	A		D			A	
X36		A	A			B				A			C			D			D	-	A	
X37	C			D				D		D			C			D				-	A	
X38	B	B			B					D			C	B					D		A	
X39	D	D	C							A								D	D	-		
X40	D	D	C				A			A			A			C		D	D		A	
Total incorrect	7	10	10	2	5	6	1	4	0	20		0	19	5	6	3	0	9	9	3		
Total correct	13	10	10	18	15	14	19	16	20	0		20	1	15	14	17	20	11	11	17		

3. Using the item analysis test matrix as a guide (Table 9-5), we can prepare an individual matrix for test items that require closer scrutiny. An individual item matrix is shown in Table 9-6

Table 9-6

Individual item matrix: Item 3

Responses ⟶	A	B	C	D*	Blank	Total
High	4	0	0	6	0	10
Low	2	1	2	4	1	10
Total	6	1	2	10	1	20

*Correct response.

4. Individual item matrices can be used to obtain the item difficulty and item discrimination as well as to examine the item for "goodness." The following is an example of item 3.

$$\text{diff} = \frac{NR_{hi} + NR_{lo}}{N_{hi} + N_{lo}} = \frac{6 + 4}{10 + 10} = \frac{10}{20} = 0.50$$

$$\text{diff} = 50\%$$

$$r_{disc} = \frac{NR_{hi} - NR_{lo}}{N_{hi}} = \frac{6 - 4}{10} = \frac{2}{10} = 0.20$$

$$r_{disc} = 0.20$$

WITH AN ITEM DIFFICULTY OF 50%, AN ITEM DISCRIMINATION OF 0.20, AND ON THE BASIS OF THE INDIVIDUAL ITEM MATRIX, WHAT WOULD YOU CONCLUDE ABOUT ITEM 3? _____

_____

_____

_____

It is an item of average difficulty, indicating it can give us much information about the achievement of the class on the item. The item discriminates slightly, between the high and low scorers, favoring the high scorers, since the index is positive. On the basis of the item difficulty and discrimination index, the item is worth retaining. All the options proved attractive to at least some of the students. Option "A" functions as a good distractor, although it seems more attractive to the high scorers than to the low scorers. Since it lowers the discrimination of the item, it would be well to reread the item to make sure option "A" is not as equally a good choice as the keyed option, "D."

From the item analysis test matrix you can determine the speed with which the students take the test. Students leaving items blank at the end of the test may not be able to complete the test in the time allotted. The student X_{31} left the last four items unanswered. If the difficult items are distributed throughout the test, we can assume he did not have time to complete the four items. When too many students find insufficient time to complete the test, an item difficulty and discrimination may give distorted information about the value of the test items. If the test's purpose is to measure the student's speed as one aspect of performance, however, then we must take this into consideration in our analysis of the item.

PREPARE AN INDIVIDUAL ITEM MATRIX FOR ITEM 40. ANALYZE THE ITEM FOR DIFFICULTY, DISCRIMINATION, AND "GOODNESS."

Item matrix: Item 40

Responses →	A	B	C	D	Blank	Total
High						
Low						
Total						

diff = _____

r_{disc} = _____

Your item matrix should match the one shown below. Did you remember to place an asterisk next to the correct option?

Responses→	A	B	C*	D	Blank	Total
High	2	0	7	0	1	10
Low	6	0	1	0	3	10
Total	8	0	8	0	4	20

$$\text{diff} = 8/20 = 0.40 = 40\%$$

$$r_{disc} = 6/10 = 0.60$$

The item does a good job of discriminating between the high and low scorers. Option "A" is a good distractor, which the low scorers find attractive. It should be studied in order to understand why the students are being misled. Neither options "B" nor "D" are adding to our understanding of the students' difficulties. Three of the ten low scorers left item 40 blank. We need to determine whether they ran out of time or if the item is too difficult. Checking the item difficulty we find it to be on the difficult side. But we should also check the test matrix (Table 9-5) to determine whether the same students are also leaving the last several items in the test unanswered. On the whole, item 40 is a good item if we reconsider options "B" and "D."

STATISTICS APPLIED TO THE TEACHER-MADE ESSAY TEST

To apply statistical procedures to essay items we must first quantify each essay. Chapter 1 dealt with the question of quantification. The problem of content validity is an essential aspect of an essay test. Since the test is limited, as a rule, to relatively few items, the items must sample as wide a universe of the instructional objectives as possible.

We are faced with another aspect of reliability regarding essay tests that has only been discussed peripherally in the preceding sections. In addition to the usual sources of error, a major source is in scoring the responses. The focus is on the scorer or rater, and many factors are at work that add inconsistencies to the scores.

SUGGEST SOME FACTORS THAT INFLUENCE YOUR SCORING OF ESSAY QUESTIONS. _____

_____

_____

The list is as unlimited as are variations among humans: penmanship of the student; his name; his syntax, spelling, and punctuation; how the scorer feels at the moment; the test paper that follows an unusually good paper or an extremely poor paper; a position or point of view the student takes that is at variance with the scorer's.

There are several ways to establish rater reliability: the stability coefficient and the coefficient of rater agreement. The stability coefficient indicates the relationship between the teacher's scoring of the essay on one occasion and the scoring of the same essay on a second occasion. We are asking whether we can rely on the teacher to be consistent in his scoring of the same set of responses over a period of time.

The coefficient of rater agreement is a correlation between the raw scores on a set of essay papers scored by one teacher with the raw scores on the same set of papers scored by a second teacher. Either of these types of correlations can be used to check the degree of scoring consistency. The Pearson Product-Moment Correlation or rank order correlation are appropriate statistical techniques in either case.

CENTRAL TENDENCY AND VARIABILITY STATISTICS APPLIED TO TESTS

After completing the evaluation of the measurement instrument, we are now able to evaluate the performance of the class and individual students using the statistics introduced in Parts I and II. Is the performance to be analyzed from a norm-referenced or criterion-referenced data base? The answer determines how we apply central tendency and variability statistics, z scores and percentiles, and standard errors of measurement to understand individual and group performance.

Feedback of the results based on the above statistics should be shared with the individual students. The student should be informed of the questions he missed and those he answered correctly and how his performance relates to his past performances and to the established criterion performance. The student may also want to compare his performance to a relevant norming group.

The teacher needs the class mean, median, and standard deviation as well as items missed and options selected for planning the next instructional steps. On the level of the school district, statistical information and item analysis are useful for planning curricula, selecting instructional materials, and setting district norms.

Cases 17 and 18 continue and extend the concepts related to teacher-made tests.

REFERENCES

Bloom, Benjamin S., Hastings, J. Thomas, and Madaus, George F. *Handbook on Formative and Summative Evaluation of Student Learning.* New York: McGraw-Hill, 1971. The reader will find Chapters 5–10 invaluable in developing test items to measure specific levels of learning.

Bloom, Benjamin S., ed. *Taxonomy of Educational Objectives: The Classification of Educational Goals.* Handbook 1. *Cognitive Domain.* New York: McKay, 1956. This work orders the cognitive levels of learning in a taxonomic system that is applicable to instruction and evaluation.

Krathwohl, David R., Bloom, B. S., and Masia, B. B. *Taxonomy of Educational Objectives: The Classification of Educational Goals.* Handbook 2. *Affective Domain.* New York: McKay, 1964. This handbook orders the affective levels of learning in a taxonomic system that is applicable to classroom instruction and evaluation.

Mehrens, William A., and Lehmann, Irwin J. *Measurement and Evaluation in Education and Psychology.* New York: Holt, Rinehart and Winston, 1973. Chapters 7 through 11 describe test construction from the planning stages through the final scoring and analysis of the test. Chapters 8 and 9 emphasize the essay and objective test item forms.

10.
USE OF STATISTICS IN EVALUATION OF STANDARDIZED TEST SCORES

Standardized tests are another means used to measure academic performance as well as other traits of students. With these data individuals and classes are evaluated, and subsequent instruction is planned. We shall begin the discussion with a standardized test administered to Ronald's class in the fall of the school year. Ronald received a total raw score of 36 points on two parts of Form S in the *Differential Aptitude Test* (*DAT*). How can this information assist you, as his teacher, in assessing Ronald's performance and in designing subsequent instruction around the resulting evaluation?

STANDARDIZED TESTS can be generally defined as assessment instruments produced commercially. They usually have wider application than merely a single classroom. A test is standardized to the extent that it has available norming data, reliability and validity information, and additional statistical data on item analyses, standard error of measurement, and so forth.

Answers to eight questions will help you derive fuller meaning from Ronald's performance:
1. What is the purpose of the test?
2. What is the rationale upon which the test items are predicated?
3. What does the test include?

4. What statistical data about the test are made available?

5. What norming information is provided?

6. What does the profile of an individual performance suggest?

7. What does Oscar K. Buros, in *The Seventh Mental Measurements Yearbook* (Highland Park, N.J.: Gryphon Press, 1972), report about the test?

8. How can I best interpret the score and plan subsequent instruction in the light of the above seven answers?

Answers to the first six questions should be provided by the test publishers in the manual that accompanies each set of tests. The function of the manual is to help the user make intelligent decisions based on the test data. The manuals for "typical" standardized tests used in schools are written for teachers and administrators. Once the teacher's reticence to delve into the formal test language is overcome, he will find that the manuals are readable and contain invaluable information. The manual also includes information for administering and scoring the tests.

The answer to the seventh question is found in a set of volumes edited by Buros. A number of years ago, Buros, a noted specialist in tests and measurement, undertook the task of gathering scholarly and impartial views on the standardized tests on the market. Test users, he felt, would be in a better position to make decisions about what tests to use or about the current test they were using if they were apprised of the strengths and weaknesses of all these tests. The materials are updated periodically. The current yearbook, *The Seventh Mental Measurements Yearbook,* comprises two volumes.

The answer to the eighth question is dependent upon the seven preceding answers. We shall examine each question in turn. Following the explanations of each question, Ronald's raw score on the *DAT* will be discussed in light of those explanations.

1. WHAT IS THE PURPOSE OF THE TEST?

Standardized tests are used for many purposes. If a teacher wants to know, for example, why Ronald is not doing well in English, a diagnostic test or an aptitude test, depending upon the type of difficulty he demonstrates, would be an appropriate instrument. The teacher may want to find out more about Ronald's interests, his attitudes, or his personality characteristics. If so, the test selected must be suited to the specific purpose for which it will be used. The test manual should clearly state what the test will measure and to what purpose the results can be applied.

BELOW ARE STATEMENTS FROM THE MANUALS OF THREE STANDARDIZED TESTS. FOR WHAT PURPOSE WOULD EACH BE A SUITABLE MEASUREMENT INSTRUMENT?

a. The tests "were developed in 1947 to provide an integrated, scientific, and well-standardized procedure for measuring abilities of boys and girls in Grades 8 through 12 for purposes of educational and vocational guidance."

b. "The tests will be designed to measure attainment of major educational objectives, regardless of particular curriculum programs and methods."

c. "It is designed to measure those attitudes of a teacher which predict how well he will get along with pupils in interpersonal relationships, and indirectly how well satisfied he can be with teaching as a vocation."

WHAT DOES IT PURPORT TO MEASURE, AND FOR WHAT PURPOSE CAN THE RESULTS BE USED?

a. _____

_____

_____

b. _____

_____

_____

c. _____

_____

_____

----

a. The *Differential Aptitude Tests* (*DAT*) (quotation from G. K. Bennet, H. G. Seashore, and A. G. Wesman, *Differential Aptitude Tests Manual*, 5th edition [New York: The Psychological Corporation, 1974], 1) purport to measure abilities associated with success in school. The results of the measurement can be used to plan future educational and vocational programs for the students.

b. The *Cooperative Primary Tests* (*CPT*) (quotation from *Cooperative Primary Tests Handbook* [Princeton, N.J.: Cooperative Test Division, Educational Testing Services, 1967], 6) purport to measure achievement. The results can be used to determine attainment of instructional objectives that are common to most curriculum programs.

c. The *Minnesota Teacher Attitude Inventory* (*MTAI*) (quotation from W. W. Cook, C. H. Leeds, and R. Callis, *Minnesota Teacher Attitude Inventory Manual* [New York: The Psychological Corporation, 1951], 1) purports to measure attitudes that correlate with teacher-pupil interaction. The results can be used to predict the teacher's satisfaction and possible professional success.

Interpretation of a raw score is contingent on the purpose of a standardized test. One must always be apprised of the test's ability to fulfill its purpose. Buros can be an invaluable guide for obtaining such information. (See the discussion of the seventh question.) A review of some of the statistical data presented in the manual (the fourth question) is also helpful.

Interpretation of Ronald's Score Based on the Purpose of DAT

Ronald's raw score of 36 points represents the combined Verbal Reasoning and Numerical Ability tests in the *DAT* battery of tests. Since verbal reasoning and numerical ability are purported to be the two mental abilities most likely to predict academic success (at least as schools are now oriented), these areas are included in the battery of tests. If your purpose in using the *DAT* is to plan Ronald's educational program and select the level of class work best fitting his performance level and ability, then the test would fit your purpose.

2. WHAT IS THE RATIONALE UPON WHICH THE TEST ITEMS ARE PREDICATED?

To fulfill the purpose of the test, the test constructor chooses a rationale that is used as a basis for selecting test items. Below are statements from the three manuals cited previously that either explicitly or implicitly indicate the test's rationale.

MATCH THE RESPECTIVE TESTS (*DAT, CPT, MTAI*) WITH THE STATEMENTS BELOW.

1. ". . . attitudes afford a key to the prediction of the type of social atmosphere a teacher will maintain in the classroom."
Name of test _____

2. "The tests are predicated on the assumption that a principal aim of primary schooling for children from all backgrounds is to develop basic verbal and quantitative skills."
Name of test _____

3. "Aptitude is the result of the interaction of heredity and environment . . . aptitude embraces any characteristic which predisposes to learning . . . they are aptitude tests which describe the student's potentiality for learning in a number of academic subjects or vocational endeavors."
Name of test _____

The rationale for the *MTAI* is found in the first statement; *CPT* for the second statement; and *DAT* for the third statement.

Interpretation of Ronald's Score Based on the Rationale of DAT

The rationale presented by the authors of *DAT* are in harmony with the purpose of the tests. The test items to which Ronald responded were selected from a wide range of possible items that could "describe the student's potentiality."

3. WHAT DOES THE TEST INCLUDE?

In Chapter 1, a distinction was made between a raw score representing a single trait or a composite of several traits. It is essential to clarify which of these the obtained raw score represents. Test manuals should be specific about the meaning of the raw score. The *DAT* battery includes eight separate tests, each measuring a different trait, but nine scores are possible. The ninth raw score is a composite of the Verbal Reasoning and the Numerical Ability tests, yielding a factor called Scholastic Ability.

The *Cooperative Primary Tests* are composed of a battery of five tests plus a pilot test. Separate scores are obtained on each. The tests can be broken into component parts. Although a single raw score is obtained, for example, on the Listening Test, the three components comprising it can be analyzed by test items: items covering word meaning, sentence meaning, and paragraph meaning.

The *Minnesota Teacher Attitude Inventory* yields a single score. This can be termed the "garbage can" approach. All factors having some relevance to teachers' attitudes toward school, children, and general education are thrown in a large pot. The output is the single raw score. Breaking down specific attitudes is difficult with this type of score, although several studies have indicated that a number of factors can be identified.

Interpretation of Ronald's Scholastic Ability Score as One Score in a Test Battery

Ronald received the following raw scores on the *DAT* battery. It was from the S form for eighth graders.

Tests	Raw scores
Verbal Reasoning	24
Numerical Ability	12
VR + NA (Scholastic Ability)	36
Abstract Reasoning	32
Clerical (speed and accuracy)	54
Mechanical	42
Space Relations	15
LU- I (Spelling)	87
LU - II (Grammar)	39

Ronald's 36 points represent a composite of two of the abilities measured in the battery of *DAT* tests. The 36 points can yield additional information if we break up the score into its component scores: Verbal Reasoning, 24 points; Numerical Ability, 12 points. This will tell us how much each component contributes to the total.

4. WHAT STATISTICAL DATA ABOUT THE TEST ARE MADE AVAILABLE?

Two types of statistical data should be provided for the test user: one to assist in interpreting the individual raw scores; the other to help evaluate the worth of the test for the user's purpose. A test manual should provide the following data:

a. mean of each test for specific norming groups;
b. standard deviations for specific norming groups;
c. reliability;
d. validity;
e. standard error of measurement;
f. several types of converted scores, such as z scores, other standard scores, grade equivalents, age equivalents, percentile bands, and stanines;
g. data from several norming groups (see the fifth question);
h. profile charts and their interpretation, if a battery of tests is involved (see the sixth question);
i. expectancy tables, if predictive validity has been established.

Interpretation of Ronald's Score Using Statistical Data

Statistical data on the *DAT* and Ronald's score are shown below:

$$\text{raw score (VR + NA)} = X = 36$$
$$\text{stanine} = 6$$
$$\text{percentile} = 65$$
$$\text{percentile band} = 55\text{--}70$$
$$\bar{X} = 33.6$$
$$SD = 15.7$$
$$r_{oe} = 0.92$$
$$SE_{meas} = 4.4$$
validity = The manual offers evidence from many studies.

WHAT DO THESE DATA CONTRIBUTE TO AN INTERPRETATION OF RONALD'S SCORE ($X = 36$)? _____

_____

_____

_____

With the above data a number of statements can be made about the test and about Ronald's performance. The split-half reliability (0.92), based on correlating responses to odd and even items, is at an acceptable level. In relation to the norming group from which the statistics are derived, Ronald's score in regard to the standard error of measurement could fall between 40.4 points and 31.6 points (36 + 4.4 and 36 - 4.4). In either case it would place him above the 50 percentile of the norming group or in the 55 to 70 percentile band. The manual indicates that validity studies do show a significant positive correlation between the Scholastic Ability scores and subsequent academic performance.

5. WHAT NORMING INFORMATION IS PROVIDED?

The more norming information that is provided in the manual, the greater the likelihood of comparing your student's obtained score with a similar group's performance. Heterogeneous groups may give a broad comparative picture. Local norms provide further information. If Ronald is in eighth grade, he could be compared with a sample of eighth-grade boys and girls throughout the entire United States; with a sample of all secondary school students in the United States; with eighth-grade boys attending consolidated schools in the rural Northwest; or with boys in their eighth year in his own school system.

Interpretation of Ronald's Score in Terms of a Norming Group

Ronald's composite raw score of 36 points on the VR + NA tests was compared to a norming group composed of eighth-grade boys taking the tests in the fall of the school year from "76 public and parochial school systems throughout the United States (*DAT Manual*, p. 5)." His ranking at the sixty-fifth percentile and at stanine 6 are based on the above norming group. (See Table 10-1 for stanine and percentile norms for boys from the *DAT*, Form S, eighth grade, fall.)

6. WHAT DOES THE PROFILE OF AN INDIVIDUAL PERFORMANCE SUGGEST?

If a raw score is part of a test battery, we are able to identify the individual's weaknesses and strengths. A profile provides information needed to

Table 10-1

Differential Aptitude Test norms: In stanines and percentiles

Stanine Norms for Forms S and T

FALL
GRADE **8**

BOYS

Raw Scores

Stanine	Verbal Reasoning	Numerical Ability	VR+NA	Abstract Reasoning	Clerical S and A[a]	Mechanical Reasoning	Space Relations	Spelling	Language Usage	Stanine
9	39-50	31-40	68-90	44-50	56-100	59-70	45-60	87-100	43-60	9
8	32-38	26-30	57-67	41-43	50-55	55-58	39-44	77-86	37-42	8
7	25-31	21-25	45-56	37-40	45-49	50-54	32-38	66-76	30-36	7
6	20-24	16-20	35-44	33-36	40-44	46-49	25-31	55-65	25-29	6
5	14-19	12-15	26-34	26-32	35-39	39-45	20-24	48-54	20-24	5
4	10-13	8-11	20-25	18-25	30-34	33-38	16-19	42-47	15-19	4
3	8-9	6-7	17-19	11-17	25-29	28-32	14-15	36-41	12-14	3
2	6-7	4-5	13-16	7-10	18-24	24-27	11-13	29-35	9-11	2
1	0-5	0-3	0-12	0-6	0-17	0-23	0-10	0-28	0-8	1

Percentile Norms for Forms S and T

BOYS (N=7000+) — Raw Scores

Percentile	Verbal Reasoning	Numerical Ability	VR+NA	Abstract Reasoning	Clerical S and A[a]	Mechanical Reasoning	Space Relations	Spelling	Language Usage	Percentile
99	43-50	35-40	75-90	46-50	60-100	62-70	49-60	93-100	48-60	99
97	39-42	31-34	68-74	44-45	56-59	59-61	45-48	87-92	43-47	97
95	34-38	28-30	61-67	42-43	52-55	56-58	41-44	81-86	39-42	95
90	30-33	25-27	54-60	40-41	49-51	54-55	38-40	75-80	35-38	90
85	27-29	23-24	49-53	38-39	47-48	52-53	35-37	70-74	32-34	85
80	25-26	21-22	45-48	37	45-46	50-51	32-34	66-69	30-31	80
75	23-24	19-20	42-44	36	43-44	49	30-31	62-65	28-29	75
70	21-22	18	39-41	34-35	41-42	47-48	28-29	59-61	26-27	70
65	20	16-17	36-38	33	40	46	26-27	56-58	25	65
60	19	15	34-35	32	39	45	24-25	54-55	24	60
55	17-18	14	31-33	30-31	38	43-44	22-23	52-53	22-23	55
50	**15-16**	**13**	**29-30**	**29**	**36-37**	**41-42**	**21**	**50-51**	**21**	**50**
45	14	12	27-28	27-28	35	40	20	48-49	20	45
40	13	11	25-26	25-26	34	38-39	19	47	19	40
35	12	10	24	23-24	32-33	36-37	18	45-46	18	35
30	11	9	22-23	20-22	31	35	17	43-44	16-17	30
25	10	8	20-21	17-19	30	33-34	16	42	15	25
20	9	7	19	14-16	28-29	31-32	15	40-41	14	20
15	8	6	17-18	11-13	26-27	29-30	14	37-39	12-13	15
10	7	5	15-16	9-10	23-25	26-28	13	33-36	11	10
5	6	4	13-14	7-8	16-22	23-25	11-12	28-32	9-10	5
3	5	3	12	5-6	6-15	20-22	10	23-27	7-8	3
1	0-4	0-2	0-11	0-4	0-5	0-19	0-9	0-22	0-6	1
Mean	18.2	15.4	33.6	27.4	36.8	41.9	24.1	53.8	23.1	Mean
SD	9.5	7.6	15.7	11.1	10.9	10.5	9.9	16.0	9.5	SD

[a] S = speed; A = accuracy.

Source: Reproduced by permission. Copyright © 1973, 1974 by The Psychological Corporation, New York, N.Y. All rights reserved.

plan the type of instruction best suited to the individual. The test manual should explain how a profile can be interpreted. Figure 10-1 shows Ronald's partial profile based on his *DAT* scores.

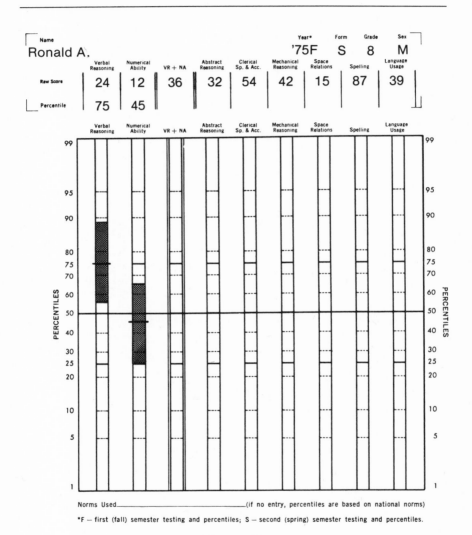

Figure 10-1

Ronald's *DAT* profile (Reproduced by permission. Copyright © 1972, 1973 by The Psychological Corporation, New York, N.Y. All rights reserved.)

COMPLETE THE PROFILE (FIGURE 10-1) BY DETERMINING THE
SEVEN MISSING PERCENTILES AND SHADING IN THE PROFILE
COLUMNS. (COMPARE THE PROFILE YOU COMPLETED IN
FIGURE 10-1 WITH THE PROFILE IN FIGURE 10-2.) RONALD'S
SCORES ARE FOUND EARLIER IN THE CHAPTER; THE NORM-
ING DATA ARE FOUND IN TABLE 10-1.

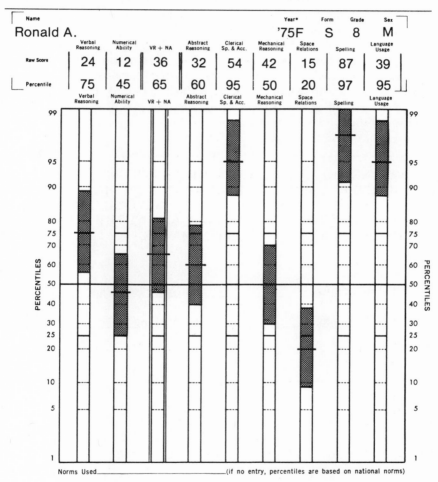

Figure 10-2

Response: Ronald's *DAT* profile (Reproduced by permission. Copyright © 1972, 1973 by The Psychological Corporation, New York,
N.Y. All rights reserved.)

Interpretation of Ronald's Profile

The manual provides a chart for recording a student's profile in percentiles and suggests a formula for determining whether differences between the scores represent important differences in ability. Figure 10-1 illustrates a *DAT* profile chart. To prepare, first draw a heavy short line across the column at the level corresponding to the percentile. The percentile of nine tests is marked in the appropriate column. Darken the space of the column one-half inch above and one-half inch below the heavy short line. (See Verbal Reasoning and Numerical Ability in Figure 10-1.)

If there is no overlap between the shaded areas of any two scores, then important differences in ability are indicated. If the overlap between two shaded areas is less than half their lengths, then you should take into account what you know about the student in interpreting the difference in the two abilities. If the overlap is greater than half the lengths, you can assume that there is little difference in level of ability.

EXAMINE THE COMPLETED PROFILE COLUMNS: UNDER "A" LIST SEVERAL ABILITIES THAT APPEAR TO SHOW AN IMPORTANT DIFFERENCE; UNDER "B" LIST SEVERAL DIFFERENCES IN ABILITIES THAT MAY POSSIBLY AFFECT THE INTERPRETATION OF THE STUDENT'S PERFORMANCE.

A

Verbal Reasoning _____ and Space Relations _____

Verbal Reasoning _____ and Spelling _____

(VR + NA) _____ and Space Relations _____

_____ and _____

_____ and _____

_____ and _____

_____ and _____

_____ and _____

_____ and _____

_____ and _____

B

Verbal Reasoning	and	Numerical Ability
_____	and	_____
_____	and	_____
_____	and	_____
_____	and	_____
_____	and	_____

A. No Overlap—Shows Important Differences:
Verbal Reasoning—Space Relations; Spelling
Numerical Ability—Clerical; Spelling; Grammar
(VR + NA)—Space Relations; Clerical; Spelling; Grammar
Abstract Reasoning—Space Relations; Clerical, Spelling; Grammar
Clerical—Space; Mechanical Reasoning
Space Relations—Spelling; Grammar.
B. Overlap Less than One-Half Length:
Verbal Reasoning—Numerical Ability; Clerical; Grammar; Mechanical
Reasoning
Numerical—Space
Mechanical Reasoning—Space.

7. WHAT DOES BUROS REPORT ABOUT THE TEST?

Buros solicits from specialists in the field of tests and measurement, as well as those in psychology and education who use a particular test widely, a review of standardized tests. A review is not repeated in a subsequent yearbook unless the test has undergone revision or further information about the value of the test is available. If a test was reviewed in an earlier yearbook, the latest yearbook will refer to the test, citing the issue in which it was reviewed. The following yearbooks have been published: 1938, 1940, 1949, 1953, 1959, 1965, and 1972.

The reviewers discuss the strengths and weaknesses of the test, the manual and the support it gives the user, inadequacies of the reliability, validity, item analyses, and cautions in using and interpreting the scores. It helps the user to interpret the scores with care and to be intelligent consumers of standardized tests.

READ THE REVIEWS OF THE *DAT'S* IN BUROS (1965: No. 767, pp. 1001–1007; 1969: No. 605, pp. 669–676; 1972: No. 673, Vol. 2, pp. 672–674). SUMMARIZE THE WEAKNESSES AND STRENGTHS.

Weaknesses: _____

_____

_____

_____

_____

Strengths: _____

_____

_____

_____

_____

8. HOW CAN I BEST INTERPRET THE SCORE AND PLAN SUBSEQUENT INSTRUCTION IN THE LIGHT OF THE ABOVE SEVEN ANSWERS?

Review the responses to the seven questions. You are now ready to interpret Ronald's performance. Cases 19 and 20 are based on the data presented in the chapter. It should be kept in mind that we are missing two important pieces of information that would ordinarily be in your possession: the test itself and Ronald's responses to the test items.

SELECTING A TEST OR TESTING PROGRAM

Administrators and teachers are expected to make decisions about the type of standardized tests used in the school district. The phrase "for what purpose" underlies all decisions concerning test selection. Tests are used for making classroom instructional decisions, for guidance purposes, for administrative purposes, and to evaluate the ongoing educational program. To make wise decisions you should review the Buros volumes, read the test manual, examine the test questions, refer to other teachers and administrators who use the tests, read reports and studies about the tests in such journals as *Journal of Applied Psychology, Journal of Counseling Psychology,* and *Journal of Consulting Psychology,* and find out from the publisher of the test the type of assistance that is provided the user in addition to the test manual. Test information has the potential of improving many facets of the educational program if it is wisely selected and wisely used.

REFERENCES

Anastasi, Anne. *Psychological Testing,* 3d edition. New York: Macmillan, 1968. Chapter 3, on the interpretation of test scores, and Chapter 21, on norms and their use, are of particular concern to the reader.

Edwards, Allen J. *Individual Mental Testing.* Part I, *History and Theories.* Scranton, Pa.: Intext Educational Publishers, 1971. The book discusses the significant contributors to the field of mental testing that range from Alfred Binet to such contemporaries as J. P. Guilford and Jean Piaget.

Gronlund, Norman E. *Readings in Measurement and Evaluation.* New York: Macmillan, 1968. Part Five, on selecting standardized tests, contains a number of short articles on what to look for in making test selections. Part Seven includes a number of readings on using the results of measurement that are of interest to teachers and administrators.

Tarczan, Constance. *An Educator's Guide to Psychological Tests: Description and Classroom Implications.* Springfield, Ill.: Charles C. Thomas, Publisher, 1972. Part IV, on standardized tests used in psychological test batteries, describes in simple terms the psychological tests widely used in schools. Information about each test includes a brief history, purpose, standardization, reliability, administration and time, content and subtests, and classroom implications.

Thorndike, Robert L., and Hagan, Elizabeth. *Measurement and Evaluation in Psychology and Education,* 3d edition. New York: John Wiley and Sons, 1969. Chapter 8 contains information about specific tests and discusses how to plan a school testing program.

11.

USE OF STATISTICS IN EVALUATION OF OBSERVATION PROCEDURES

Much concerning evaluation relies on information gathered from observation. The teacher observes how well students respond orally, the way they interact with each other, their attitudes toward rules and regulations, their work habits, and their social behavior. Principals, too, use observation to obtain data for evaluating school operations: students' conduct in the halls, lunchroom, and on the playground; teachers' performance in the classroom and at faculty meetings; and custodians' maintenance of the physical plant. And parents evaluate their children's education through observation of teaching and learning in the classroom, through their children's attitude toward school and through comments by other parents based on impressions from personal observation. Teachers, administrators, and parents make value judgments and educational decisions on the basis of observations that may or may not be valid or reliable. The problem posed below illustrates this difficulty.

BILL'S MOTHER IS AN ARDENT PROPONENT OF OPEN-CLASS-ROOM INSTRUCTION, AND GERRY'S MOTHER FEELS THAT LEARNING TAKES PLACE BEST IN A TRADITIONAL, TEACHER-ORIENTED, GROUP-PACED CLASS. TOGETHER THEY OBSERVE AN OPEN CLASSROOM AND A TRADITIONAL CLASSROOM WHAT WILL EACH OBSERVE?

Open classroom: _____

_____

_____

_____

_____

Traditional classroom: _____

_____

_____

_____

_____

Open classroom: It is likely that Bill's mother will observe children making many of their own decisions and working cooperatively with each other,
while Gerry's mother will see purposeless chatter, time being wasted, and
aimless activities.
Traditional classroom: Gerry's mother will observe order and purposeful
learning; Bill's mother will see regimentation and conformity in learning.

The above form of observation lacks a focus. Just as we do not ask
students to write everything they know about a topic to determine achievement, so too do we realize that unfocused observation seldom yields more
than personal biases.

HOW CAN OBSERVATIONS BE MADE A USEFUL PROCEDURE FOR COLLECTING INFORMATION? _____

_____

_____

Observations need to be structured and directly related to specific objectives.

Carefully constructed items in observation instruments help the observer
to characterize an event, behavior, or trait in a way that is consistent from
one observer to the next. Though there are many types of observation instruments, this chapter discusses only two—checklists and rating scales—for
they serve as exemplars and have applicability to other forms of observation.

TYPE OF OBSERVATION INSTRUMENTS

Checklists and *rating scales* are the most frequently used observation procedures for collecting information about classroom activity. Their usefulness extends beyond measurement of achievement; if properly constructed they yield data on specific learning difficulties, attitudes, degree of psychomotor development, and textbooks and other instructional materials, and they point up teaching strengths and weaknesses. Whatever information we gather, it is only as good as the instrument's reliability and validity.

CHECKLIST is a data-collecting instrument containing items that focus on observable characteristics of an object, event, or behavior. The observer checks the appropriate items on the checklist as they are observed.

Example: A checklist for evaluating a textbook may consist of several categories (such as physical characteristics of text, design elements, and methodology) and under each category a number of specific items. The observer checks the items that pertain to the textbook.

_____ The author(s) includes instructional objectives.
_____ The textbook contains study guide suggestions.
_____ The text includes a glossary of terms.

FREQUENCY CHECKLIST has similar characteristics to the simple checklist; however, the observer checks the frequency of an event or characteristic occurring within a given frame of reference.

Example: occurrence of a behavior within a given time; word usage within a given number of pages.

RATING SCALE requires the observer to make a quantitative, descriptive, or value judgment along a continuum in response to each item.

Example: The observer responding to items a and b makes a value judgment about the "goodness" or appropriateness of relevant characteristics of a textbook. The observer exercises a descriptive judgment in item c and a quantitative judgment in item d.

Item a. The instructional objectives are clearly stated.

/_____/_____/_____/
Poorly   Marginal   Adequate   Clearly
stated   stated

Item b. The study guide questions are helpful in guiding the student.

/_____/_____/_____/
Of no   Some   Considerable   Great
value   value   value   value

Item c. Instructional objectives

/_____/_____/
None   Implied   Explicit
provided

Item d. Study guide questions

/_____/_____/_____/
None   Few   Frequent   Many
provided

Figure 11.1 illustrates how three types of observation instruments attempt to gather information about a student's oral reading ability.

Item	Checklist	Frequency checklist	Rating scale
1. Pronounces *s*'s correctly	✓	/	⨀————————————⌐ Poor Average Good
2. Pauses at correct places	✓	///	⌐———————⨀———————⌐ Never Seldom Frequently Always
3. Reads with feeling	✓	⊬⊬⊢	⌐———————————————⨀ Poor Fair Good Excellent

Figure 11-1

Comparison of observation instruments for
students reading for a five-minute period

DO YOU OBTAIN THE SAME INFORMATION FROM EACH OF
THE THREE TYPES OF OBSERVATION INSTRUMENTS? YES _____
NO _____. WHY? _____

_____

_____

_____

No. Different amounts and types of information were obtained. In the
simple checklist a single observation of the characteristic is sufficient to
check the item, whether the behavior occurred only once or many times. If
we read down the checklist from the first through the third items, we find
it difficult to determine the significance of the check marks. The frequency checklist contains additional information: the number of occurrences in a given time interval. We do not know, however, from the
information given how many possible opportunities the student had to display the behavior within the time interval. The single tally mark for the
first item tells us one thing about the performance if the student only had
a single opportunity to pronounce the s sound, or it tells us something else
about the performance if the student had seven such opportunities within
the time interval. The rating scale involves a judgment to be made on the
part of the observer. It indicates that, though the student has trouble with
s's, he reads with feeling.

DO YOU, AS THE OBSERVER, PERFORM THE SAME TASK
USING EACH TYPE OF INSTRUMENT?   YES_____. NO_____.
WHY? _____

_____

_____

No. In the simple checklist the observer merely records once each characteristic he observes. In the frequency checklist he specifies the number of
times an action or event was observed. In the rating scale he rates the
observation.

GIVEN THE FOLLOWING SITUATION, EXAMINE THE ITEM BE-
LOW, AND THEN SCORE SUSAN'S PERFORMANCE, USING EACH
OF THE OBSERVATION EXAMPLES:
   Susan, a second grader, was reading a paragraph orally to the class.
The paragraph contained six instances where the reader should have
lowered her voice for the proper emphasis. Susan lowered her voice in two
of the six instances.

Checklist:	Frequency checklist:	Rating scale:
Lowers voice for proper emphasis	Lowers voice for proper emphasis	Lowers voice for proper emphasis
_____	_____	/_____/_____/
		Poor Average Good

1. Did you give Susan a check in the checklist? Yes_____. No_____.
Why? _____

2. What information helped make the frequency checklist meaningful?
_____

3. What problems did you encounter in using the rating scale? _____
_____

_____

4. Construct a different scale for the rating scale that may reduce the above difficulty?

/_____/_____/

Your responses to the above questions probably ran along the following lines:

                                                    ?
_____ √ _____   _____ // _____   /_____/_____/
                                             Poor Average Good

1. Yes. A single check is placed in the checklist because the observer heard Susan lower her voice for the proper emphasis.

2. There are two tallies in the frequency checklist, indicating that this may be more than mere chance behavior. Knowing that Susan had six opportunities in the passage she was reading to lower her voice for proper emphasis gives us additional information about how she performs on this skill. She is only performing successfully one-third of the time.

3. On the rating scale we are expected to make a judgment about the performance. Is one-third of the time indicative of poor, average, or good performance? We need to know more about Susan's previous performance as well as something about the expectations for second graders. A different scale might help us to avoid making a value judgment by selecting scales that elicit quantitative values.

4. /_____/_____/_____/
   Never   Sometimes   Frequently   Always
   lowers voice   lowers voice

There are guidelines for selecting one type of observation form above another: the form chosen should be the one that provides the most information without introducing observer biases. It is not always possible to remove these biases because the type of information sought may itself be value laden.

Carefully constructed items in the checklist can, generally, reduce observer bias. Checklists are highly suitable for measuring attainment of a specific skill, such as the ability to thread a projector, focus a microscope, or maintain the building safety code. A frequency checklist adds another dimension to the simple checklist, for it includes additional information without introducing biased judgment. The rating scale requires the observer to place a value judgment on the behavior, whether that judgment be quantitative, descriptive, or value. Although the judgments add information, they also increase chances of error and differences in judgment between one observer of the same event and another observer.

Each type of observation procedure has advantages and disadvantages. For some situations the checklist may be the appropriate instrument, for others the frequency checklist, and for still others the rating scale.

REVIEW THE THREE ITEMS IN FIGURE 11-1 AND SELECT THE MOST APPROPRIATE OBSERVATION PROCEDURE FOR EACH SITUATION AND EXPLAIN YOUR CHOICE.

1. Pronounces s's correctly: _____

_____

_____

2. Pauses at correct places: _____

_____

_____

3. Reads with feeling: _____

_____

_____

---

1. The simple checklist will give you the information you need for the first item. Children who say their s's correctly usually do so consistently. If this were a speech correction class, then the frequency checklist is suitable, but, where a simpler procedure will do, it should be used in preference to a more complex one.

2. The frequency checklist is suited to the second item. We obtain a picture of how well the student "pauses at correct places" by comparing the number of correct pauses with the total possible correct pauses in the assigned reading. The rating scale could also apply, but more judgment on the part of the rater is involved. One has to ask if there is a likelihood of two observers checking different places on the continuum for the same ob-

served event. If so, consideration should be given either to rewording an item in a rating scale or using another procedure.

3. The third item is value laden; thus it is best served by a rating scale. To ensure consistency among different raters, it is necessary to coach each rater in the accepted meaning of the terms "poor," "fair," "good," and "excellent."

QUANTIFYING OBSERVATION INSTRUMENTS

Quantifying the checks, tallies, or ratings puts the data in a form that facilitates evaluation. When quantified the observation yields a single score or a number of subscores if the items on the instrument are subsumed into subcategories or components. Chapter 1 discussed total scores and sub-scores, and other chapters in Part I showed ways to analyze quantified data statistically.

To quantify a checklist, add all the checks. The total number of possible checks depends on the total number of items in the checklist. If items are positively worded, the more items checked, the more positive the perform-ance or behavior. If items are negatively worded, the less items checked, the more positive the performance or behavior.

As an example, the driver education teachers use a checklist containing fifteen safety actions the student driver must perform before putting the car in motion. These are:

_____ 1. adjust seat

_____ 2. adjust rearview mirror

_____ 3. adjust sideview mirror

_____ 4. fasten seat belt

_____ 5. lock door

_____ 6. check that gear is in neutral

_____ 7. insert key

_____ 8. depress gas pedal

_____ 9. turn key to start motor

_____10. remove foot from gas pedal

_____11. check instrument pan-el (gas, oil, etc.)

_____12. check front, side, and rear views

_____13. release emergency brake

_____14. use turn signal

_____15. shift to first or drive

The students' performance on the checklist depends on the number of items checked. Ten, twelve, or all the items may be necessary for driver safety. The teacher establishes the criteria for determining safety in preference to norma-tive standards. The student is evaluated on whether he has achieved the requisite number of checks that constitute the criterion standard. Items left unchecked tell the student what actions he needs to practice. A breakdown of the number of times an item is checked for a whole class tells the teacher where the instructional emphasis should be placed.

Quantifying a frequency checklist differs according to the kinds of data collected. If the observer obtains data on an event with a given number of possibilities of occurrence, he would prepare the quantitative data in one way. If the event can occur any number of times, then he must use another method for quantifying the data. As an example of the first case, the student is given ten opportunities at bat to get a hit. We can obtain the percent of times he gets a hit in ten attempts. To obtain the percent, the number of hits is divided by the total possible hits he could get; the resulting decimal is put into percent. Let us say the student got four hits; that is, he hit the ball 40 percent of the time: $(4/10 = 0.40 = 40\%)$.*We may want to compare the performance of one student with that of the total class. In this case we would divide the number of hits of the one student by the number of hits obtained by the total class. If the class, including the one particular student, had eighty hits, then his percent would be $(4/80 = 0.05 = 0.05 \times 100 = 5\%)$.

Where the number of occurrences of an event or behavior is not given or predetermined, then we need to follow the second method: quantifying the frequency of an occurrence for a student in terms of the total number of occurrences for the class. Let us say we are observing the number of times the students leave their seats. There is an undetermined number of times this activity can occur, holding constant the teacher's telling the class to rise or line up. As we observe the class we record the frequency with which each child leaves his seat. This gives us the total for each child and for the class. We can also compare two different classes or a particular student as he behaves in one class with his behavior in another class. Behavior in this instance is the number of times he leaves his seat. In both comparisons, however, we need to make sure the time factor is kept constant, that is, the length of time of the observation is the same. If we compare two different classes, there should be approximately the same number of students in each. It should be noted that in the cases cited above no value statement has been made concerning the student's behavior related to the number of times he leaves his seat.

We quantify rating scales by assigning numerical values to fixed points on the continuum. Three examples for assigning numerical values to items on a textbook rating scale are shown:

Item: The print is clear and readable

1. /_____/_____/
   Good   Average   Poor

Good = 1
Average = 2
Poor = 3

---

*Reminder: To convert a decimal into percent, multiply the decimal by 100 and add the percent sign: $0.40 \times 100 = 40\%$.

2. /_____/_____/_____/
  Always   Frequently   Seldom   Never

$$Always = 4$$
$$Frequently = 3$$
$$Seldom = 2$$
$$Never = 1$$

3. /_____/_____/_____/
  Excellent   Good   Fair   Poor   Unacceptable

$$Excellent = 4$$
$$Good = 3$$
$$Fair = 2$$
$$Poor = 1$$
$$Unacceptable = 0$$

To obtain a quantitative measure of four mathematics textbooks, each text is rated, the numerical values for each item are summed, and the total scores are compared.

At times one characteristic of a textbook, represented by an item on a rating scale, is of greater importance than other characteristics. For example, the accuracy of presenting a concept certainly overrides the attractiveness of the diagrams. Yet we may give excess weight to the less important characteristic if both items are rated equally "good," and we tend to lose the impact of poorly presented concepts if the diagrams are rated high.

HOW CAN YOU ACCOUNT DIFFERENTIALLY FOR CHARACTERISTICS THAT VARY IN IMPORTANCE? _____

_____

_____

_____

- -

Using two items on the rating scale to rate an important characteristic weights the characteristic differentially. One item reads: "Mathematical concepts are accurately developed"; the second item reads: "Examples to further develop a mathematical concept are adequate."

After the observations are quantified, the scores can be analyzed statistically for the mean, standard deviation, and group norms.

VALIDITY OF OBSERVATION INSTRUMENTS

We need to raise the questions concerning validity in conjunction with the checklist and rating scale: Do the scores obtained from the observations represent the behavior, trait, or event they are designed to measure? What predictions can be made on the basis of the obtained scores? Applying the two questions concerning validity to an observation instrument that rates the effectiveness of teachers, as an example, we ask if the obtained scores distinguish between effective and noneffective teaching, and if effective teaching in subsequent teaching situations can be predicted from the obtained rating or the number of checks on the checklist.

Content validity is dependent on the items included in the checklist or rating scale. The items should sample as much of the relevant aspects of the object, event, or behavior as is necessary to yield comprehensive measurement. When one is evaluating a lesson using an observation instrument, the teacher's instructional objectives are important guides for formulating rating scale and checklist items. The school system's philosophy, curriculum goals and objectives, and statement of staff responsibility also need to be considered in constructing items.

YOU HAVE BEEN ASKED TO DESIGN A RATING SCALE FOR GATHERING INFORMATION ON VARIOUS INTERMEDIATE LITERATURE TEXTBOOKS FROM WHICH THE SELECTION FOR THE SCHOOL IS BASED. WHAT ITEMS SHOULD BE INCLUDED?

First, you need to check the school system's statement of philosophy concerning its language arts or literature program. In addition, there are salient characteristics that describe instructional materials. Recheck your list to see if you included such features as the following: design of the textbook (goals and instructional objectives, scope, sequence, methodology, and evaluation materials for determining students' progress); content of the book (topics covered, types of literature, representativeness of the literature, inclusion of language arts skills); instructional aids (discussion questions, vocabulary tips, charts, pictures, diagrams); physical characteristics of the book (readability, attractiveness, durability); and learner verification studies (publisher's evidence that the text was field-tested or in some manner validated with learners). Recently ethnic, racial, and sex biases have been included as features of instructional materials requiring evaluation; hence items related to these biases should be included in the instrument.

Designing a checklist for gathering information about students' performance in a driver training course would, of course, involve many different items. The selected items must include the relevant aspects of acceptable driving procedures.

RELIABILITY OF OBSERVATION INSTRUMENTS

In addition to the sources of error common to all measurement instruments, the observer plays a prominent part in contributing to the possibility of unreliability of observation instruments. Sources of error stem from the inability of items consistently to measure a defined behavior; lack of consistency of checking or rating by a single observer from one observation to a second observation of the same behavior or event (observer stability coefficient); and lack of reliability between two observers checking or rating the same behavior (coefficient of observer agreement).

Reliability Coefficient

It is difficult to obtain the reliability coefficient of an observation instrument uncontaminated by the errors the observer introduces. Data obtained from test-retest and parallel instruments are subject to errors by the observer. Data used to derive the internal consistency of an instrument suffer from the same source of error. Until the reliability of the checker or rater is established, the usual procedures for ascertaining reliability of an instrument are of limited value.

Stability Coefficient

The Pearson Product-Moment Correlation is used to obtain information about the stability of the scorer or rater to obtain consistent data over time. Where the event is itself stable, such as a textbook, the stability coefficient yields information about the scorer's stability. The scorer rates a series of textbooks on one occasion and again on a second occasion. The ratings are correlated, and the obtained correlation coefficient establishes the stability of the rater.

Where the event or behavior is not stable from one time to the next, such as the teacher's behavior, the stability coefficient gives us information about the instrument's ability to yield stable data, once the reliability of the observer has been established.

For example, Observer 1 used Checklist M to gather data on the behavior fifteen teachers employed to motivate students. At a later date the same observer observed the same fifteen teachers, recording motivational behavior using the same checklist. The formula for determining the stability coefficient of the event using the same observer is illustrated below.

| | Observer 1 | |
Teacher	Occasion A	Occasion B
1	X	X
2	X	X
3	X	X
4	X	X
.		
.		
.		
14	X	X
15	X	X

$$r = \frac{\Sigma (X_a - \bar{X}_a)(X_b - \bar{X}_b)}{N(SD_a)(SD_b)}$$

where X_a = raw scores on the first occasion

X_b = raw scores on the second occasion

The obtained correlation between the motivational behavior on the first and second occasions gives us information on the degree of consistency of the instrument to yield data on motivational behavior.

Coefficient of Observer Agreement

Even though the reliability of an observation instrument has been shown to be acceptable, each scorer or rater introduces his own errors. We need to make certain the score we have obtained has not been inadvertently biased by the observation of the observer. Using the same observer on different occasions does not necessarily get at the question of bias.

To determine the coefficient of observer agreement, two observers observe simultaneously the acts of motivation of each of the fifteen teachers. A correlation between each of their observations of the same event or behavior is obtained. The following is an example.

| | | Checklist M | |
Teacher	Date	Observer 1	Observer 2
1	January 8	X	X
2	January 9	X	X
3	January 10	X	X
4	January 12	X	X
.			
.			
.			
14	January 27	X	X
15	January 29	X	X

$$r = \frac{\Sigma (X_1 - \bar{X}_1)(X_2 - \bar{X}_2)}{N(SD_1)(SD_2)}$$

where X_1 = the raw scores obtained by the first observer

X_2 = the raw scores obtained by the second observer

If the obtained correlation is high, the instrument can be used by both observers in the future with some assurance that their personal observations as scorers are not unduly biasing the results.

Where scores for more than two raters of the same event are correlated, the Pearson Product-Moment statistic is not applicable. Other statistical techniques are employed. More advanced statistics texts discuss these procedures.

STUDENT INPUT IN OBSERVATIONS

Observation instruments such as those described in this chapter can become vehicles for involving students in monitoring their own performance and evaluating both the process and the product. With the guidance of the teacher, students can become aware of the many facets of a learning situation, their own actions and thought processes, and how these sum up achievement and desired behavior. The students also become sensitive to evaluation procedures as dependent upon the concepts of reliability and validity.

Case 21 serves as a review of Chapter 11. In working through Case 22 the readers have an opportunity to develop an observation instrument and to implement it in a school setting.

REFERENCES

Cooper, John O. *Measurement and Analysis of Behavioral Techniques.* Columbus, Ohio: Charles E. Merrill Publishing Co., 1974. Chapter 2 introduced techniques for recording a variety of observed activities. The appendix describes timed devices used in recording observations.

Hynes, Roger, and Lippitt, Ronald A. "Systematic Observational Techniques." In *Handbook of Social Psychology,* Vol. I. Ed. G. Lindzey. Cambridge, Mass.: Addison-Wesley, 1954. This is a classic treatment of the topic.

Mehrens, William A., and Lehmann, Irvin J. *Measurement and Evaluation in Education and Psychology.* New York: Holt, Rinehart and Winston, 1973. Chapter 12 discusses observation tools and techniques and includes cautions and suggestions for developing and using observation instruments.

Thorndike, Robert L., and Hagan, Elizabeth. *Measurement and Evaluation in Psychology and Education.* 3d edition. New York: John Wiley and Sons, 1969. Chapter 13 examines problems in obtaining sound ratings and ways of improving the effectiveness of ratings.

Appendix

GUIDE

FOR THE USE OF TABLE OF SQUARES

AND SQUARE ROOTS OF NUMBERS

The accompanying table of squares and square roots lists whole numbers from 1 to 1,000. The left-hand column shows the numbers. The next column to the right gives the square of the numbers. The third column gives the square root of the numbers.

To Find the Squares and Square Roots of Whole Numbers where $N = 20$:

1. Locate 20 in the "Number" column.

2. The square of 20 (20^2) is shown in the corresponding "Square" column: ($20^2 = 400$).

3. The number in the corresponding "Square root" column is the square root of 20: $\sqrt{20} = 4.472$.

To Find the Squares and Square Roots of Three-Digit Numbers between 1.00 and 9.99 where $N = 8.73$:

1. Move the decimal point two places to the right; the number now reads 873.

2. Locate 873 in the "Number" column.

3. Find the square of 873 in the corresponding column: $873^2 = 762129$. Move the decimal point four places to the left; the number now reads 76.2129, that is, $8.73^2 = 76.2129$.

4. Find the square root of 873 in the corresponding column: $\sqrt{873} = 29.547$. Move the decimal point in the answer one place to the left: 2.9547; or $\sqrt{8.73} = 2.9547$.

To Find the Squares and Square Roots of Three-Digit Numbers between 10.1 and 99.9 where $N = 32.6$:

1. Move the decimal point one place to the right; the number now reads 326.

2. Locate 326 in the "Number" column.

3. Find the square of 326 in the corresponding column: $326^2 = 106276$. Move the decimal point two places to the left; the number now reads 1062.76, that is, $32.6^2 = 1062.76$.

4. To find the square root of 32.6 we need to interpolate.

   a. Look up the square roots of the numbers 32 and 33; we know that the square root of 32.6 lies somewhere between the two values.

   $$\sqrt{32.0} = 5.657 \text{ ----------------- } 5.657$$
   $$\sqrt{32.1} = 5.657 + (0.009 \times 1) = 5.666$$
   $$\sqrt{32.2} = 5.657 + (0.009 \times 2) = 5.675$$
   $$\sqrt{32.3} = \quad .$$
   $$\sqrt{32.4} = \quad .$$
   $$0.088 \quad \sqrt{32.5} = \quad .$$
   $$\sqrt{32.6} = 5.657 + (0.009 \times 6) = 5.711$$
   $$\sqrt{32.7} = \quad .$$
   $$\sqrt{32.8} = \quad .$$
   $$\sqrt{32.9} = \quad .$$
   $$\sqrt{33.0} = 5.745 \text{ ---------------- } 5.745$$

   b. Find the difference between the square root of 32 and the square root of 33: $(5.745 - 5.657 = 0.088)$.

   c. Divide the difference between the values of the two square roots by 10 (rounded to the nearest thousandth): $(0.088/10 = 0.009)$. The product (0.009) is the unit of increment added to the square root value of a number as the number lying between 32 and 33 increases by one-tenth.

   d. In the case of our example, 32.6, multiply 0.009 by 6 (6 increments) and add the value to the square root of 32: $5.657 + (0.009 \times 6) = 5.657 + 0.054 = 5.711$.

   $$\sqrt{32.6} = 5.711$$

Table of squares and square roots of numbers from 1 to 1000

Number	Square	Square root	Number	Square	Square root
1	1	1.000	51	2601	7.141
2	4	1.414	52	2704	7.211
3	9	1.732	53	2809	7.280
4	16	2.000	54	2916	7.348
5	25	2.236	55	3025	7.416
6	36	2.449	56	3136	7.483
7	49	2.646	57	3249	7.550
8	64	2.828	58	3364	7.616
9	81	3.000	59	3481	7.681
10	100	3.162	60	3600	7.746
11	121	3.317	61	3721	7.810
12	144	3.464	62	3844	7.874
13	169	3.606	63	3969	7.937
14	196	3.742	64	4096	8.000
15	225	3.873	65	4225	8.062
16	256	4.000	66	4356	8.124
17	289	4.123	67	4489	8.185
18	324	4.243	68	4624	8.246
19	361	4.359	69	4761	8.307
20	400	4.472	70	4900	8.367
21	441	4.583	71	5041	8.426
22	484	4.690	72	5184	8.485
23	529	4.796	73	5329	8.544
24	576	4.899	74	5476	8.602
25	625	5.000	75	5625	8.660
26	676	5.099	76	5776	8.718
27	729	5.196	77	5929	8.775
28	784	5.292	78	6084	8.832
29	841	5.385	79	6241	8.888
30	900	5.477	80	6400	8.944
31	961	5.568	81	6561	9.000
32	1024	5.657	82	6724	9.055
33	1089	5.745	83	6889	9.110
34	1156	5.831	84	7056	9.165
35	1225	5.916	85	7225	9.220
36	1296	6.000	86	7396	9.274
37	1369	6.083	87	7569	9.327
38	1444	6.164	88	7744	9.381
39	1521	6.245	89	7921	9.434
40	1600	6.325	90	8100	9.487
41	1681	6.403	91	8281	9.539
42	1764	6.481	92	8464	9.592
43	1849	6.557	93	8649	9.644
44	1936	6.633	94	8836	9.695
45	2025	6.708	95	9025	9.747
46	2116	6.782	96	9216	9.798
47	2209	6.856	97	9409	9.849
48	2304	6.928	98	9604	9.899
49	2401	7.000	99	9801	9.950
50	2500	7.071	100	10000	10.000

Table of squares and square roots (*continued*)

Number	Square	Square root	Number	Square	Square root
101	10201	10.050	151	22801	12.288
102	10404	10.100	152	23104	12.329
103	10609	10.149	153	23409	12.369
104	10816	10.198	154	23716	12.410
105	11025	10.247	155	24025	12.450
106	11236	10.296	156	24336	12.490
107	11449	10.344	157	24649	12.530
108	11664	10.392	158	24964	12.570
109	11881	10.440	159	25281	12.610
110	12100	10.488	160	25600	12.649
111	12321	10.536	161	25921	12.689
112	12544	10.583	162	26244	12.728
113	12769	10.630	163	26569	12.767
114	12996	10.677	164	26896	12.806
115	13225	10.724	165	27225	12.845
116	13456	10.770	166	27556	12.884
117	13689	10.817	167	27889	12.923
118	13924	10.863	168	28224	12.961
119	14161	10.909	169	28561	13.000
120	14400	10.954	170	28900	13.038
121	14641	11.000	171	29241	13.077
122	14884	11.045	172	29584	13.115
123	15129	11.091	173	29929	13.153
124	15376	11.136	174	30276	13.191
125	15625	11.180	175	30625	13.229
126	15876	11.225	176	30976	13.266
127	16129	11.269	177	31329	13.304
128	16384	11.314	178	31684	13.342
129	16641	11.358	179	32041	13.379
130	16900	11.402	180	32400	13.416
131	17161	11.446	181	32761	13.454
132	17424	11.489	182	33124	13.491
133	17689	11.533	183	33489	13.528
134	17956	11.576	184	33856	13.565
135	18225	11.619	185	34225	13.601
136	18496	11.662	186	34596	13.638
137	18769	11.705	187	34969	13.675
138	19044	11.747	188	35344	13.711
139	19321	11.790	189	35721	13.748
140	19600	11.832	190	36100	13.784
141	19881	11.874	191	36481	13.820
142	20164	11.916	192	36864	13.856
143	20449	11.958	193	37249	13.892
144	20736	12.000	194	37636	13.928
145	21025	12.042	195	38025	13.964
146	21316	12.083	196	38416	14.000
147	21609	12.124	197	38809	14.036
148	21904	12.166	198	39204	14.071
149	22201	12.207	199	39601	14.107
150	22500	12.247	200	40000	14.142

Table of squares and square roots (*continued*)

Number	Square	Square root	Number	Square	Square root
201	40401	14.177	251	63001	15.843
202	40804	14.213	252	63504	15.875
203	41209	14.248	253	64009	15.906
204	41616	14.283	254	64516	15.937
205	42025	14.318	255	65025	15.969
206	42436	14.353	256	65536	16.000
207	42849	14.387	257	66049	16.031
208	43264	14.422	258	66564	16.062
209	43681	14.457	259	67081	16.093
210	44100	14.491	260	67600	16.125
211	44521	14.526	261	68121	16.155
212	44944	14.560	262	68644	16.186
213	45369	14.595	263	69169	16.217
214	45796	14.629	264	69696	16.248
215	46225	14.663	265	70225	16.279
216	46656	14.697	266	70756	16.310
217	47089	14.731	267	71289	16.340
218	47524	14.765	268	71824	16.371
219	47961	14.799	269	72361	16.401
220	48400	14.832	270	72900	16.432
221	48841	14.866	271	73441	16.462
222	49284	14.900	272	73984	16.492
223	49729	14.933	273	74529	16.523
224	50176	14.967	274	75076	16.553
225	50625	15.000	275	75625	16.583
226	51076	15.033	276	76176	16.613
227	51529	15.067	277	76729	16.643
228	51984	15.100	278	77284	16.673
229	52441	15.133	279	77841	16.703
230	52900	15.166	280	78400	16.733
231	53361	15.199	281	78961	16.763
232	53824	15.232	282	79524	16.793
233	54289	15.264	283	80089	16.823
234	54756	15.297	284	80656	16.852
235	55225	15.330	285	81225	16.882
236	55696	15.362	286	81796	16.912
237	56169	15.395	287	82369	16.941
238	56644	15.427	288	82944	16.971
239	57121	15.460	289	83521	17.000
240	57600	15.492	290	84100	17.029
241	58081	15.524	291	84681	17.059
242	58564	15.556	292	85264	17.088
243	59049	15.588	293	85849	17.117
244	59536	15.620	294	86436	17.146
245	60025	15.652	295	87025	17.176
246	60516	15.684	296	87616	17.205
247	61009	15.716	297	88209	17.234
248	61504	15.748	298	88804	17.263
249	62001	15.780	299	89401	17.292
250	62500	15.811	300	90000	17.321

Table of squares and square roots (*continued*)

Number	Square	Square root	Number	Square	Square root
301	90601	17.349	351	123201	18.735
302	91204	17.378	352	123904	18.762
303	91809	17.407	353	124609	18.788
304	92416	17.436	354	125316	18.815
305	93025	17.464	355	126025	18.841
306	93636	17.493	356	126736	18.868
307	94249	17.521	357	127449	18.894
308	94864	17.550	358	128164	18.921
309	95481	17.578	359	128881	18.947
310	96100	17.607	360	129600	18.974
311	96721	17.635	361	130321	19.000
312	97344	17.664	362	131044	19.026
313	97969	17.692	363	131769	19.053
314	98596	17.720	364	132496	19.079
315	99225	17.748	365	133225	19.105
316	99856	17.776	366	133956	19.131
317	100489	17.804	367	134689	19.157
318	101124	17.833	368	135424	19.183
319	101761	17.861	369	136161	19.209
320	102400	17.889	370	136900	19.235
321	103041	17.916	371	137641	19.261
322	103684	17.944	372	138384	19.287
323	104329	17.972	373	139129	19.313
324	104976	18.000	374	139876	19.339
325	105625	18.028	375	140625	19.365
326	106276	18.055	376	141376	19.391
327	106929	18.083	377	142129	19.416
328	107584	18.111	378	142884	19.442
329	108241	18.138	379	143641	19.468
330	108900	18.166	380	144400	19.494
331	109561	18.193	381	145161	19.519
332	110224	18.221	382	145924	19.545
333	110889	18.248	383	146689	19.570
334	111556	18.276	384	147456	19.596
335	112225	18.303	385	148225	19.621
336	112896	18.330	386	148996	19.647
337	113569	18.358	387	149769	19.672
338	114244	18.385	388	150544	19.698
339	114921	18.412	389	151321	19.723
340	115600	18.439	390	152100	19.748
341	116281	18.466	391	152881	19.774
342	116964	18.493	392	153664	19.799
343	117649	18.520	393	154449	19.824
344	118336	18.547	394	155236	19.849
345	119025	18.574	395	156025	19.875
346	119716	18.601	396	156816	19.900
347	120409	18.628	397	157609	19.925
348	121104	18.655	398	158404	19.950
349	121801	18.682	399	159201	19.975
350	122500	18.708	400	160000	20.000

Table of squares and square roots (*continued*)

Number	Square	Square root	Number	Square	Square root
401	160801	20.025	451	203401	21.237
402	161604	20.050	452	204304	21.260
403	162409	20.075	453	205209	21.284
404	163216	20.100	454	206116	21.307
405	164025	20.125	455	207025	21.331
406	164836	20.149	456	207936	21.354
407	165649	20.174	457	208849	21.378
408	166464	20.199	458	209764	21.401
409	167281	20.224	459	210681	21.424
410	168100	20.248	460	211600	21.448
411	168921	20.273	461	212521	21.471
412	169744	20.298	462	213444	21.494
413	170569	20.322	463	214369	21.517
414	171396	20.347	464	215296	21.541
415	172225	20.372	465	216225	21.564
416	173056	20.396	466	217156	21.587
417	173889	20.421	467	218089	21.610
418	174724	20.445	468	219024	21.633
419	175561	20.469	469	219961	21.656
420	176400	20.494	470	220900	21.679
421	177241	20.518	471	221841	21.703
422	178084	20.543	472	222784	21.726
423	178929	20.567	473	223729	21.749
424	179776	20.591	474	224676	21.772
425	180625	20.616	475	225625	21.794
426	181476	20.640	476	226576	21.817
427	182329	20.664	477	227529	21.840
428	183184	20.688	478	228484	21.863
429	184041	20.712	479	229441	21.886
430	184900	20.736	480	230400	21.909
431	185761	20.761	481	231361	21.932
432	186624	20.785	482	232324	21.954
433	187489	20.809	483	233289	21.977
434	188356	20.833	484	234256	22.000
435	189225	20.857	485	235225	22.023
436	190096	20.881	486	236196	22.045
437	190969	20.905	487	237169	22.068
438	191844	20.928	488	238144	22.091
439	192721	20.952	489	239121	22.113
440	193600	20.976	490	240100	22.136
441	194481	21.000	491	241081	22.159
442	195364	21.024	492	242064	22.181
443	196249	21.048	493	243049	22.204
444	197136	21.071	494	244036	22.226
445	198025	21.095	495	245025	22.249
446	198916	21.119	496	246016	22.271
447	199809	21.142	497	247009	22.293
448	200704	21.166	498	248004	22.316
449	201601	21.190	499	249001	22.338
450	202500	21.213	500	250000	22.361

Table of squares and square roots (*continued*)

Number	Square	Square root	Number	Square	Square root
501	251001	22.383	551	303601	23.473
502	252004	22.405	552	304704	23.495
503	253009	22.428	553	305809	23.516
504	254016	22.450	554	306916	23.537
505	255025	22.472	555	308025	23.558
506	256036	22.494	556	309136	23.580
507	257049	22.517	557	310249	23.601
508	258064	22.539	558	311364	23.622
509	259081	22.561	559	312481	23.643
510	260100	22.583	560	313600	23.664
511	261121	22.605	561	314721	23.685
512	262144	22.627	562	315844	23.707
513	263169	22.650	563	316969	23.728
514	264196	22.672	564	318096	23.749
515	265225	22.694	565	319225	23.770
516	266256	22.716	566	320356	23.791
517	267289	22.738	567	321489	23.812
518	268324	22.760	568	322624	23.833
519	269361	22.782	569	323761	23.854
520	270400	22.804	570	324900	23.875
521	271441	22.825	571	326041	23.896
522	272484	22.847	572	327184	23.917
523	273529	22.869	573	328329	23.937
524	274576	22.891	574	329476	23.958
525	275625	22.913	575	330625	23.979
526	276676	22.935	576	331776	24.000
527	277729	22.956	577	332929	24.021
528	278784	22.978	578	334084	24.042
529	279841	23.000	579	335241	24.062
530	280900	23.022	580	336400	24.083
531	281961	23.043	581	337561	24.104
532	283024	23.065	582	338724	24.125
533	284089	23.087	583	339889	24.145
534	285156	23.108	584	341056	24.166
535	286225	23.130	585	342225	24.187
536	287296	23.152	586	343396	24.207
537	288369	23.173	587	344569	24.228
538	289444	23.195	588	345744	24.249
539	290521	23.216	589	346921	24.269
540	291600	23.238	590	348100	24.290
541	292681	23.259	591	349281	24.310
542	293764	23.281	592	350464	24.331
543	294849	23.302	593	351649	24.352
544	295936	23.324	594	352836	24.372
545	297025	23.345	595	354025	24.393
546	298116	23.367	596	355216	24.413
547	299209	23.388	597	356409	24.434
548	300304	23.409	598	357604	24.454
549	301401	23.431	599	358801	24.474
550	302500	23.452	600	360000	24.495

Table of squares and square roots (*continued*)

Number	Square	Square root	Number	Square	Square root
601	361201	24.515	651	423801	25.515
602	362404	24.536	652	425104	25.534
603	363609	24.556	653	426409	25.554
604	364816	24.576	654	427716	25.573
605	366025	24.597	655	429025	25.593
606	367236	24.617	656	430336	25.612
607	368449	24.637	657	431649	25.632
608	369664	24.658	658	432964	25.652
609	370881	24.678	659	434281	25.671
610	372100	24.698	660	435600	25.690
611	373321	24.718	661	436921	25.710
612	374544	24.739	662	438244	25.729
613	375769	24.759	663	439569	25.749
614	376996	24.779	664	440896	25.768
615	378225	24.799	665	442225	25.788
616	379456	24.819	666	443556	25.807
617	380689	24.839	667	444889	25.826
618	381924	24.860	668	446224	25.846
619	383161	24.880	669	447561	25.865
620	384400	24.900	670	448900	25.884
621	385641	24.920	671	450241	25.904
622	386884	24.940	672	451584	25.923
623	388129	24.960	673	452929	25.942
624	389376	24.980	674	454276	25.962
625	390625	25.000	675	455625	25.981
626	391876	25.020	676	456976	26.000
627	393129	25.040	677	458329	26.019
628	394384	25.060	678	459684	26.038
629	395641	25.080	679	461041	26.058
630	396900	25.100	680	462400	26.077
631	398161	25.120	681	463761	26.096
632	399424	25.140	682	465124	26.115
633	400689	25.159	683	466489	26.134
634	401956	25.179	684	467856	26.153
635	403225	25.199	685	469225	26.173
636	404496	25.219	686	470596	26.192
637	405769	25.239	687	471969	26.211
638	407044	25.259	688	473344	26.230
639	408321	25.278	689	474721	26.249
640	409600	25.298	690	476100	26.268
641	410881	25.318	691	477481	26.287
642	412164	25.338	692	478864	26.306
643	413449	25.357	693	480249	26.325
644	414736	25.377	694	481636	26.344
645	416025	25.397	695	483025	26.363
646	417316	25.417	696	484416	26.382
647	418609	25.436	697	485809	26.401
648	419904	25.456	698	487204	26.420
649	421201	25.475	699	488601	26.439
650	422500	25.495	700	490000	26.458

Table of squares and square roots (*continued*)

Number	Square	Square root	Number	Square	Square root
701	491401	26.476	751	564001	27.404
702	492804	26.495	752	565504	27.423
703	494209	26.514	753	567009	27.441
704	495616	26.533	754	568516	27.459
705	497025	26.552	755	570025	27.477
706	498436	26.571	756	571536	27.495
707	499849	26.589	757	573049	27.514
708	501264	26.608	758	574564	27.532
709	502681	26.627	759	576081	27.550
710	504100	26.646	760	577600	27.568
711	505521	26.665	761	579121	27.586
712	506944	26.683	762	580644	27.604
713	508369	26.702	763	582169	27.622
714	509796	26.721	764	583696	27.641
715	511225	26.739	765	585225	27.659
716	512656	26.758	766	586756	27.677
717	514089	26.777	767	588289	27.695
718	515524	26.796	768	589824	27.713
719	516961	26.814	769	591361	27.731
720	518400	26.833	770	592900	27.749
721	519841	26.851	771	594441	27.767
722	521284	26.870	772	595984	27.785
723	522729	26.889	773	597529	27.803
724	524176	26.907	774	599076	27.821
725	525625	26.926	775	600625	27.839
726	527076	26.944	776	602176	27.857
727	528529	26.963	777	603729	27.875
728	529984	26.981	778	605284	27.893
729	531441	27.000	779	606841	27.911
730	532900	27.019	780	608400	27.928
731	534361	27.037	781	609961	27.946
732	535824	27.055	782	611524	27.964
733	537289	27.074	783	613089	27.982
734	538756	27.092	784	614656	28.000
735	540225	27.111	785	616225	28.018
736	541696	27.129	786	617796	28.036
737	543169	27.148	787	619369	28.054
738	544644	27.166	788	620944	28.071
739	546121	27.185	789	622521	28.089
740	547600	27.203	790	624100	28.107
741	549081	27.221	791	625681	28.125
742	550564	27.240	792	627264	28.142
743	552049	27.258	793	628849	28.160
744	553536	27.276	794	630436	28.178
745	555025	27.295	795	632025	28.196
746	556516	27.313	796	633616	28.213
747	558009	27.331	797	635209	28.231
748	559504	27.350	798	636804	28.249
749	561001	27.368	799	638401	28.267
750	562500	27.386	800	640000	28.284

Table of squares and square roots (*continued*)

Number	Square	Square root	Number	Square	Square root
801	641601	28.302	851	724201	29.172
802	643204	28.320	852	725904	29.189
803	644809	28.337	853	727609	29.206
804	646416	28.355	854	729316	29.223
805	648025	28.373	855	731025	29.240
806	649636	28.390	856	732736	29.257
807	651249	28.408	857	734449	29.275
808	652864	28.425	858	736164	29.292
809	654481	28.443	859	737881	29.309
810	656100	28.460	860	739600	29.326
811	657721	28.478	861	741321	29.343
812	659344	28.496	862	743044	29.360
813	660969	28.513	863	744769	29.377
814	662596	28.531	864	746496	29.394
815	664225	28.548	865	748225	29.411
816	665856	28.566	866	749956	29.428
817	667489	28.583	867	751689	29.445
818	669124	28.601	868	753424	29.462
819	670761	28.618	869	755161	29.479
820	672400	28.636	870	756900	29.496
821	674041	28.653	871	758641	29.513
822	675684	28.671	872	760384	29.530
823	677329	28.688	873	762129	29.547
824	678976	28.705	874	763876	29.563
825	680625	28.723	875	765625	29.580
826	682276	28.740	876	767376	29.597
827	683929	28.758	877	769129	29.614
828	685584	28.775	878	770884	29.631
829	687241	28.792	879	772641	29.648
830	688900	28.810	880	774400	29.665
831	690561	28.827	881	776161	29.682
832	692224	28.844	882	777924	29.698
833	693889	28.862	883	779689	29.715
834	695556	28.879	884	781456	29.732
835	697225	28.896	885	783225	29.749
836	698896	28.914	886	784996	29.766
837	700569	28.931	887	786769	29.783
838	702244	28.948	888	788544	29.799
839	703921	28.965	889	790321	29.816
840	705600	28.983	890	792100	29.833
841	707281	29.000	891	793881	29.850
842	708964	29.017	892	795664	29.866
843	710649	29.034	893	797449	29.883
844	712336	29.052	894	799236	29.900
845	714025	29.069	895	801025	29.917
846	715716	29.086	896	802816	29.933
847	717409	29.103	897	804609	29.950
848	719104	29.120	898	806404	29.967
849	720801	29.138	899	808201	29.983
850	722500	29.155	900	810000	30.000

Table of squares and square roots (*continued*)

Number	Square	Square root	Number	Square	Square root
901	811801	30.017	951	904401	30.838
902	813604	30.033	952	906304	30.854
903	815409	30.050	953	908209	30.871
904	817216	30.067	954	910116	30.887
905	819025	30.083	955	912025	30.903
906	820836	30.100	956	913936	30.919
907	822649	30.116	957	915849	30.935
908	824464	30.133	958	917764	30.952
909	826281	30.150	959	919681	30.968
910	828100	30.166	960	921600	30.984
911	829921	30.183	961	923521	31.000
912	831744	30.199	962	925444	31.016
913	833569	30.216	963	927369	31.032
914	835396	30.232	964	929296	31.048
915	837225	30.249	965	931225	31.064
916	839056	30.265	966	933156	31.081
917	840889	30.282	967	935089	31.097
918	842724	30.299	968	937024	31.113
919	844561	30.315	969	938961	31.129
920	846400	30.332	970	940900	31.145
921	848241	30.348	971	942841	31.161
922	850084	30.364	972	944784	31.177
923	851929	30.381	973	946729	31.193
924	853776	30.397	974	948676	31.209
925	855625	30.414	975	950625	31.225
926	857476	30.430	976	952576	31.241
927	859329	30.447	977	954529	31.257
928	861184	30.463	978	956484	31.273
929	863041	30.480	979	958441	31.289
930	864900	30.496	980	960400	31.305
931	866761	30.512	981	962361	31.321
932	868624	30.529	982	964324	31.337
933	870489	30.545	983	966289	31.353
934	872356	30.561	984	968256	31.369
935	874225	30.578	985	970225	31.385
936	876096	30.594	986	972196	31.401
937	877969	30.610	987	974169	31.417
938	879844	30.627	988	976144	31.432
939	881721	30.643	989	978121	31.448
940	883600	30.659	990	980100	31.464
941	885481	30.676	991	982081	31.480
942	887364	30.692	992	984064	31.496
943	889249	30.708	993	986049	31.512
944	891136	30.725	994	988036	31.528
945	893025	30.741	995	990025	31.544
946	894916	30.757	996	992016	31.559
947	896809	30.773	997	994009	31.575
948	898704	30.790	998	996004	31.591
949	900601	30.806	999	998001	31.607
950	902500	30.822	1000	1000000	31.623

Case Studies

CASE 1 — CHAPTER 1

Fifth-grade students were assigned oral book reports. You are measuring three components of oral reporting: interest in reading; understanding of plot development; and oral presentation.

1. Prepare a minimum of three subcomponents of each component.

   a. Interest
      1. _____
      2. _____
      3. _____
      4. _____
      5. _____
   b. Understanding
      1. _____
      2. _____
      3. _____
      4. _____
      5. _____
   c. Oral presentation
      1. _____
      2. _____
      3. _____
      4. _____
      5. _____

2. Can you observe the performance specified in the subcomponents?
   Yes_____ No_____

3. Would you assign weights to the components or to the subcomponents first? Components_____ Subcomponents_____ Why? _____
   _____

4. Is the total score as useful in interpreting the student's performance as the subscore? Yes_____No_____

5. Which score (total or subscore) provides you with the greater amount of feedback information? Total_____ Subscore_____ Explain. _____
   _____
   _____
   _____
   _____

CASE 2 — CHAPTER 1

A three-member student committee prepared the bulletin board just outside the school office. The theme, scientific in nature, focused on Archimedes' principle of floating bodies. It served as part of the students' class requirement.

1. Before setting up components for quantifying the product, what information would you need?_____

_____

_____

2. Is it better to use several components with no subcomponents or components each with subcomponents? Components only_____ Components and subcomponents _____ Why? _____

_____

_____

3. Select a component for evaluating the bulletin board and set up subcomponents in order to gather quantitative data on the product.
Component _____

____ _____

____ _____

____ _____

____ _____

4. Assign weights to each subcomponent. (Use the blank space to the left of your responses in the third question.)
5. Justify your assignment of weights. _____

_____

_____

_____

CASE 3 — CHAPTER 2

A set of twenty raw scores ($N = 20$) represents students' performance on an essay assigned to a tenth-grade English class. The purpose of the assignment was to measure the students' written form of communication. There were 50 possible points distributed in the following manner:

20 points—development of idea
10 points—clarity of expression
10 points—grammatical usage
5 points—uniqueness of presentation
5 points—punctuation, capitalization,
and spelling.

The class membership totaled twenty students.

N is used in statistics to symbolize the total number of students, test items, or other data; n is used to distinguish a subset from the total number (N).

Example: The class has a total of twenty students ($N = 20$), but only ten students are in the upper 50 percent of the class ($n = 10$).

Assuming the assignment to be *valid* and the scores to be accurate quantitative measures of the performance of the class, answer the following questions on the basis of the set of scores shown below:

Raw Scores for Case 3

$X_1 = 48$	$X_6 = 29$	$X_{11} = 25$	$X_{16} = 14$
$X_2 = 47$	$X_7 = 29$	$X_{12} = 25$	$X_{17} = 14$
$X_3 = 47$	$X_8 = 28$	$X_{13} = 25$	$X_{18} = 10$
$X_4 = 31$	$X_9 = 27$	$X_{14} = 25$	$X_{19} = 10$
$X_5 = 30$	$X_{10} = 25$	$X_{15} = 15$	$X_{20} = 10$

1. Summarize the performance of the class on the basis of the information available. _____

_____

_____

_____

_____

2. From the information given, describe the score of X_{15}. _____

_____

_____

_____

3. X_{10} is in the top 50 percent (upper half) of the class. X_{11} is in the bottom 50 percent (lower half) of the class. Is there a noticeable difference between the performances of X_{10} and X_{11}? Yes_____ No_____ Explain. _____

_____

_____

_____

4. Suggest another way to report the scores of the class members. (This may resolve the difficulty in responding to the third question above.) _____

_____

_____

_____

5. What further information would you need to determine how many of the students show mastery of written communication skills? _____

_____

_____

> VALID means in this case that the given score measures that which it purports to measure.
>
> *Example:* In the case above we are assuming that the five areas contributing to the total score do measure written communication.

CASE 4 — CHAPTER 2

The following scores were obtained from a fourth-year arithmetic class on a *speed test* that covered the addition and subtraction operations. There were twenty items in the test, ten on addition and ten on subtraction. Below are the raw scores.

Raw Scores on Speed Test

$X_1 = 20$	$X_6 = 19$	$X_{11} = 19$
$X_2 = 19$	$X_7 = 19$	$X_{12} = 20$
$X_3 = 4$	$X_8 = 19$	$X_{13} = 17$
$X_4 = 20$	$X_9 = 20$	$X_{14} = 15$
$X_5 = 19$	$X_{10} = 20$	$X_{15} = 8$

> SPEED TEST is usually a timed test. The important attributes being measured are speed and accuracy of performance on a particular skill.

Assuming the test was properly administered, with each student given the same amount of time, discuss the following questions.

1. What step needs to be undertaken first in order to make the data easier to understand?_____

2. What happened to the X subscript arrangement when you completed the first question above? _____

3. On the basis of the performance as indicated by the raw scores, is the class ready to proceed to the next concept in arithmetic? Yes_____ No _____ Explain. _____

4. X_2 is the sixth from the top scorer. X_{13} is the fourth from the bottom scorer. Does the difference in their scores indicate a difference in performance? Yes_____ No_____ Explain. _____

5. In the fourth question above is it necessary to know the subscore as well as the total score of X_2? Yes_____No_____ Explain. _____

6. In the fourth question of Case 1 it was determined that reporting the component scores (subscores) might have given a more complete picture of the

students' writing ability. Would you get a more complete picture of the arithmetic performance of X_{14} if subscores had been reported? Yes_____
No_____ Explain. _____
_____

7. What factors do you need to consider in planning for the future arithmetic instruction of X_3? _____
_____
_____

8. The score of X_{15} can be viewed as indicating poor performance. What information would you need to justify this statement? _____
_____
_____

9. The score of X_{15} can indicate that he understands his arithmetic and can perform the problems accurately. Justify this statement. _____
_____
_____
_____
_____

10. In evaluating the results of a speed test, such as the fourth-grade arithmetic test, select the frame of reference for interpreting the test results (normative-referenced, criterion-referenced, self-referenced) and explain what information it would give you for planning the next lesson. _____
_____
_____

Name_____   Date _____

CASE 5 — CHAPTER 3

The junior high boys in a gym class were tested on the number of pushups they could perform. The teacher recorded the following scores:

```
_____ John G .......... 10
_____ Greg D .......... 10
_____ Arnold L ......... 4
_____ Aaron S .......... 19
_____ Bob R .......... 17
_____ Barry F .......... 19
_____ Carl H .......... 17
_____ Dick T .......... 10
_____ Earl F .......... 47
_____ Fred P .......... 20
_____ Phil O .......... 21
_____ George A ......... 29
_____ William C ........ 20
_____ Howard L ........ 18
 X₂  Tim F .......... 31
_____ Ken D .......... 16
_____ Lenny S .......... 18
_____ Norman G ........ 15
_____ Thomas J......... 20
```

The teacher wanted to graph the boys' performance in order to study the strengths and weaknesses of the class. Since working with names is tedious, he assigned "X sub" labels to each.
1. How would you suggest he assign these labels? Alphabetically_____ Ordered scores_____
2. In the space to the left of each boy's name assign an X label.
3. Arrange a frequency table of the data to facilitate construction of a graph.

Student	Number of pushups (X)	(f)
	47	1

201

4. Would it help to arrange the scores in intervals? Yes_____ No_____
Why? _____
_____
_____

5. Construct the appropriate graph (based on your answer to the fourth question) and label the horizontal and vertical axes.

6. What is the range of the most representative scores of the class? _____
7. What are the extreme or deviant scores? _____
8. If the average performance for eighth-grade boys is approximately sixteen pushups, what could the teacher conclude generally and numerically about his class? _____
_____
_____

9. Discuss Tim F.'s score (X_2). _____
_____
_____
_____

10. What type of program might you suggest for Arnold L.? _____
_____
_____
_____
_____

11. If the scores were grouped by interval ($i = 10$) starting with 0–9 and ending with 40–49, could you answer:
    a. The seventh question?   Yes_____ No_____
    b. The eighth question?   Yes_____ No_____
    c. The ninth question?   Yes_____ No_____
    d. The tenth question?   Yes_____ No_____

CASE 6 — CHAPTER 3

An ad hoc committee of teachers and parents was formed to study the impact of an after-school recreation program on the extent of vandalism to the school building and to determine at the end of the nine-month trial period the parents' view of the program. Vandalism is measured in terms of the number of broken windows each month starting in September, custodial time required to remove graffiti from the inside walls, and the number of adult supervisors required to maintain a sufficient level of discipline to keep the program operating. The following data were obtained:

Month	Number of broken windows	Hours of custodial time	Number of supervisors
September	8	6	4
October	8	6	4
November	5	5	4
December	3	2	4
January	2	5	4
February	1	4	4
March	3	3	3
April	4	2	3
May	4	2	3

1. Construct and label graphs using the pertinent data above to determine if trends in reduction of vandalism are evident.

2. What are some of the conclusions you can come to about the impact of the after-school recreation program on vandalism to the school building? _____
_____
_____
_____

_____
_____
_____

3. Data were obtained from the parents on their views concerning the program. Prepare your own nominal or ordinal data of the parents' responses and represent the data on a graph.

CASE 7 — CHAPTER 4

On a spelling test, the following scores were recorded:

$X_1 = 35$	$X_6 = 19$	$X_{11} = 15$	$X_{16} = 7$
$X_2 = 24$	$X_7 = 18$	$X_{12} = 15$	$X_{17} = 7$
$X_3 = 23$	$X_8 = 16$	$X_{13} = 14$	$X_{18} = 6$
$X_4 = 20$	$X_9 = 16$	$X_{14} = 13$	$X_{19} = 4$
$X_5 = 20$	$X_{10} = 16$	$X_{15} = 10$	$X_{20} = 2$

The students could earn a maximum of thirty-five points on the test.
1. Compute the following statistics:
   a. Mode = _____
   b. Mdn = _____
   c. $\bar{X}$ = _____
   d. SD = _____ (round off to the nearest hundredth)
   e. SD_{tm} = _____ (round off to nearest hundredth)
2. What do the three central tendency statistics tell you about the distribution of the scores? _____

_____

3. In the light of the SD, $\bar{X}$, and range, would you conclude that the scores are highly variable, or do they show little variability? _____

_____

4. Compare the deviation of the scores of X_2 and X_{18} to the mean? _____

_____

5. How many scores deviated less than 1 SD from the mean? _____
6. How many scores deviated 1 SD or more *above* the mean? _____
7. As the teacher, would you be concerned about the performance of X_{15}. Why? _____

_____

_____

_____

_____

CASE 8 — CHAPTER 4

The first-grade teachers and principals of a school district are reviewing the spring reading test scores. The following information is available to them. School district norms: $\overline{X} = 50.0$, and $SD = 7.1$.

School	$\overline{X}$	SD
A	52.0	7.2
B	40.0	3.5
C	54.3	8.6
D	47.1	10.0
E	57.0	4.0

1. The reading scores from what school(s) are most similar to the norms of the school district? _____

_____

2. Besides the fact that School B is below the school district's mean norm, what other information can the principals and teachers surmise about that school? _____

_____

3. Can the principals and teachers conclude that there are a few extreme scores in School E that account for the very high mean score of the school? Yes_____ No_____ Explain. _____

_____

4. How would you describe the reading achievement of first-graders in School D?_____

_____

_____

_____

CASE 9 — CHAPTER 5

Peter K. has been struggling along in his junior high school mathematics class. He works hard, but takes longer to understand the subject than most of the group. Following a two-week instructional period in introductory trigonometry, the teacher tested the achievement of the class using a departmental test that emphasized problems of practical application. A total of 40 points was possible on the test, 4 points for each of the 10 problems. Peter received 29 points. Departmental norms were used to compare Peter's performance with that of the norming group. The mode, median, and mean of the norming group were 30 points, respectively. The standard deviation was 6 points.

1. Compute the following scores for Peter
    a. z score = _____
    b. percentile = _____
    c. stanine = _____
    d. *T score = _____
2. Does a negative z score indicate poor performance? Yes_____ No_____
    Explain. _____
    _____
    _____
    _____

3. Evaluate Peter's achievement on the basis of
    a. the statistical findings: _____
    _____
    _____

    b. his past performance: _____
    _____
    _____

_____
*See footnote on page 66 for T score transformation formula.

CASE 10 — CHAPTER 5

Below are the scores of one class on a departmental *English Achievement Test*. Because of the composition of the class and because of its past perform- ance, the school system is using these scores to establish system-wide norms.

Scores of norming group on the *English Achievement Test*

50	29	25	17
48	28	25	15
36	27	20	14
32	26	20	10
30	25	18	5

1. Compute the $\bar{X}$ and *SD* of the norming group. (Use the teacher-made statistic for calculating the *SD*.) Determine the Mdn and the mode.
   a. $\bar{X}$ =_____
   b. mode = _____
   c. Mdn =_____
   d. SD_{tm} = _____(round off to tenths)
2. Complete the norming table for the English Department. The table shows percentile band rank in 5-point intervals using the high and low score in each interval as the limits.

Norming table for the departmental *English Achievement Test*

Raw scores	Percentile (rounded off to nearest whole number) band
46–50 _____	97–99
41–45 _____	93–96
36–40 _____	_____
31–35 _____	71–82
26–30 _____	54–67
21–25 _____	_____
16–20 _____	21–33
11–15 _____	10–18
6–10 _____	4–9
1– 4 _____	2–3

3. Sally N. received 31 points on the *English Achievement Test*. On the basis of the norming group, evaluate Sally's performance._____
_____
_____

4. The 50 percentile was the average rank for Sally's class. If you were the teacher, would you be disappointed or encouraged by the findings? _____
_____
_____

5. A new student entered at midyear at which time he was given the department's *English Achievement Test.* He scored at the 46.41 percentile.

    a. What is the student's stanine? _____

    b. Compute his z score: _____

    c. Determine his raw score: _____

CASE 11 — CHAPTER 6

A school system began instruction in musical instruments in the fourth grade. A policy of come one, come all was followed. At the end of each year the attrition rate was phenomenal. Last year the music department decided to select only students whose parents scored high on a test of musical interest. The attrition rate was markedly reduced.

1. What is the predictor variable?_____

2. What is the criterion variable? _____

3. Defend or refute the following statements predicated on the situation above:

    a. The music department has found an adequate solution to the problem of selection. _____

_____

_____

    b. Students' interest in continuing instruction in musical instruments is positively correlated with parents' scores on the tests of musical interest.

_____

_____

4. Suggest another criterion measure that could serve as a guide for selecting students for musical study. _____

_____

_____

_____

CASE 12 — CHAPTER 6

A college of education developed a test for measuring the interest of teacher candidates in children. The college hoped to use the test as a predictor for selecting students to its teacher education program. Ten students took the test. After two years of teaching, their effectiveness as teachers was scored by their respective school principals on an observation schedule. The scores on both measures are listed below.

Predictor			Criterion			Cross products
X	$(X-\bar{X})$	$(X-\bar{X})^2$	Y	$(Y-\bar{Y})$	$(Y-\bar{Y})^2$	$(X-\bar{X})(Y-\bar{Y})$
100			10			
85			4			
80			5			
70			7			
60			8			
60			3			
50			2			
45			9			
30			5			
20			7			
$\bar{X}=$			$\bar{Y}=$			$\Sigma(X-\bar{X})(Y-\bar{Y})=$ ___

1. Construct a scattergram using data from the two variables. (Label the X axis and the Y axis.)

2. Describe the correlation as shown in the scattergram. _____

_____

3. Compute the means: $\bar{X}=$ _____; $\bar{Y}=$ _____

4. Compute the standard deviations using the regular statistical formula (to the nearest tenth): $SD_X=$ _____; $SD_Y=$ _____

5. Compute the sum of the cross products: $\Sigma(X-\bar{X})(Y-\bar{Y})=$ _____

6. Compute the correlation coefficient: $r =$ _____

7. Would you recommend the use of the *Teacher Attitude Test* (the test used to measure interest in children) as a basis for selecting students to participate in the teacher education program? Yes_____ No_____ Explain. _____

_____

_____

8. A cutoff score for admission to the program was set at 60 points on the *Teacher Attitude Test*. A score of 7 or above was accepted as an adequate description of teachers' effectiveness. How many students were inappropriately accepted in the program?_____ How many inappropriately rejected? _____

9. What percent of the total number were appropriately accepted and rejected? _____%

10. What can you conclude about the predictive ability of an instrument with a correlation of 0.14? _____

_____

_____

CASE 13 — CHAPTER 7

A biology teacher developed a twenty-item checklist for measuring the ability of his students to prepare slides from different cultures. Each item on the checklist purported to measure a step in the preparation of a slide, and a student received 1 point for each item that the teacher checked off as a step accurately performed.

1. The teacher wanted to determine the reliability of the checklist. Comment on the appropriateness of each concept of reliability for the biology teacher's purpose.

    a. Stability reliability: _____

_____

_____

    b. Equivalency reliability: _____

_____

    c. Internal consistency reliability: _____

_____

2. Given the following data, compute the reliability using the teacher-made formula: $\bar{X} = 10$; $SD = 5$; $N = 20$. $r_{tm} =$ _____

3. On the basis of the reliability coefficient found in the second question, would you have confidence in the checklist as an instrument for measuring the ability of the biology students to prepare slides? Yes_____ No_____
Explain. _____

_____

_____

_____

4. Three members of the class obtained scores of 8 points on the checklist. How would you interpret their performance on the basis of the $\bar{X}$ and SD of the class? _____

_____

_____

5. Compute the standard error of measurement of the checklist.
$SE_{meas} =$ _____

6. One of the students obtained a raw score of 13 points. With what confidence can you assume the interval covering the true score lies between 10.75 and 15.25 points? _____

CASE 14 — CHAPTER 7

The school librarian, in cooperation with the instructional materials committee, wants to determine the faculty's attitude toward the library as a resource learning center before making any changes during the next school year. The librarian and the committee prepared an instrument entitled *Learning Center Resource Utilization Inventory*. Each teacher was asked to fill out and return the inventory at the regular weekly faculty meeting. One week later the committee members distributed the same inventory to the faculty with the instructions that it should be returned the following day. After all the inventories were in, the committee computed the reliability coefficient and other relevant statistics.

1. Discuss the sources of inconsistency that could affect the reliability of the inventory. _____
_____
_____
_____

2. Is the test-retest reliability a proper approach to use in determining the reliability of the inventory? Yes_____ No_____ Explain. _____
_____
_____

3. What is the SE_{meas}, when $r_{12} = 0.64$; $SD = 15$? $SE_{meas} =$ _____
4. If you were a member of the instructional materials committee, how much weight would you give to the responses in planning for changes in the library during the next year? _____
_____
_____
_____
_____
_____
_____

CASE 15 — CHAPTER 8

Given the following tests, what type of validity or validities—content validity; criterion-related validity (predictive or concurrent); construct validity—would you try to establish? Explain your response.

1. Instrument: *High School Departmental Algebra Term Test*_____
_____
_____

2. Instrument: *Interest Inventory Test*_____
_____
_____

3. Instrument: *Physical Fitness Test* _____
_____
_____

4. Instrument: *Intermediate Reading Achievement Test*_____
_____
_____

5. Instrument: *Primary Reading Readiness Test* _____
_____
_____

CASE 16 — CHAPTER 8

Scores were obtained from a manual dexterity test. They were used to predict success in a machine shop class. Success was defined on a 10-point performance rating scale with a criterion score of 6 indicative of adequate success in the shop class. The scores on the predictor and criterion are shown below.

	Predictor: Manual dexterity score			Criterion: Rating in machine shop			
Students	X	$(X - \bar{X})$	$(X - \bar{X})^2$	Y	$(Y - \bar{Y})$	$(Y - \bar{Y})^2$	xy *
Roger	25			8			
Carlos	20			9			
Pete	18			8			
Randy	16			5			
Leon	16			7			
Alvin	14			4			
Bert	10			7			
Don	8			5			
Manuel	8			3			
Harry	5			4			

*$xy = (X - \bar{X})(Y - \bar{Y})$

1. Compute the validity coefficient: $r_{xy} =$ _____

(You will need to calculate the mean of the predictor and the mean of the criterion, the standard deviations of each, and the sum of the cross products: $\Sigma(X - \bar{X})(Y - \bar{Y})$.)

2. If you were going to use the scores on the manual dexterity test as a basis for admission to the shop class, what else would you want to know about the test? _____

_____

_____

3. What level of confidence could you place in the validity coefficient? (Use Table 8-1.) _____

_____

4. This question is for readers who completed the section in Chapter 8 on the regression line equation. A new boy entered the school. He was given the manual dexterity test in order to determine if he should be placed in the machine shop course. He obtained a score of 15 points on the test. Predict his $\hat{Y}$ score (rating on the criterion), rounding to the nearest whole number. Remember, you will need to solve for the slope of the equation (b_{yx}) and the Y intercept (a). In addition, you will use $\bar{X}$, $\bar{Y}$, SD_x, SD_y, r_{xy}, and the predictor score, $X = 15$. $\hat{Y} =$ _____

CASE 17 — CHAPTER 9

Use Table 9-5 for responding to the following questions.

1. Complete the cells in item 40. Total correct _____ Total incorrect
_____

2. Prepare individual item matrices for items 9 and 10.

Item 9

Responses →	A	B	C	D	Blank	Total
High						
Low						
Total						

Item 10

Responses →	A	B	C	D	Blank	Total
High						
Low						
Total						

3. Determine the item difficulty and item discrimination for the above.
   a. Item 9:   diff = _____; r_{disc} = _____
   b. Item 10:   diff = _____; r_{disc} = _____

4. Although items 9 and 10 have the same indexes of discrimination, each item presents a different problem. Explain. _____
_____
_____

5. Using only Table 9-5, derive the item difficulty and discrimination index for item 2. Did you find a short-cut method? diff = _____; r_{disc} = _____
_____

6. Would you retain item 2? Yes_____ No_____ Why? _____
_____
_____

7. Would you retain item 6? Yes_____ No_____ Why? _____
_____
_____
_____

CASE 18 — CHAPTER 9

At the end of a unit the physics teacher administered a 40-item multiple-choice test to his class of thirty-one students. Each item had five options. The test had a mean of 25, a standard deviation of 7.0, a median of 22, and the performance of the class ranged from 7 to 38 points.

1. Determine the internal consistency reliability of the test using the teacher-made formula. $r_{tm} = $ _____

2. How would you determine the validity of the physics test? _____
_____
_____
_____

3. In preparing an item analysis, how many scores would you use for the top group of scorers and how many for the bottom group of scorers? Top scorers _____ Bottom scorers_____

4. If the test has an average item difficulty of 31 percent with a range of item discriminations from ⁻0.25 to 0.80, how could the average item discrimination index be improved? _____
_____
_____

5. If the average item difficulty is 46 percent, is this consistent with the information we obtained from the mean? Yes_____ No_____ Why? _____
_____
_____

6. The student X_3 obtained a raw score of 28 points, while X_8 obtained a raw score of 23 points. Do the two students appear to differ in their performance? (In your response consider the SE_{meas}, the test item analysis, and other relevant information.) Yes_____ No_____ Explain. _____
_____
_____
_____
_____

7. Using the information presented as a basis for your reply, do you think the teacher-made test would be an acceptable instrument for measuring student performance in physics? Yes_____ No_____ Explain. _____
_____
_____
_____
_____
_____

CASE 19 — CHAPTER 10

Before working on this case, refer to the *DAT* battery. The tests are available in the test files of most college libraries.

1. Do the test items appear to fulfill the purpose of the test? Yes_____
No_____ Explain. _____
_____

2. Does the battery of eight tests cover a range of abilities that gives you sufficient information about a student in order to make educational decisions?
Yes_____ No_____ Explain. _____
_____
_____

3. Is the reliability of the test satisfactory? Yes_____No_____ Explain.
_____

4. Would you feel confident in using the *DAT* after reviewing it in Buros?
Yes_____ No_____ Explain. _____
_____
_____

5. If Ronald's true score lies in the upper range of the SE_{meas} on scholastic ability (VR + NA), would that have changed the differences between his scholastic ability score and the other ability scores? (Refer to the lists under A and B in Chapter 10.) Yes_____ No_____ Explain. _____
_____
_____

6. How does Ronald's score of 36 points representing scholastic ability compare with the norming group shown in Table 10-1? _____
_____
_____
_____

7. Separate the scholastic ability score into its components and explain each component's contribution to the 41 points. _____
_____
_____
_____

8. Examine Ronald's profile.
    a. Identify a possible problem. _____
_____
_____

b. What questions would you ask or what further information would you seek to confirm whether the above is a real problem? _____

_____

_____

_____

_____

9. Ronald says he would like to be an accountant. Would you encourage him to pursue this interest? Yes_____ No_____ Explain. _____

_____

_____

_____

_____

10. In what way could Ronald's lower performance in Space Relations as compared to his performance on the other tests in the *DAT* battery affect his total school performance? _____

_____

_____

_____

_____

CASE 20 — CHAPTER 10

1. Ronald makes the honor roll each grading period. Mathematics is not his strongest subject, but he works hard and receives average to above average grades in this area. Is this consistent with his profile? Yes_____ No_____ Explain. _____

_____
_____
_____
_____
_____
_____

2. Although Ronald makes the honor roll, his performance on tests and on other assignments is routine, unimaginative, and indicates little creativity. Is this consistent with his profile? Yes_____ No_____ Explain. _____

_____
_____
_____
_____
_____

3. You are planning Ronald's instructional program. What recommendations would you make to help him develop more creativity in his school performance? _____

_____
_____
_____

CASE 21 — CHAPTER 11

A teacher wants to collect data on the "responsiveness" of each class member to her assignment. She hypothesized that the data would help to determine her effectiveness in creating an assignment. She developed a ten-item checklist as shown below.

Responsiveness Checklist

_____ 1. Student appears attentive during explanation.

_____ 2. Student is interested enough to ask questions for clarification of assignment.

_____ 3. Student asks pertinent question(s) going beyond the assignment.

_____ 4. Student gets to work on the assignment without delay.

_____ 5. Student makes sarcastic remark about "more work" or casts aspersion on the assignment.

_____ 6. Student turns in assignment on time.

_____ 7. Student's paper indicates understanding of assignment.

_____ 8. Student's paper handles the assignment in a highly creative fashion.

_____ 9. Student subsequently participates actively in discussion based on the assignment.

_____10. Student shows continued interest in the assigned topic.

1. Justify or refute the teacher's hypothesis that the responsiveness of the class can be an indicator of her effectiveness in making an assignment. _____

_____

_____

_____

_____

2. Is the checklist an appropriate observation procedure for collecting the data she wants? Yes_____ No_____ Why? _____

_____

_____

_____

3. Are the items representative of the type of behavior of students that indicates responsiveness to an assignment? Yes_____ No_____ Why? _____

_____

_____

4. Suggest other items that may aid in getting at the desired data. _____

_____

_____

_____

_____

5. Which item requires revision?_____ Why? _____

6. How would you decide what constitutes a high "responsiveness" score or a low "responsiveness" score? _____

_____

_____

_____

_____

7. Suggest a way to determine the reliability of the instrument. _____

_____

8. How would you determine your effectiveness as an observer? _____

_____

CASE 22 — CHAPTER 11

Select the area that fits your interest.

For Primary Classes

1. Devise a rating scale for measuring students' "cooperativeness" behavior as members of the class.
2. Use the instrument in a normal classroom setting.
3. Develop a scale of "cooperativeness."
4. Determine the coefficient of observer agreement.
5. Have another person use your instrument on a different class to determine whether your scale is applicable to another class.
6. Set up norms in the light of the data you have obtained.

For Intermediate Classes

1. Devise a rating scale for measuring ability of students to give demonstrations in science.
2. Use the instrument in a normal classroom setting.
3. Develop a quantitative scale for evaluating a student's ability to perform the scientific demonstration.
4. Determine the coefficient of observer agreement.
5. Have another person use your instrument on a different class to determine whether your quantitative scale is applicable to another class.
6. Set up norms in the light of the data you have obtained.

For Secondary Classes

1. Devise a rating scale for measuring a skill related to your subject area. For example, in physical education, batting performance; in social science, map-reading skills; in mathematics, graphing; in English, contributions as a panel member.
2. Use the instrument in a normal classroom setting.
3. Develop a quantitative scale for evaluating students' ability or performance.
4. Determine the coefficient of observer agreement.
5. Have another person use your instrument to determine whether your quantitative scale is applicable to another class.
6. Set up norms in the light of the data you have obtained.

For Administrators

1. Devise a rating scale for measuring general behavior around the building (halls, washrooms, lunchroom, learning center, student lounge, playground).
2. Use the instrument to collect data on students' behavior.
3. Develop a quantitative scale for evaluating the behavior around the building.
4. Determine the coefficient of observer agreement.
5. Have another administrator use your instrument in another school to determine whether your quantitative scale is applicable to another school.
6. Set up norms in the light of the data you have obtained.

Case Study Responses

CASE 1 — CHAPTER 1

1. Plausible responses:
    a. Interest
        1. outwardly enthusiastic
        2. goes beyond the book to add new information
        3. takes the book seriously
        4. recommends book to others
        5. plans to read more on topic or works by the same author
        6. shows charts, maps, pictures, models
    b. Understanding
        1. clearly presents sequence of story plot
        2. indicates role of major characters
        3. identifies climax
        4. analyzes ending
        5. describes style of writing
        6. explains symbolism
        7. presents unique interpretation of author's intent
    c. Oral presentation
        1. speaks clearly
        2. shows no outward nervous manifestations
        3. demonstrates poise
        4. speaks fluently
        5. holds interest of class
        6. presents report to class rather than to teacher
        7. establishes rapport with listeners
        8. maintains eye contact with listeners
2. Yes. If No is checked, the component cannot be measured; it should not, therefore, be included.
3. Components. Each component must be assigned its appropriate importance in relation to the total assignment. Following this the subcomponent can be weighted accordingly.
4. No. A student may be able to understand a story, but not do well in presenting it orally. Oral presentation is an important objective to measure.
5. Subscore. The subscores pinpoint the weakness and strength of individuals and of the class. The information can be used to give direction to subsequent instructional planning.

CASE 2 — CHAPTER 1

1. The response should include such information as type of class, age group, past performance, classroom setting, instructional objectives.
2. Components and subcomponents. There are broad areas involved in measuring a bulletin board assignment: artistic aspects; scientific accuracy; affective aspects of group interaction and participation. Each component may have a number of subcomponents.
3. and 4. Component: Group participation

Subcomponents and their weights:
10   cooperativeness (carried out responsibilities willingly)
5   leadership (took initiative to get group moving)
5   enthusiasm (added spirit to the group)
10   contributor to group ideas
5   coordinator of group activities once they were planned

Component: Aesthetics
Subcomponents and their weights:
2   use of space
2   use of color
2   balance
5   unique use of materials
3   illusion of movement in display
5. Weights are dependent on one's instructional objectives. If the teacher was hoping to develop group spirit, he might have given more weight to the subcomponent "enthusiasm."

CASE 3 — CHAPTER 2

1. There is a wide range in the scores, from 48 points (high scorer) to 10 points (low scorer), which represents a 38-point spread. Some scores are very high; a number are low. Three-fourths of the class received at least 50 percent of the possible points.
2. X_{15} is sixth from the bottom. He received 15 out of a possible 50 points, or 30 percent of the points.
3. Yes. If the points are distributed differently over the various components, then their performances would be different.
No. There is little difference in their position based on the total essay score in relation to the class.
4. By reporting points received in each component, a distinction can be made between the strengths and weaknesses of X_{10} in comparison with X_{11}.
5. The number of points that represents the criterion level or mastery for each component should be available.

CASE 4 — CHAPTER 2

1. Order scores from high to low.
2. The X subscripts are no longer in order. Since they represent students, it is not important for the subscripts to be in numerical order.
3. Yes. All but two appear to have sufficient mastery of the materials, at least on the basis of their raw scores.
4. Not necessarily. The number of problems each missed, one and three, respectively, does not indicate misunderstanding, since they did answer most of the problems correctly. What appear as mistakes could have been due to

insufficient time to complete all the problems, or it could indicate carelessness.

5. No. Though the test measured two components of the number operation, in the case of X_{13} and X_2, their scores indicate achievement in both components.

6. Yes. If all the errors are in one component, the subscore would give this information. If the errors were distributed between the components, it may be due to careless computation on the part of X_{15} rather than to a lack of understanding of addition and subtraction operations.

7. The score indicates he made many errors in both components of the test, which goes beyond carelessness in computation. We need to know if all the correct answers were in one component or distributed, although in either case he is still having difficulty with addition and subtraction. If the mistakes are concentrated in one component, then X_3 does have some basic knowledge in the other component, which can be the basis for building on what strengths he has. He definitely is not ready to proceed to new work based on his present performance, although instruction can be planned to build on his strengths.

8. It is essential to have the subscores of X_{15}. Should the eight correct answers be distributed evenly between addition and subtraction, X_{15} is only working 40 percent of the addition problems and 40 percent of the subtraction problems correctly. This is not a satisfactory level of mastery.

9. There are two plausible explanations: First, if all eight correct answers were in one component, then X_{15} answered 80 percent of the problems correctly, which may be a satisfactory mastery level for the one component. This means, however, that X_{15} was unable to get any correct answers on the other component. Second, for this explanation we need to know more about how X_{15} works. If he is a meticulous worker, who proceeds slowly and checks each problem before going to the next one, he may have answered the questions correctly on all of the eight problems he had time to complete. Given more time, he may be able to answer all twenty problems correctly.

10. For a speed test, analysis of test results based on normative-referenced groups may not always be appropriate. You may want to determine whether the students have attained mastery of addition and subtraction operations in terms of speed and accuracy before you introduce other concepts that are based on competency in addition and subtraction. In this case, criterion-referenced comparisons are appropriate. Self-referenced comparisons give you data on whether the students are improving despite the fact that they may not have reached the desired criterion level.

CASE 5 — CHAPTER 3

1. Ordered scores.
2. and 3.

Student	Number of pushups (X)	f
X_1 Earl F.	47	1
X_2 Tim F.	31	1
X_3 George A.	29	1
X_4 Phil O.	21	1
X_5 Fred P.	20	
X_6 William C.	20	3
X_7 Thomas J.	20	
X_8 Aaron S.	19	
X_9 Barry F.	19	2
X_{10} Howard L.	18	
X_{11} Lenny S.	18	2
X_{12} Bob R.	17	
X_{13} Carl H.	17	2
X_{14} Ken D.	16	1
X_{15} Norman G.	15	1
X_{16} John G.	10	
X_{17} Greg D.	10	3
X_{18} Dick T.	10	
X_{19} Arnold L.	4	1

4. No. It would not help to arrange the scores in intervals in this case. Nineteen scores are not too difficult to handle. We may lose some important information if the scores are grouped in intervals, especially since the teacher intends to work with the boys individually on their strengths and weaknesses.
5. Frequency polygon

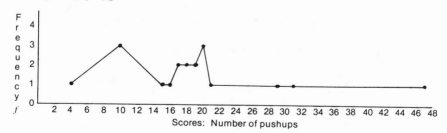

Scores: Number of pushups

6. 15 through 21
7. 4 and 47
8. A large proportion of the class performs better than average on the skill of

pushups: fifteen out of the nineteen boys, or approximately 79 percent of the class.

9. Although Tim's performance is well above that of most of his peers, his ability is in no way unusual.

10. A number of characteristics that affect physical performance must be understood in order to suggest a program for Arnold L.: Is he much younger than the group? Is he slower in physical development than the other boys? Has he been in the same gym class with the other boys? Is he unusually shy about performing in front of others? Have the boys previously labeled him in an adverse way? Has his cumulative health record been reviewed? On the basis of the information gathered, the appropriate steps can be planned.

11. The following are the proper responses for these questions:

a. Yes. The two deviant scores, one at the low end of the scale and the other at the high end would appear in intervals at the extremes of the scale.

b. No. The information is lost in the interval 10–19. The interval does not indicate what scores within it are less than 15.

c. Yes and No. Although the score of X_2 would appear in an interval by itself, separated from X_3, you cannot tell whether 20 points separate their performance or whether their performance is in fact very similar.

d. Yes. Whether grouped in an interval on a graph or shown as a separate score on a graph, Arnold's score would clearly indicate an extremely low performance.

CASE 6 — CHAPTER 3

1. Graphs need to be constructed to show the number of broken windows by month and custodial hours by month. The data on the number of supervisors required is self-evident; and a graph of the data would add little to what can be inferred from the numbers.

2. Much information can be inferred from the graphs.

a. The number of broken windows declines from October through February, at which time there is a rise in the number of broken windows. The rise is less, however, than for the first three months of the program.

b. The decline in the number of broken windows from December through February is a typical trend during the winter months when there is less ball playing around the school building.

c. If the decline during the winter months is a typical trend, then we need to compare the periods of September through November and March through May. There are 50 percent fewer broken windows during the last two months of the program, a period when students play outdoors, than there are during the first two months of the program, also a period of outdoor activities.

d. The number of custodial hours required to remove writing from the inside walls shows a slow but steady decline, except for the month of December, when there is a marked decline. The decline in December can be

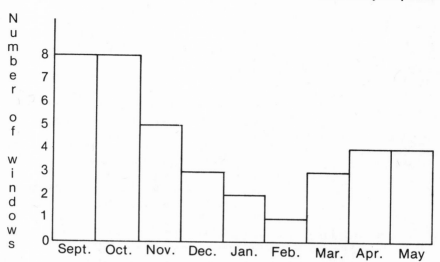

Number of broken windows per month during the trial period of the
after-school recreation program

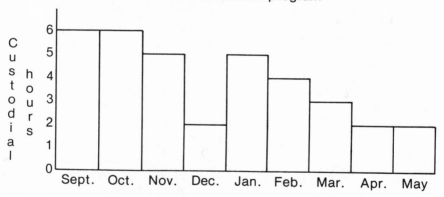

Number of custodial hours per month during the trial period of the
after-school recreation program

attributed to the two-week Christmas vacation when students are not
using the building.

e. During the last three months of the trial period, one less supervisor was
needed to monitor the after-school recreation program.

f. Putting the data from the three sources together, we can make a cautious statement about the decline of vandalism as it may be related to the
recreation program.

3. Each reader's response will differ according to the data presented. If
nominal data were used, the responses would have been arranged in exclud-

ing categories, such as, continue the program—discontinue the program. If ordinal data were used, the responses would be ordered on a continuum, with a designated number of categories. An example of categories showing a rank order could include: highly favorable, favorable, unfavorable. The bar graph for both types of data would be appropriate.

CASE 7 — CHAPTER 4

1. Central tendency and deviation statistics:
   a. Mode = 16
   b. Mdn = 15.5
   c. $\bar{X} = 15$
   d. $SD = 7.59$
   e. $SD_{tm} = 7.43$
2. The mode, Mdn, and $\bar{X}$ are within a point or less of each other. The Mdn is the point dividing one-half the number of scores from the other half. With the mean only $\frac{1}{2}$ point below the Mdn, scores do not cluster at one end of the scale but the distribution of scores is, rather, symmetrical.
3. The distribution has a range of 33 points (35 - 2) and a $\bar{X}$ of 15. It indicates that the scores spread over nearly the full possible range. It is difficult to say just how variable the SD of 7.59 is without having another distribution as a comparison. For classroom distributions a ratio of 3:1 between the $\bar{X}$ and SD can, however, be used as a guide ($\bar{X}:SD$ or $\bar{X}/SD$). In this case the ratio is 2:1, a rather large index of variability.
4. Each score varies 9 points from the mean, but X_2 is 9 points above the mean, and X_{18} is 9 points below the mean. In standard deviation units, that is, z scores, the difference in scores can be shown in this way:

$$z = (24 - 15)/7.59 = {}^+1.19 \text{ for } X_2$$

$$z = (\ 6 - 15)/7.59 = {}^-1.19 \text{ for } X_{18}$$

A negative z score indicates that the score is below the mean.
5. 12. 1 SD above the $\bar{X}$ and 1 SD below the $\bar{X}$ equal:

$$(15 + 7.59) \text{ and } (15 - 7.59) \text{ or } 22.59 \text{ to } 7.41$$

Twelve scores fall between 22.59 and 7.41.
6. 3. There are three scores above 22.59: X_1, X_2, and X_3.
7. No. the performance of X_{15}, while below the mean, is certainly within a normal range. Although the z score of X_{15} is negative, it is less than 1 SD from the mean:

$$z = (10 - 15)/7.59 = {}^-0.66$$

CASE 8 — CHAPTER 4

1. School A.
2. Students in School B vary little in their performance; thus we can say that the first graders in School B are fairly homogeneous, but tend toward the lower end of the performance scale.
3. No. This would not be an accurate conclusion. The relatively small variability (in comparison with the statistic of the school district) indicates that students in School E are similar to each other in performance, but tend toward the upper end of the performance scale. Comparison of the statistics for Schools B and E bears this out.
4. The performance of children in School D varies considerably within the group. Although there is only a 2.9 point difference between the mean of School D and that of the school district, the variability of performance indicates a large spread in the distribution with fewer scores clustered around the mean as in Schools B and E.

CASE 9 — CHAPTER 5

1. Peter's derived scores:
   a. z score = $^-0.17$ $(29 - 30)/6 = ^-1/6 = ^-0.666 \ldots$
   b. percentile = 43.25 $50.00\% - 6.75\% = 43.25\%$
   c. stanine = 5   from Figure 5-8
   d. T score = 48 $(^-0.17) (10) + 50 = ^-1.7 + 50 = 48.3$, or rounded to 48 points
2. No. A negative z score only indicates the score is below the mean. It is the extent of the deviation below the mean that is important for interpreting a student's performance in relation to the norming group. Peter's score is within the average range of performance, further supported by a stanine 5.
3. Peter's achievement can be evaluated as follows:
   a. His performance exceeds 43 percent of his peers. The median indicates that half the class obtained 75 percent of the total possible points on the test. Peter scored just below this group.
   b. On the basis of Peter's past performance, the teacher should be encouraged. Peter has moved at a pace more in keeping with his peers than he has in the past.

CASE 10 — CHAPTER 5

1. Statistics on the *English Achievement Test*:
   a. $\overline{X} = 25$
   b. Mode = 25
   c. Mdn = 25
   d. $SD_{tm} = 11.07$ or 11.1
2. Percentile bands for the norming table:
   36-40—84-91 percentile
   21-25—36-50 percentile

3. Sally ranks in the band represented by the 71 to the 82 percentile band. Her score ($z = 0.54$) is less than 1 SD above the mean, although she is 6 raw score points above the mean. In terms of her peers, Sally is performing just above the middle range of the norming group.

4. It all depends on the type of test, difficulty level of the items, past performance of other similar classes on the same material, the instructional objectives, and whether this was intended as a diagnostic achievement test or a final test of English achievement.

5. The students' statistics follow:

   a. stanine = 5

   b. $z = {}^-0.09$ (50% - 46.41%) = 3.59%, the corresponding value on the normal distribution table is 0.09. Since the percentile was below 50, the z score is negative.

   c. $X = 24$ $({}^-0.09)(11.1) + 25 = {}^-0.999 + 25 = 24.001$ or $X = 24$.

CASE 11 — CHAPTER 6

1. The predictor is parental interest in music.

2. The criterion is the attrition rate or the number of students who fail to continue in the music program or, conversely, the number of students who choose to continue.

3. The points below can be made in defense or refutation of the statements:

   a. It is an adequate solution in terms of reducing attrition, but a very poor predictor in terms of the goals of an educational institution. Pupils are being prejudged on the basis of parental interest.

   b. This may be so, but we are not distinguishing between interest as a positive attitude based on a liking for the instrument and interest as a negative response based on the need or desire to avoid parental punishment for refusing to practice or continue music lessons.

4. Any reasonable suggestion is worth exploring, such as a student's overt physical responses to music, his willingness to participate in musical activities, and so forth.

CASE 12 — CHAPTER 6

1. Scattergram: Interest in children correlated with teaching effectiveness

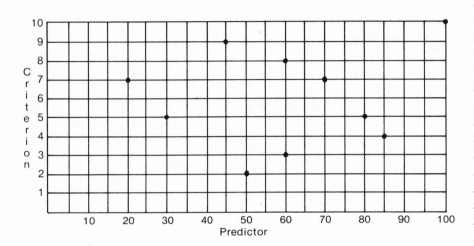

2. There appears to be no relationship, or near zero correlation, between the interest of teacher candidates in children and their subsequent rating as teachers.
3. $\bar{X} = 60$; $\bar{Y} = 6$
4. $SD_X = 23.6$; $SD_Y = 2.5$
5. $\Sigma(X - \bar{X})(Y - \bar{Y}) = 85$
6. $r = 0.14$. The formula is:

$$r = \frac{\Sigma(X - \bar{X})(Y - \bar{Y})}{N(SD_X)(SD_Y)}$$

7. No. A random selection of teacher candidates could have been as effective as the *Teacher Attitude Test* in predicting subsequent teaching effectiveness.
8. Inappropriately accepted: 3; inappropriately rejected: 2.
9. 50%
10. A correlation of 0.14 is not much better than chance.

CASE 13 — CHAPTER 7

1. The following comments would be helpful to the biology teacher:
   a. Test-retest would be appropriate if we can be certain that the second preparation of the slide did not carry over some learning from the first preparation of the slide.

b. Parallel checklists would also be appropriate if we could be assured that the students had not gained additional skills in preparation of slides from their performance on the first checklist.

c. K-R 20, Hoyt's analysis of variance, and the teacher-made formula are appropriate for determining the checklist's reliability if we are assured the skills involved in preparing a slide are interrelated. The split-half or odd-even reliability is not appropriate since there are so few items in the original checklist.

2. $r_{tm} = 0.80$

$$r_{tm} = 1 - \left[\frac{10(20-10)}{20(5^2)} \right] = 1 - \left[\frac{(10)(10)}{20(25)} \right] =$$

$$r_{tm} = 1 - \left[\frac{100}{500} \right] = 1 - 0.20 = \underline{0.80}$$

3. Yes. For a teacher-made checklist, a reliability in the 0.80's is considered adequate; however, the teacher needs to keep in mind that there will be a certain degree of error in each student's score.

4. The three students are performing within the normal range of the class. They are a bit below the mean, with a z score of ‾0.40, which is at the 34.46 percentile. We do need to consider the question of criterion- versus norm-referenced comparisons. There is a preset standard of performance for the preparation of a slide. Either the slide meets that standard or it does not. It is not so important, therefore, to know where the students stand in relation to each other (that is, to the class), but rather whether each student meets the standard. While the three students may be performing near the mean of the class, they may have a relatively poor score in terms of the accepted performance standard for mastering the skills involved in the preparation of slides.

5. $SE_{meas} = 2.25$

$$SE_{meas} = SD \sqrt{1 - r_{tm}}$$
$$SE_{meas} = 5 \sqrt{1 - 0.80} = 5 \sqrt{0.20}$$
$$SE_{meas} = 5(0.45) = 2.25$$

6. Approximately two-thirds of the time (68.26 percent) the true score will fall between 10.75 and 15.25 points.

$$X = 13 \pm 2.25$$

CASE 14 — CHAPTER 7

1. Sources of inconsistency could come from the inventory itself, from the teachers responding to the inventory, and from the administration and scoring of the inventory. We need to determine whether the items in the inventory were clearly stated and understood in the same way by all the teachers. The

teachers' second response to the instrument might have been affected by discussion and arguments between the first administration and the second. The differences between the first administration and the second were so great that it is more than possible the responses were affected by these differences.

2. No. In this situation the test-retest reliability is not proper. The issue of changing the purpose of a library requires extensive discussion among the staff. The teachers are bound to discuss the issue among themselves and bring to their responses on the second administration of the instrument changes in their own thinking. Therefore stability reliability is inappropriate.

3. $SE_{meas} = 9$

$$SE_{meas} = 15 \sqrt{1 - 0.64} = 15 \sqrt{0.36} =$$

$$SE_{meas} = 15 (0.6) = 9$$

4. As a member of the instructional materials committee, I would not accept the test-retest reliability as an indicator of the instrument's ability to measure with stability the teachers' attitude. I would also have to discount, therefore, the standard error of measurement. I would consider using the instrument as a way to focus discussion among the faculty about the role and purpose of the library and the advantages and disadvantages in shifting emphasis to a learning resource center.

CASE 15 — CHAPTER 8

1. Content validity. A term test is usually an achievement test. It is used to determine the degree to which the objectives of the course have been realized. The content of the test (test items) should measure the achievement of these objectives.

2. Construct and predictive validities. Interest is a psychological construct. To determine whether the test measures what it purports to measure, the validity of the construct (interest), as defined by the test items, must be established. If the test is used to predict future behavior on another variable, information about its predictive validity is helpful.

3. Content and/or predictive validity. A physical fitness test can measure physical achievement that results from participation in a physical fitness program. This would call for establishing content validity. A physical fitness test could also measure one's physical potential. In this case, a correlation between physical fitness and concurrent and/or future physical stamina should be established.

4. Content and concurrent validities. We should determine whether the test items measure the level of reading called "intermediate" achievement. The level is defined by curriculum specialists and current school norms.

5. Content, predictive, and construct validities. We need to validate the content of a readiness test to determine whether the items elicit reading readiness behavior. A readiness test is used to indicate possible success in future performance after exposure to an instructional program. Readiness is a construct that also needs to be validated in terms of this particular test.

CASE 16 — CHAPTER 8

1. The validity coefficient is: $r_{xy} = 0.74$ (*SD*'s rounded to the nearest hundredths).

$\bar{X} = 14.0$

$\bar{Y} = 6.0$ $\qquad r_{xy} = \dfrac{86}{10\,(5.92)\,(1.95)}$

$SD_x = 5.92 \qquad r_{xy} = 0.74$

$SD_y = 1.95$

$\Sigma xy = 86.0$

2. Among the things we would want to know about the test, in addition to the validity coefficient, are reliability of the predictor, reliability of the criterion, standard error of measurement, confidence we can have in the observer's rating of the machine shop tasks.

3. An observed validity coefficient of 0.74 with 8 degrees of freedom occurs only 5 percent of the time. We can, therefore, be confident that the obtained validity coefficient is not due to chance factors 95 percent of the time.

4. $Y = 6$. To compute Y from the predictor score, $X = 15$, we need the following in addition to the data used in the first problem.

$b_{yx} = 0.74 \left[\dfrac{1.95}{5.92} \right]$

$b_{yx} = 0.24$ (rounded to the nearest hundredth)

$a = 6 - [(0.24)(14)]$

$a = 2.64$

$\hat{Y} = 2.64 + [(0.24)(15)]$

$\hat{Y} = 6.24$ or 6 (rounded in whole numbers)

CASE 17 — CHAPTER 9

1. Total correct: 8; total incorrect: 12.
2. Item matrices:

Item 9

Responses →	A	B	C	D*	Blank	Total
High	0	0	0	10	0	10
Low	0	0	0	10	0	10
Total	0	0	0	20	0	20

Item 10

Responses →	A	B	C*	D	Blank	Total
High	4	2	0	1	3	10
Low	4	4	0	2	0	10
Total	8	6	0	3	3	20

3. The item difficulty and item discrimination are:
   a. Item 9:   diff = 100% ; → r_{disc} = 0.00

   b. Item 10: diff =   0% ; → r_{disc} = 0.00

4. The matrix for item 9 indicates an extremely easy item. The options in no way distract or force the learner to make a choice. Item 10 appears to have no definite correct response. The keyed response is the least attractive option. As a result, students choose the other options that appear more plausible, or, in the case of the high scorers, three left the item blank. This may indicate that no correct option is available. While neither item could discriminate between the high and low scorers, one is too difficult and the other too easy.

5. diff = 50% ; → r_{disc} = 0.40. For item difficulty, count the blank cells and divide by N. For item discrimination, subtract the number of blank cells of the low scorers from the blank cells of the high scorers and divide by $N/2$.

6. Yes. Both the item difficulty and discrimination levels are in the acceptable range. All the options were selected, showing that they were plausible, even if they were not the best options.

7. No. Item 6 has a negative discrimination index. Option B is highly attractive to the high scorers and may well be a higher cognitive level response to the question. The teacher may not have anticipated this when writing and keying the item.

CASE 18 — CHAPTER 9

1. $r = 0.81$

$$r = 1 - \left[\frac{25\,(40 - 25)}{40\,(49)} \right] = 1 - 0.19 = 0.81$$

2. There are a number of ways. Among them are: have other teachers look over the test; prepare a text matrix to see how closely test items measure the instructional objectives; compare pupil performance on this test with pupil performance on another test measuring achievement in physics.

3. Top scorers: 8; bottom scorers: 8. To determine these scores, first round off the total class to the nearest whole number divisible by four, and then multiply the number by 25 percent.

$$N = 31 \text{ (number of students)}$$
$$(N + 1) = (31 + 1) = 32 \text{ (32 is divisible by 4)}$$
$$25\% \text{ of } 32 = 0.25 \times 32 = 8$$

4. The average item discrimination index could be improved by dropping the negatively discriminating items. A discrimination index of 0.80 is rather high, and so we need to determine how many items have discrimination indexes as high as 0.80. If it is only one or two items, that is acceptable. The item difficulty indicates that there may be too many difficult items. Because of some negatively discriminating items, a check should be made to see if the negative indexes are also associated with items shown to be difficult. If so, this would indicate that the items or the key correct option should be examined.

5. Yes. The median was a little below the mean. Less than one-half the class was able to reach the mean. An average difficulty of 46 percent reflects the above information.

6. Statistics on X_3: $z = 0.43$; 67 percentile; $(28 - 25)/7 = 0.43$
Statistics on X_8: $z = {}^-0.29$; 39 percentile; $(23 - 25)/7 = {}^-0.29$
$SE_{meas} = 7 \sqrt{(1 - 0.81)} = (7)(0.44) = 3.08 \text{ or } 3$

The possible range for $X_3 = 25$ to 31 points; for $X_8 = 20$ to 26 points. If the true performance of X_3 was at the lower range and the true performance of X_8 at the higher range, there is little difference between the boys' raw scores. From the standpoint of the normal curve, their z scores do not indicate a great difference. Each is less than a half SD from the mean. The type of test items missed by each student will give information in comparing their raw scores. What type of questions did each miss? Did X_3 miss difficult items, easy items, some of each? How does this compare with the items X_8 missed? Were the items missed discriminating in a positive direction? Does the performance on the test indicate whether X_3 and X_8 have achieved the basic instructional objectives, most of them, some of them? Were they missing items of higher or lower cognitive levels?

7. Yes. After the negatively discriminating items have been revised as indicated, on the basis of the r, $\overline{X}$, SE_{meas}, and item analysis, you could assume that this is an acceptable achievement measurement instrument.

CASE 19 — CHAPTER 10

1. Yes. Educational success (as our educational system is presently set up) is predicated on verbal and quantitative ability. These are being measured by the test, as claimed in the test manual. Another purpose of the DAT is to assist in vocational guidance.

2. No. Other factors than cognitive and psychomotor abilities are needed to give the proper guidance. The whole range of factors affecting performance, such as attitudes, interests, study habits, and motivation, would help to

guide students educationally and vocationally. It is recommended that the test data be used in conjunction with information about the other traits.

3. Yes. The reliability coefficients cited in the manual are sufficiently high to accept the test as a reliable instrument.

4. Yes. The tests are thought to be among the best in the field of aptitude battery tests. The revised 1964 test and the new manual have corrected many of the former deficiencies noted in the earlier yearbook by Buros. Caution must be exercised when interpreting the new raw scores for use in vocational guidance. Not enough direction is given the interpreter of the test.

5. Yes. The difference would not, however, be too striking: $36 + 4.4$ $(SE_{meas}) = 40.4$ points at the 75 percentile. The difference between Scholastic Ability and Language Usage II may no longer be important.

6. Ronald is at the 65 percentile. He is above the mean with a z score of 0.15. This is within the typical range of the group with whom he is being compared.

7. Ronald's verbal ability is higher than his quantitative ability. The overlap is less than half the length of the shaded area. This difference should be taken into consideration, although caution should be exerted in making any definite statements concerning the differences unless they are substantiated by other evidence. When two scores are combined as Scholastic Ability, the score does not reveal the difference between these two important abilities.

8. An examination of Ronald's profile produces the following information:

    a. The low score in Space Relations stands out as a marked difference in ability compared to the other test scores in the battery. Mechanical Reasoning and Numerical Ability are also substantially lower than some of Ronald's other abilities. One might suspect perceptual difficulties. On the other hand, there may well be a testing or scoring discrepancy since Ronald does score high in Clerical Speed and Accuracy. Close observation is mandatory.

    b. If you think that it is warranted after close observation, you could test Ronald along perceptual lines to see if there is a significant correlation between his lack of ability in Space Relations and his perception. He should also be retested in Space Relations to determine whether the first score was representative of his ability.

9. Yes, with reservations. Ronald's score in Clerical Speed and Accuracy indicates he can work quickly and accurately. His scores in Verbal Reasoning and Language Usage I and II would help him to prepare accounting reports. But one would have to determine if the lack of ability in Space Relations would keep him from handling accounts neatly. Also, if the accounting involved much mathematics, he might not be able to meet the demands.

10. Lack of ability in Space Relations may affect his work in the science laboratory, in mechanical drawing, in shop courses, and possibly in descriptive geometry. In the lower grades it might have an effect on his reading, although this is not borne out by his Verbal and Language scores. His work in art may reflect limitations in Space Relations ability.

CASE 20 — CHAPTER 10

1. Yes. Ronald's Numerical Ability score is not much below the median. Because he is a hard worker, he could easily achieve in classwork well above his peers. His scores in Verbal Reasoning and Abstract Reasoning would also help account for his higher performance in mathematics.
2. No. The fact that Ronald makes the honor roll may be an indictment of the school's evaluation procedures. The system may be rewarding rote performance, which is then reflected in high grades. Students with verbal ability augmented by effective language usage tend to be rewarded in most school situations, regardless of the quality of the work.
3. Ronald's Verbal Reasoning ability should be used in a constructive manner, through assignments that will challenge and use his talent. Open-ended writing tasks, exposure to imaginative literature, and science problems requiring intuitive attempts at solution should be made a part of his instructional program.

CASE 21 — CHAPTER 11

1. The hypothesis can be both justified and refuted. In justification, there should be a direct relationship between the manner in which an assignment is made and the effect it has on students as measured by their behavior. The student can manifest either positive or negative behavior toward the assignment. In refutation, it should be noted that, by the intermediate years, students have developed attitudes toward assignments based on previous experiences (either pleasant or unpleasant) that color their behavior toward the teacher's assignments. The students' reactions may be to the past and not directly related to the action of the present teacher. This is especially so earlier in the school year.
2. Yes. A checklist, with items clearly worded, can be an appropriate observation procedure for measuring behavior related to an assignment, if the items include descriptions of typical positive behavior.
3. Yes. Most items are positive behavior manifestations that are indicative of a responsive student.
4. Examples of additional items include: student uses outside references in writing assignment; student speaks with teacher about the assignment; student relates a personal experience similar to the topic of the assignment; student voluntarily brings in some items related to the topic.
5. Number 5. It is negatively worded, while the other nine items are positively worded. The wording of items in a checklist should all be in the same direction, that is, either all positively or all negatively worded.
6. There are several methods available for determining a high or low "responsiveness" score. First, have an observer use the checklist to collect data on two groups of students: those who are usually highly responsive and those who are usually unmotivated, lethargic, and lack enthusiasm. The mean $(\overline{X})$ of each group will help determine what constitutes a high score and what

constitutes a low score. Second, if there are no previous data to work with, choose those items most likely to be related to usual responses of students to an assignment, such as items 1, 4, 6, 7, and 9. Let us assume an average-motivated student responds positively to these five items. Five points will then represent the mean. Qualitative values are assigned, using the mean score as average performance:

$$0-1 \quad = \text{unresponsive}$$
$$2-3 \quad = \text{low responsiveness}$$
$$4-6 \quad = \text{average responsiveness}$$
$$7-8 \quad = \text{above average responsiveness}$$
$$9-10 = \text{high responsiveness}$$

These values would be altered as data from students' scores are collected. With the additional information, meaningful norms are developed.

7. Two observers should use the checklist to collect data. The data on a number of different observations by both observers of the teacher(s) presenting assignments are correlated. Internal consistency reliability using the K-R 20 formula or the teacher-made formula is appropriate.

8. Obtain an interrater reliability between a trained observer and yourself. The coefficient of stability would not be an appropriate statistic since it is impossible to collect data on the same event a second time.

CASE 22 — CHAPTER 11

Responses to the area you selected in Case 22 should be studied by a committee of peers. You need to ask continuously if the instrument is reliable, if it has validity, and if the information generated is of value in planning further instruction or instituting changes that will generate behavior in and around the school building.